Bilibid Diary

Bilibid Diary

The Secret Notebooks of

Commander Thomas Hayes

POW, the Philippines, 1942–45

Edited by A. B. Feuer

Archon Books   1987

Set in Baskerville by Brevis Press, Bethany, Connecticut.
Designed by Nora Jacobson.

The opinions expressed in Commander Hayes's diaries are
his personal opinions at the time of writing and do not
necessarily reflect the opinions or the policy of the
editor, the publisher, or the Department of the Navy.

Printed in the United States of America

The paper in this book meets the guidelines
for permanence and durability of the
Committee on Production Guidelines for Book Longevity
of the Council on Library Resources. ∞

Library of Congress Cataloging-in-Publication Data

Hayes, Thomas, 1898–1945.
   Bilibid diary.
   1. Hayes, Thomas, 1898–1945.   2. World War, 1939–1945—
Personal narratives, American.   3. Bilibid Prison (Manila,
Philippines)   4. World War, 1939–1945—Prisoners and
prisons, Japanese.   5. Prisoners of war—Philippines—
Manila—Biography.   6. Prisoners of war—United States—
Biography.   I. Feuer, A. B., 1925–   .   II. Title.
D805.P6H36   1987   940.54′72′52095991   87–14564
ISBN 0–208–02169–8 (alk. paper)

Dedicated to the Defenders of Bataan and Corregidor

Contents

Foreword

Several days after Pearl Harbor, World War II came to the Philippines. On December 10, 1941, high-flying Japanese bombers hit Manila and virtually leveled the Cavite Navy Yard. Overwhelmed, U.S. Navy medical personnel and their Army compatriots ministered to the casualties as the islands prepared for a full-scale Japanese invasion.

In the weeks that followed, Americans and Filipinos fought against increasingly hopeless odds as defense lines stretched to the breaking point. Olongapo was evacuated and many of the naval personnel joined the Fourth Marines at Mariveles on the Bataan Peninsula. On New Year's Day, 1942, this unit and many others left the mainland to make a last stand on Corregidor.

By the time the siege of that porkchop-shaped island ended on May 6, 1942, the United States had suffered the worst military defeat in its history and Japanese might had all but extinguished American power in the Far East.

For those who surrendered, the real ordeal had barely begun. Although the Corregidor defenders had been spared the infamous Bataan Death March, they faced a grim future. Some were held in such notorious hellholes as Cabanatuan and Camp O'Donnell. The "lucky" ones ended up at the old Spanish-built criminal prison called Bilibid in downtown Manila.

The POWs handled the months of starvation, disease, forced labor, and boredom in their own ways. Some merely struggled to survive as day followed day in monotonous, undefined rhythm. Many, too sick to cope, simply gave up on the moldy, musty rice ration and were buried in a cemetery near the prison wall. A few kept journals, either mindful of recording individual ordeals or simply to keep their minds active.

The journals of Commander Thomas Hirst Hayes, Medical Corps, U.S. Navy, span almost the entire thirty-one months of his captivity. Begun the day he walked into a prison the Filipino authorities had condemned as unfit for human habitation, Hayes wrote almost every day. The original journal begins with a handwritten, small green notebook and ends on whatever scraps of paper he could press into service. The entries are seldom terse or laconic and never dispassionate. Most of them eloquently cover the full range of human emotions, from Hayes's elation at having eaten an adequate ration, or having put one over on his hated Japanese overseers, to his sober realization that starvation would certainly overtake him before the end of the war.

A man of strong opinions, Hayes could level harsh judgment at his comrades. Many failed to pass the rigid standards he set for himself. Through his observations, the twin myths of prisoner solidarity and cooperation are shattered. Interservice rivalries erupt in the prison hospital. Starving men steal or hoard food. Inmates consort with the enemy for special favors. Discipline breaks down. As he chronicles the glaring defects in human nature, Hayes justly recognizes that these frailties have been aggravated by the despair of prison life.

And always there exists in these journals the theme of a man struggling with the burden of command. As Hayes assumes leadership of the Bilibid Prison Hospital, he also assumes responsibility for the welfare of its inmates. Despite criticism and personal unpopularity, he chooses to exercise his will the Navy way and by the book. Moreover, he never wavers up to his own tragic and ironic death aboard a Japanese prison ship almost on the eve of rescue.

The recovery of Hayes's nearly intact journal by Bilibid's liberators over forty-two years ago is itself a small miracle. The big miracle is that an edited version of a rare and truly unique World War II document has finally been published.

Jan K. Herman
Historian
Naval Medical Command
U.S. Navy

Acknowledgments

I am deeply indebted to Mr. Jan Herman at the U.S. Naval Medical Command in Washington for his generosity and patience while I rummaged through the Bilibid correspondence, and his permission to use the surviving diary and notes of Commander Hayes for the preparation of this account.

I would also like to thank Dr. Alfred Smith of Richmond, Virginia for reminiscences of his experience at Bilibid Prison, and Eugene Rogers of Chesapeake, Virginia for his recollections of the "hell ships."

A special thanks to Dr. Paul Ashton of Santa Barbara, California for reading this manuscript, and his personal impressions of Tom Hayes and others mentioned in the diaries.

Other material used includes "The Prisoners' Voyage of Doom," by J. V. Crews and R. J. Hostetter, which appeared in volumes 20 and 21 of the *Hospital Corps Quarterly*; and *The Oryoku Maru Story*, by Charles M. Brown. I would also like to thank the Scripps Howard Foundation for their permission to use the series of articles written by war correspondent George Weller entitled "The Cruise of Death." These materials are extensively quoted in Parts IV and V of this book.

The accompanying photographs are used by courtesy of the National Archives, the Naval Medical Command Archives, Dr. Paul Ashton, and Charles M. Brown.

Introduction

Thomas Hirst Hayes was born in Philadelphia, Pennsylvania on February 8, 1898, and graduated from the George Washington University Medical School in 1920. He was commissioned a lieutenant (jg.) in the Medical Corps of the U.S. Navy on July 10, 1924.

During his early years of service, Hayes was stationed at naval hospitals in Pensacola, Boston, Norfolk, and the Virgin Islands. In 1931, Hayes attended a course of postgraduate instruction in orthopedic surgery at Harvard Medical School, and then reported aboard the USS *Sapelo* for an eighteen-month tour of duty. He spent the three years following that on the staff of the Norfolk Naval Hospital and in 1936 returned to the Virgin Islands where he was attached to an aircraft squadron. In 1937 Hayes was transferred back to Norfolk.

In August 1940, Lieutenant Commander Hayes was assigned to the USS *Milwaukee* and served aboard that ship until May 1941. With the clouds of impending war gathering over the Pacific, he was ordered to the Sixteenth Naval District, Cavite, Philippine Islands, and reported for duty in August 1941.

When the war began four months later and the Japanese invaded the Philippines, Hayes was assigned to the Fourth Marine Regiment as its chief medical officer. He was promoted to the rank of commander on January 1, 1942.

Hayes remained with the Fourth Regiment throughout the defense of Bataan and Corregidor and was captured by the Japanese when the island fortress surrendered on May 6, 1942. Commander Hayes and the other Corregidor prisoners were transferred by ship to Manila, and from there to various prisoner-of-war camps.

Hayes and his medical unit were sent to Bilibid Prison in Manila, where he remained in captivity from July 2, 1942 until December 13, 1944. During the first half of his imprisonment, Hayes was chief of surgery at the Bilibid hospital, and was later appointed senior medical officer of the prison.

Bilibid was formerly an old Spanish penitentiary which had been declared unfit for the incarceration of criminals but was reopened by the Japanese after the fall of Manila in January 1942. For the next three years it was used as an internment camp for prisoners of war.

The prison was located in downtown Manila at Azcarraga Street and Quezon Boulevard. It was constructed in the shape of a square, approximately 600 feet long on each side. A wall, twelve feet high, divided the complex into two separate compounds. In the center of the bisecting partition a circular guard tower was situated, giving the Japanese sentries a commanding view of both areas. In the upper compound stood a large uncompleted building and two jail cell blocks resembling animal cages. The jails had six cells to a side and could hold about fifteen men each.

Around the perimeter of the round guard tower, long barracks buildings were arranged like spokes in a wheel. Each barracks was 120 feet long and twenty feet wide, made of whitewashed masonry walls and cement floors. The roofs were corrugated iron and the windows had barred openings covered by heavy wooden shutters which opened outwards.

As the prisoners from Bataan and Corregidor arrived, they were marched into the upper compound. The lower compound was set aside for a prison hospital and became the central medical facility for all captured Americans on Luzon.

Also confined at Bilibid were over 200 Filipino soldiers and civilians. Several of the Filipinos were trusted by the Japanese and were permitted to come and go as they pleased. An underground spy network soon operated within the prison: messages were smuggled in and out of the front gate with astonishing regularity. Items such as food, tobacco, and newspapers were sneaked into Bilibid by trusted townspeople and outside prison working parties.

Tom Hayes was a prolific writer and kept a diary and notebooks during his Bilibid captivity. He recorded a great deal of valuable historical data pertaining to the administration of Bilibid Prison; relations between American and Japanese officials; and studies of human behavior under the pressures of imprisonment. He spared neither friend nor foe when their conduct conflicted with his own ideals.

Hayes was also very much involved with the spies and they are mentioned many times in his diary. In most cases he used only their initials in the event that the Japanese discovered his notes. In constant fear of being found out, Hayes divulges very little information concerning his espionage activities, or the people he was involved with. The stories of clandestine activities he mentions leave much to the imagination.

The diaries and notebooks of Tom Hayes have been edited and arranged chronologically here, but the full flavor of the man and his remarks, and the uncompromising conviction of his opinions, remain. As starvation and the pressures of command took their toll on Hayes the diary becomes muddled and at times it rambles between the past, present, and future. Much of the editing was an effort to put all incidents in their proper perspective and correct time frame. Nothing of importance was left out.

Before leaving Bilibid, Commander Hayes turned all his written material over to Lieutenant J. V. Crews for safekeeping. The papers were packed in hermetically-sealed containers and buried in five separate caches beneath the prison commissary area. Only a portion was ever recovered and much is still missing—including Hayes's clinical notes and many of the biographical sketches of people mentioned in his diary. There is a distinct possibility that additional information about the spy operations is among this material. Similarly missing here is a nine-month period of Hayes's imprisonment—from January to October 1943.

On December 13, 1944, Tom Hayes was among the 1,615 prisoners of war that were herded aboard the Japanese merchant ship *Oryoku Maru* for transfer to Japan. He survived the sinking of the vessel at Subic Bay, but was subsequently killed in the bombing of a second ship, the *Enoura Maru*, at Takao, Formosa, on January 9, 1945.

Chronology: Pearl Harbor to the Liberation of Bilibid Prison

7 December 1941 —Japanese carrier aircraft attack Pearl Harbor.

8 December 1941 —Japanese planes bomb U.S. airfields and military installations in the Philippine Islands.

9 December 1941 —Japanese troops occupy Makin Island in the Gilberts.

10 December 1941 —Japanese capture Guam.

12 December 1941 —Japanese Army lands at Lagaspi in southern Luzon, Philippine Islands.

20 December 1941 —Japanese troops land at Davao, Mindanao.

22 December 1941 —Japanese Army lands at Lingayen Gulf on Luzon.

23 December 1941 —Japanese capture Wake Island.

24 December 1941 —Japanese troops land at Lamon Bay, Luzon.

25 December 1941 —American and Filipino forces commence withdrawal into the Bataan Peninsula.

8 January 1942 —Japanese Army strikes at Bataan.

11 January 1942 —Japanese troops land on the Celebes Islands.

12 January 1942 —Japanese troops land on Borneo.

4 February 1942 —Sea battle at Makassar Strait, U.S. cruisers *Marblehead* and *Houston* damaged.

15 February 1942 —Singapore surrenders and Japanese land on Sumatra.

19 February 1942 —Japanese bomb Port Darwin, Australia.

28 February 1942	—Battle of the Java Sea. Combined Allied fleet defeated.
1 March 1942	—Battle of the Sunda Strait. USS *Houston* sunk.
8 March 1942	—Netherlands East Indies surrender. Japanese capture Rangoon, Burma, and attack New Guinea.
9 April 1942	—Bataan falls to the Japanese and the Battle of Corregidor begins.
18 April 1942	—General Doolittle's bombers raid Japan.
5 May 1942	—Japanese troops land on Corregidor.
6 May 1942	—General Wainwright surrenders Corregidor and the Philippine Islands fall to the Japanese.
8 May 1942	—Battle of the Coral Sea. USS *Lexington* is sunk.
4 June 1942	—Battle of Midway. Japanese lose four aircraft carriers.
5 June 1942	—Japanese occupy Attu Island in the Aleutians.
7 June 1942	—USS *Yorktown* sunk by Japanese submarine.
7 August 1942	—U.S. Marines invade Guadalcanal and Tulagi Islands.
8 August 1942	—Japanese cruiser force sinks three American cruisers in first night sea engagement of war at Savo Island.
24 August 1942	—Second Battle of the Solomon Sea. USS *Enterprise* damaged.
15 September 1942	—USS *Wasp* sunk by Japanese submarine.
11 October 1942	—Battle of Cape Esperance. Japanese fleet turned back in attempt to reinforce Guadalcanal.
24 October 1942	—Battle of Santa Cruz Islands. USS *Hornet* sunk and three Japanese carriers damaged.
13 November 1942	—Third Battle of the Solomon Sea. Heavy losses on both sides. Japanese battleship *Hiei* sunk.
15 November 1942	—Japanese attempt to bombard Henderson Field on Guadalcanal. Japanese battleship *Kirishima* and seven transports are sunk.
30 November 1942	—Battle of Tassafaronga. One U.S. cruiser sunk and three damaged.
2 February 1943	—Japanese commence evacuation of Guadalcanal.
3 March 1943	—Battle of the Bismarck Sea. Six Japanese transports and four destroyers sunk.
26 March 1943	—Battle of the Komandorski Islands. Japanese supply convoy for their troops in the Aleutians is turned back.

18 April 1943	—Japanese Admiral Yamamoto is killed when his plane is shot down.
11 May 1943	—U.S. Army invades Attu in the Aleutians.
21 June 1943	—American troops invade New Georgia Island.
6 July 1943	—Battle of the Kula Gulf. USS *Helena* and three Japanese destroyers sunk.
13 July 1943	—Battle of Kolombangara, Solomon Islands. One Japanese cruiser sunk. One U.S. destroyer sunk and three cruisers damaged.
28 July 1943	—Japanese abandon the Aleutian Islands.
6 August 1943	—Battle of Vella Gulf, Solomon Islands. Three Japanese destroyers sunk.
6 October 1943	—Battle of Vella Lavella. One Japanese destroyer sunk. Two American destroyers damaged.
1 November 1943	—U.S. Marines invade Bougainville.
2 November 1943	—Battle of Empress Augusta Bay. Japanese cruiser and destroyer sunk.
5 November 1943	—American carrier planes attack Rabaul, New Britain. Four Japanese cruisers and two destroyers damaged.
11 November 1943	—American planes again attack Rabaul sinking one Japanese cruiser and damaging two destroyers and a cruiser.
20 November 1943	—U.S. Marines invade Tarawa and Makin Islands.
26 November 1943	—Battle of Cape St. George, Solomon Islands. Two Japanese destroyers sunk.
26 December 1943	—General MacArthur invades New Britain.
1 February 1944	—U.S. Marines invade Kwajalein Island in the Marshalls.
17 February 1944	—Japanese naval base at Truk in the Caroline Islands attacked by U.S. carrier and battleship task force. Over 300 Japanese planes are destroyed along with three cruisers, four destroyers, and thirty merchant ships and auxiliary craft.
21 February 1944	—Eniwetok Island in the Marshalls is captured.
24 March 1944	—American troops invade the Admiralty Islands.
22 April 1944	—General MacArthur invades New Guinea.
27 May 1944	—U.S. troops land on Biak Island.
14 June 1944	—American Twentieth Bomber Command launches its first strike against mainland Japan attacking military targets on the island of Kyushu.

15 June 1944	—U.S. troops invade Saipan.
19 June 1944	—Battle of the Philippine Sea. Two Japanese carriers sunk and three damaged. Over 100 Japanese planes shot down.
21 July 1944	—U.S. troops invade Guam.
24 July 1944	—U.S. troops invade Tinian.
15 September 1944	—U.S. Marines land on Peleliu Island. Heavy air attacks are carried out against Japanese bases in the Philippines.
10 October 1944	—The U.S. Third Fleet bombards the Philippines, Okinawa, and Formosa. Attacking Japanese planes damage two American cruisers, but 500 Japanese aircraft are shot down.
20 October 1944	—American troops land on Leyte Island in the Philippines and General MacArthur steps ashore.
23 October 1944	—Three-day Battle of Leyte Gulf begins. Japanese losses include four carriers, three battleships, six cruisers, and a dozen destroyers.
10 December 1944	—Organized Japanese resistance on Leyte ends.
13 December 1944	—The Japanese prison ship *Oryoku Maru* sails from Manila with 1,615 prisoners of war including Commander Thomas Hayes.
15 December 1944	—American troops land on the island of Mindoro.
9 January 1945	—The American Sixth Army lands on Luzon at Lingayen Gulf and drives toward Manila. Commander Hayes is killed in the bombing of the *Enoura Maru* at Takao, Formosa.
28 January 1945	—American forces recapture Clark Field.
1 February 1945	—American prisoners of war at Cabanatuan are liberated.
3 February 1945	—American troops enter Manila. Prisoners at Santo Tomas are set free.
4 February 1945	—American prisoners of war in Bilibid are liberated.

I.

The Notebooks
July 2, 1942 to July 30, 1942

July 2, 1942

We were a tired and squalid gang that filed through the Bilibid Prison gates about three o'clock this afternoon. Our group was marched into the upper compound and I managed to assemble all my officers in one cell. Thirst was intense, but after an hour I was able to fill my canteen and get a few husky drinks down my throat. I unslung my pack and stretched out on the concrete floor in my sweat-drenched clothes, and slept.

I awakened in about an hour—it was raining. It had been pouring for some time and the cell, open on two sides to the weather, was quite wet. We had no idea what our ultimate status would be. It was quite evident we were no longer a hospital unit, but only a batch of prisoners. If this cell was to be our final destination, we could just make up our minds to a tough period of imprisonment. We had already learned that *lugao* [rice] three times a day was the daily ration, and that in itself was not very promising. However, I also noted as we passed the Navy group in the lower compound, that while all of them had lost weight, they still looked in damn sight better shape than we did.

We were soon ordered to don our packs and move into the large unfinished building. Our destination was the second floor. The deck was laid out in large sections, apparently intended for cells, but the bars had not yet been installed. Our group filled one side of the structure. The men with blankets spread them out on the deck and staked their claim to that part of the floor.

We drew a ration of rice from a gasoline tin and choked it down. I had eaten nothing since early morning when we were given a can of salmon before leaving Corregidor. One of the Filipinos had slipped me a hard biscuit which helped my hunger somewhat. Lieutenant Wanger soon brought us a big tin of coffee and everybody took heart considerably.

Commanders Lee Sartin and Maurice Joses arrived about this time and welcomed us heartily. Sartin assured me that he was trying to have my medical personnel attached to his unit. I also learned that Bilibid was "an accommodating place" for prisoners, from which drafts were sent out to the provinces on working details. The lower compound was a central prison hospital, staffed by the captured medical unit from Canacao. Sartin was in command of the hospital and Joses was his executive officer.

For the past six months we had been attached to the Army, and while our relationships were apparently good, we were always considered outsiders. The Army made us feel like we were "poor relations" or refugees working for our room and board.

I did my best to maintain good working relations between us, but will never forget that we were denied quarters with Army officers and were made to sleep in the toilet—later a passageway. Not that we minded, but space was available if they had seen fit to let us have it. Although we worked day and night in their hospital, my officers and I were not allowed to eat with the Army for quite some time. However, as their need for us grew, we gradually assumed undeniable importance in their setup. Finally we were accepted—never wholeheartedly, but nevertheless accepted. Whenever the Army needed help, they knew where to come—and they got it—gracefully and competently rendered.

It wasn't long before the shoe was on the other foot and the Navy sat in the saddle. We suddenly amounted to something. We were no longer just refugees and poor relations. The Army couldn't understand why.

They may have understood if they knew that the reason a Navy medical unit was placed in charge of the Bilibid hospital was because the Army had their chance and failed. The stories concerning the Army's regime at Bilibid exceeded everything I had ever heard about foul-ups and crookedness in this war. The Army medical officers actually "sold" medicine to the patients. One medic even "charged" for special attention to the sick.

By nine o'clock at night I was assured that my medical personnel would be attached to the hospital staff and remain at Bilibid. We were later informed that all prisoners except the Army and Navy medical units were to leave for the prison camp at Cabanatuan. I immediately began to sense that there was some fast politics at work. The arrangement here was similar to other Japanese camps. While Sartin was in command of the hospital, the Japanese appointed Chief Machinist Warrant [Officer] G. B. Gooding as Camp Warden—in charge of all the prisoners. Gooding was an emotionally unstable chap in a job entirely beyond his depth and capabilities. His assistant was an Army captain [Winship]. Gooding attached several other Army personnel to his staff as "yes-men"—one of whom he planted in the medical officers' quarters to eavesdrop on all that went on.

About two o'clock in the morning I was informed that dental

officers would not be considered medical personnel—although I had every assurance that they would be. I had reason to believe that the Army was deliberately unloading their dental officers, but I thought that our dental group was safe.

However, by four o'clock it was evident that all my dental officers except two were to leave for Cabanatuan. The two dentists remaining were the "politicians" I had with me, and the only no-good personnel I was associated with during the war. They had worked a "rabbit's foot" sure as hell. I later learned that they were friends with the Camp Warden. When the smoke cleared away, it was evident that Gooding and Winship had retained their friends and made up the required Cabanatuan draft quota with dental officers.

Both Gooding and Winship denied knowledge of any complicity—that was a lie. Later in the day I heard their excuses. Gooding claimed that he made an error because the dental officers on his list were shown only by rank and not noted as medical department people. Winship denied any knowledge of the incident at all. It seemed rather pointed to me that the two dental officers who remained were the ones who always resented my keeping Bob Herthneck as my regimental dental officer. They cracked at me through him and got away with it—for the present anyway.

July 3, 1942

Late this morning I received word from Sartin to move my medical unit over to the hospital compound. I was returned to my job as chief of surgery. It felt good to be back with the Navy again.

During the day we were permitted to go out the front gate and pick up our belongings that had been brought to the prison from Corregidor. I found my bedroll, barracks bag, and foot locker. I also managed to grab Bob Herthneck's bedroll. I hope to send it to him at Cabanatuan.

Unfortunately, all the corned beef, canned tomatoes, coffee, soap, and canned milk that we smuggled out of Corregidor was confiscated by the Japanese. They searched every piece of baggage and we lost the entire lot.

July 4, 1942

Today I began my new duties as chief of surgery. There is a lot to be done here. Within these dingy prison barracks are crowded all the human flotsam and jetsam from Bataan and Corregidor. Filipino and American alike, side by side on the concrete deck. The mattresses they lie on are filthy, stinking, and vermin-ridden. Emaciated carcasses look up with staring eyeballs sunk deep in bony sockets. Their broken bodies, starved and bloated, hover near death. Some show anguish and apprehension, some are pleading, some even have hope; but most of them are past manifesting anything—or even caring.

My walk through the wards is one of the most depressing and heart-rending sights imaginable. The mixed smells of dirty bodies, rotting tissue, dried blood, and excrement are repulsive to every filament of the esthetic senses. The conglomerate horror of it all beats upon my sensibilities as an outrageous defiance against all the principles of civilization, and dispels any delusion I may have had of human progress.

Our job here is to do all we can with the pitiful little available to us. But even badly needed surgery will not help. These starved, tissue-dead, zombie-like creatures can't stand surgery. At best, many will die. In this prison the war has just begun.

By nightfall I had moved into the Staff Officer Quarters located in one of the long prison barracks, an end of which was separated by a partition and served as the S.O.Q. [Sick Officer Quarters]. We were not allowed regular beds. Each man was required to build a low platform about a foot from the floor. This was covered by a mattress and became a bed. During the day the mattress is rolled back and the platform can be used as a table or desk.

July 8, 1942

We are served rice three times a day by the Japanese, which is brought in from the central galley in five-gallon gasoline tins. Once or twice a week we also receive a ration of watery soup with a little eggplant cut up in it.

A "store" has been operating within the camp. Legally and technically it doesn't exist because the Japanese don't want us to buy extra food. They feel that they "lose face" by not feeding their prisoners adequately. However, on the pretext of providing supplementary articles for the sick, the store is permitted to do business. The guards and the prison commandant, Captain Kusumoto, take little notice of occasional trucks entering the compound, bringing tobacco, peanuts, coffee, and sugar. The store is run by our pay clerk. Each man deposits money with him and draws against the account. A small profit is allowed which goes toward a fund to provide extras for the sick and penniless. Gradually other items have been sneaked into the store, such as mongo beans, canned salmon, sardines, and bananas. On the surface this arrangement sounds ideal. However, we have very little money and the prices charged are beyond reason. There are only a few of us who can afford to buy in this market for very long.

The high prices, of course, are *C'est la guerre.* All food stuffs are rapidly becoming scarce and the merchants, knowing the demand, take advantage of the situation. Then, naturally, the guards have to get their cut, and a small profit added to the fund. I figure that I have enough money to buy additional rations for another three weeks.

Our salvation is the lowly mongo bean. They are reasonably cheap and can be used in many ways. The mongo is a tiny green bean about the size of a "BB" shot and has a lentil taste. We soak them in wet towels and let them sprout. They can then be stewed and poured over rice. Everybody has mongo bean cultivation underway. The men can always be seen washing the beans, putting them to sprout, or cooking them in improvised galleys. They appear in buckets, tin cans, jars, or any other container available. The mongo is rich in vitamin B-1, in which so many of us are deficient. It has been a lifesaver for us, and as long as we can get them we can stomach the rice.

Surprisingly, it was in this very prison years ago that experiments were carried out in which it was discovered that mongo beans when added to a plain rice diet prevented beriberi. The prisoners were used as guinea pigs.

Even the preparation of coffee is a group project. Everybody donates a kilo and we start with the old standard of one tablespoon per cup and one for the pot. For the first run we have fair coffee. Then for several days we boil and boil the grounds, adding more and more water. Eventually the coffee gets pretty thin and one has to use his imagination to detect the taste.

Captain Kusumoto is in favor of legalizing the store, but it will never be done unless the Japanese decide to recognize that part of the Geneva Treaty relative to the pay of prisoners. There have been hints in this direction, but to date nothing has come of it. According to the treaty, an officer is to be paid commensurate with his rank in the conquering army. That wouldn't amount to a hell of a lot here, but it would help.

July 9, 1942

We are gradually getting the more urgent cases attended to, insofar as our limited facilities will permit. The Japanese released the Corregidor medical supplies for our use and we distributed them to the wards.

I decided to build an operating room at one end of Ward Six. The plans and specifications have been submitted for approval. I hope the Japanese will give us enough material to get started. I only need a few lengths of pipe and some couplings to hook up my sterilizers. As it is, I have been using the dispensary as an operating room. Surgery as we must practice it here is very offensive to the trained sensibilities of our specialized help. Years of experience in the tropics have long since taught me that a Mayo Clinic is not necessary for excellent results. Much can be done without the O.R. ritual which is so overplayed by many of our larger institutions at the expense of good common sense.

There is constant conflict as Gooding and his cohorts attempt to invade the hospital administration. However, Sartin has everything moving along quite well. I must pay tribute to this officer who was considered unworthy of appointment to captain just before the war. For when the pressure came, Sartin shouldered the responsibilities and survived the tough going, while the "selected ones" folded up completely. This is another sad commentary on our selection system. Everyone here has nothing but praise for Sartin—from the lowest corpsman to the highest ranking member of our staff. This is partly due to his fatherly, easygoing manner and his reluctance to order anybody to do anything unpleasant, or not in accord with their own wishes. So far this has worked well here, but it would never do in the field or in action. Frankly, however, I still see this bunch not as primarily serving the patients, but rather themselves. They can do more for the patients, but many of them are too intent on their own care and comforts as a whole. They should be working harder. In a few days my men will be doing more and more. We will make this place operate like a hospital and less like a convenient place to spend the war.

Captain Kusumoto is difficult to analyze. There are certain policies of his which are fair and tempered with kindness. On the other hand, there are paradoxical streaks in his actions that make me wonder. It's rumored that his superiors have often asked him whose side he's on—theirs or the Americans. From all I can gather, he's doing the right thing by everybody. He was an athlete in the Olympics several years ago. Kusumoto's top sergeant is also a pleasant sort of guy and visits us regularly. At times he brings his brother along. They both seem very amiable and everyone likes them.

There is no doubt, however, that the basic policy of this regime is to consider us prisoners of war. We are to be held incommunicado, draw our pound of rice a day, and like it. Anything else we may get is a special favor and should be greatly appreciated as an act of benevolent kindness.

It has become evident that conspiracies are at work to prevent the equitable distribution of available food and necessities. For instance, while the bulk of the confiscated food we brought from Corregidor did find its way to the patients, I have seen certain special groups appearing with cans of it now and then. I have also noticed working parties coming back to camp, bringing with them fruit and coffee and selling it to their fellow prisoners. All this profiteering is permitted by the Camp Wardens—American officers. Honest, sympathetic Sartin, the soul of kindness and fair play, can do nothing about it. The deplorable state of the needy hurts him deeply. Sartin does have one good card to play if he can ever get it on the table. He has a letter of authority to obligate the United States for the care of his patients and personnel. If he can establish contact with neutral consular agents, there are any number of merchants who will gamble on the U.S. being able to pay, and will grant us credit and supply us with food. Of course, Japanese permission is needed also.

July 10, 1942

I brought Colonel Manuel Olympia [Philippine Army] into contact with Sartin. The Colonel will be discharged soon and has close connections on the outside. Since the sick Filipinos seem to be getting out first, I put Olympia on the sick list. He came to Corregidor as the

Senior Flight Surgeon of the Philippine Army and was assigned to me
with the 4th Regiment. He was a courteous gentleman and I treated
him as such. The American Army ignored him, practically denying
him living space and making him feel very much like an outsider. I
felt sorry for the old gent—after all, I had experienced the same cold-
blooded attitude. Our relationship remained pleasant and we have
developed a comradeship through these many months. He often remarked to me that he would never forget that I alone was a friend to
him when he arrived on Corregidor.

Olympia studied medicine in Tokyo and was knighted with the
"Order of the Rising Sun" by the Japanese emperor. At one time he
had large lumber and hemp interests in Davao where he employed
Japanese labor. Philippine law prohibits Japanese from owning land
and conducting such enterprises. However, many Filipinos hold land
and businesses for Japanese investors.

The Colonel spent many years organizing and training the Philippine Army Medical Department, and last April he was named Surgeon General. When Corregidor fell to the Japanese, our Army
changed its attitude toward Olympia. Since the Colonel speaks excellent Japanese, the Americans suddenly decided that they needed him.
Olympia became the man of the hour. The Army couldn't move or
do a damn thing without him. I certainly got a kick out of the stuffed
shirt, high-and-mighty Army boys who had accorded Olympia less
attention than one would ordinarily pay to a servant. The Colonel got
a kick out of it, too. He has not been blind to the treatment accorded
him by the American factions, and anyone who denies that there had
been a distinction made is ignorant of the facts.

I still haven't categorized Olympia. Since the surrender he has
been of more service to the Americans than any other one person I
know. In looking back over my association with him, there has never
been an instance in which he did not manifest anything but the greatest loyalty to our side. However, I have never known him to be demonstrative or express strong American sentiment. My belief is that
he's a hundred percent Filipino—be it Japanese or American policy.
I can forgive him for this because I know the disrespect that the
American Army group dealt out to him, and I don't believe he will
ever forget it. His native pride and self-esteem have been deeply of-
fended. Our American smugness and provincial self-satisfied attitude
and arrogance lost dividends in this case—as in so many others. I have
seen this obtuse behavior among our Americans abroad and have been

repeatedly ashamed of it. We have always been poor colonizers. We just can't help but look down on people and patronize them. We have neither the understanding nor the desire to understand a people or a custom other than our own. We only tolerate.

So, just how Olympia will jump when free, I hesitate to say. He and Sartin should get along well. The Colonel has often told me what a difference he has observed between our Army and Navy. I still have hopes that he will help us.

Olympia is the one counterespionage problem that I have never mentioned to St. M. [Santa Maria—Hayes's underground contact in Bilibid]. Someday when the time is favorable I'll ask her about him. I expect her analysis to be the same as mine. It would be natural for her to believe that he's on our side, but this is a world of intrigue and even a brother may be false.

July 11, 1942

We had a visit from Sikiguchi today. I immediately recognized him as the character who visited us at Corregidor soon after the surrender. "Siki" is a bullet-headed, ugly, brutal-looking Japanese officer, and is a lieutenant colonel in the medical corps. As near as I can figure out, he is the assistant to the chief of the Japanese Medical Department in the Philippines. His duties are apparently roving and take him to all prison areas. This is his first visit to Bilibid, and he let it be known in no uncertain terms that he is anti-American. He had been taught at school how merciful and pleasant the Americans were—only to come to manhood and realize how "heartless, cruel, and mercenary" we are. He insisted on telling us how infamous he is in Manila and calls himself "General Wickedness!"

"Siki" has a way of blaspheming Americans—accusing them of deliberately sinking hospital ships and committing other atrocities. He has one tirade—chastising us for not knowing a single word of Japanese and having no interpreters of our own. He asked how we can claim to give medical aid to the enemy when we can't talk to them.

"No! No!," he screamed. "You Americans never thought you would have to talk to us. You don't deal in words, but only with the sword, with the fist, with guns and cannon. Not so Japan! We have all kinds of interpreters—English, Malay, Dutch, German, Chinese, and Tagalog [Philippine]. We like to talk to people."

I can still hear him as he ranted, "Yes! Oh, yes! Now you want interpreters! Now you realize what a help they would be to you! Now you realize how much it would mean to you to be able to talk and understand us! You think we should supply interpreters! We should know English! You should have thought of this before! You were high and mighty, but what do you think of your future now?" I had heard him give this same speech to Colonel Duckworth.

However, immediately after his rehearsed tirade, he would ask information as to the amount of food and supplies, and the condition of the sick. He also offered constructive criticism. After pooling the experiences of several officers who had dealings with him, I'm inclined to think that he is as reliable and helpful as anyone I have met at Bilibid. Duckworth seems to have gotten good cooperation from Sikiguchi in spite of the theatrics. In fact, "Siki" is quite fond of "Ducky."

I must admit there are certain elements of truth in Sikiguchi's speech. I particularly refer to this matter of interpreters. I have long contended that the Army and Navy should be more proficient in languages. For years I have heard our people allude to other races with: "Why in the hell don't these bastards speak English?" It seems that anyone who doesn't speak English is a damn heathen. It's always the other guy who must build a bridge for understanding. Because of our ignorance in this respect, we have placed other nationalities in an advantageous position over us. They are able to grasp our psychology and concepts by learning our language, while we remain ignorant of theirs.

The Japanese are conversing [with] and entering into the everyday life of all the people they conquer. It's astonishing how rapidly they learn a conversant vocabulary. In addition to their interpreters, who land right along with the invading troops, every soldier attempts to acquire a workable knowledge of the language spoken. Each member of the Japanese Navy carries a small pocket-sized book listing everyday phrases and words. They also take every opportunity to enlarge on the vocabulary. We would do well to take a lesson from the enemy in this regard.

Our Army and Navy have not seen fit to require learning the politics, economy, customs, and religions of our enemies. This essential requirement has been in my mind for many years, and the need for it is evident to me in this war. In my opinion we are committing national *hari-kari* on the sword of smugness and provincialism.

However, there is one thing that I would like to tell Mister Sikiguchi. It seems that any interest in the Japanese language by our Navy has always been looked upon by them as having an ulterior motive of the most sinister kind. Any of our language students that manifested an interest in Japanese life and customs were looked upon with suspicion—and were almost expected to offer an apology. This, of course, should not have been a deterrent, but rather should have inspired us to dig even deeper under the surface of these people.

Had we followed such a policy, perhaps the popular fallacies as to their racial nearsightedness might not have had to be disproved in such a calamitous manner. The idea that the Japanese are a race of poor physical specimens, fed on soybeans and rice, would have long since been exploded. And their tough, wiry troops would not have come as a surprising revelation to so many of our soldiers.

Duckworth was invited to eat with us tonight as a guest of the Japanese—Sikiguchi, as a matter-of-fact. "Siki" had a long talk with Duckworth and tried to convince him to go to Tarlac with the other *Tai-sas* [senior commanders and colonels]. He also brought Duckworth some fruit and permitted the Colonel to make purchases in town.

Duckworth has many privileges not accorded the rest of us. He arrived in Bilibid with his personal orderly and valet, along with his administrative assistant and twenty pieces of baggage. He also brought his own bed equipped with mattress and spring. I learned that he was here ostensibly to have a hernia belt made. Since I last saw him "Ducky" had been operated on for appendicitis and there was a possible herniation through the scar. I examined him but could find no urgent demand for any belt. I'm convinced that Duckworth is nosing around for a good billet and has his eye on this place. Sikiguchi and Duckworth are a bad combination.

July 12, 1942

Several trucks from Tayabas arrived today and dropped off more than thirty dysentery derelicts—more dead than alive. We scurried around to get them bedded down, while guards yelled for working parties to scrub the trucks down with creosol. That Tayabas camp is a hellhole. They are supposed to be building a road down there, but practically everybody is sick. There can't be a lot of "pick and shovel" labor available in the group. Many of the men admitted on this date will die. They are long past help—some already moribund—all deathly sick—a pitiful situation.

The rainy season is now underway with heavy downpours and thunder and lightning practically every night. In the meantime, prison life goes on—roll call every night and morning—rice and watery soup—rumors good and bad—wishful thinking—alternating periods of hope and despair—days of scratching for existence.

Groups of men gather about open fires with improvised utensils fashioned from tin cans and pieces of wire, cooking up weird concoctions of all possible edible combinations.

Other prisoners are busy making wooden shoes, building bunks, doing laundry, carrying wood, soaking mongo beans, making crude soap. Some men read, some write, and some just sit—others break the monotony—by dying.

July 12, 1942

A clear dawn over Bilibid and no rain until dark. There is much discussion in the compound as the scuttlebutt began to flow. Bombings were heard about midnight last night and the wishful thinkers are working overtime. If they keep on as they have been, MacArthur will be calling up from the Manila Hotel and inviting us to lunch in about a week. But who can blame them? After all, what else do they have to do? There are men here who do nothing but worry and scurry over their next meal. They lie on their bunks, beat their gums, and dwell on the great question—will freedom ever come?

LaVictoire keeps himself sick, choking down large gobs of rice for fear he will have a nutritional disturbance. Food denial has become an obsession with him. He has had other flights from reality in a "neuritis" and a limp that seems to come and go. He lies on his bunk most of the time, smoking and "conserving himself"—almost cataleptic. He has adjusted less than anyone else in our medical unit. As a neuropathologist, he should have more of an insight into himself. But alas, such is the nature of the hysterias, every complaint is painfully authentic.

I was busy this morning sorting out surgical instruments for setting up my O.R. The Japanese instructed us to pick out what we need from the equipment they brought over from Corregidor. The rest will be taken to other camps. I was quite liberal with our hospital, but still left plenty for other locations. Since Bilibid is the central prison hospital, I figured that most of the surgery cases will come to us anyhow.

The Filipino women in the upper compound made six dozen plaster rolls for us. Rumor has it that they may be freed tomorrow and sent home. I hope so. This incarceration has been harder on them than anyone else, shut up as they are in their building. They are eating well, however. The Filipino boys coming in from working parties bring them fruit and milk. The Japanese guards also buy a few things for the women.

The *Tai-sas* no longer have to show up for *bango* [roll call]. That makes me the senior staff officer present at *bango* from now on. Sartin was inclined not to take advantage of this Japanese concession to him as commanding officer, but Joses and Duckworth talked him into it. The Japanese go in for rank in a big way. The fact that a person is looked upon as "high up" gives him valuable prestige. We convinced Sartin that he must play the "rank with privilege" game.

God, but that Communicable Disease Ward is terrible! Human wrecks piled into a long adobe building, lying on dirty mattresses spread on the concrete floor. Most of the men are too prostrate to give a damn about their surroundings. Brokenshire is doing a good job there with what little medicine and equipment he has available.

Our good Japanese sergeant leaves us tonight. He has only been here a week, but in that short time we have fared much better than before. We have soup with a few more vegetables included, and occasionally a piece of meat for seasoning. The sergeant is also a good rumor artist. He insists that our planes bombed Cavite, that soon he will leave to go home and American occupation troops will come. Experience has taught me that the Japanese soldier, even the officers, know very little more than we do about how the war is going. Also, when rumors are highly favorable for our side, especially when disseminated by the Japanese, one must remember the German method of propaganda which is based on building up the hopes, and then with a crash of truth, letting you down. The effect is very demoralizing.

I made contact with St. M. today and believe she will be leaving here soon. I gave her a message for Leach. She will probably be able to contact him at Santo Tomas [internment camp for civilians].

Four of us tossed a baseball around for awhile this afternoon. We need a certain amount of exercise to keep in shape. While our low calorie diet doesn't permit us to do anything strenuous, we can do that much in hopes of gradually building up our strength. Keeping fit and well must be our first consideration after taking care of the patients.

Tonight we are sitting in our barracks, trying to dodge the steady drip of rain through the leaky roof. A few cribbage games are in progress—along with the ever present bull sessions. Jim Pfeiffer diligently works over his Japanese notebook. He has done remarkably well with his language attempts. The mosquitoes are very bad tonight.

July 15, 1942

Our deaths continue daily. We bury the dead in the upper compound near the prison wall. A man is kept busy cutting headstones for the graves and marking them by name, rank and organization. His work is piled up for months to come. There is no way he can keep pace with the grim reaper. Dysentery and nutritional deficiencies continue to decimate the men. No end appears in sight.

The Japanese had a long talk with Sartin and Duckworth today. Kusumoto wants them to divide the medical forces. Duckworth, however, doesn't want any of the Army officers that are now in the upper compound. He wants us to take the Army medics. Sartin told Kusumoto that we didn't need them, but Kusumoto insisted. I mentioned to Sartin that I had a plan to absorb the Army boys, and yet keep them out of our hair where they can't throw a monkey wrench into our operation. We also will be able to keep them under surveillance.

Duckworth suggested sending all the Army medical officers to Cabanatuan, but Sartin is too kindhearted for that. He stands out like a nobleman among thieves.

We received an unexpected delivery of meat and vegetables this afternoon—that means soup again tomorrow. We never seem to get enough of those items. The thin soup poured over our rice certainly helps to choke it down. Yesterday Cecil Welch mixed a few vegetables with a can of corned meat and two duck eggs. He made hash from them and we had two tablespoons each to eat with our rice. To us it was a feast.

The Japanese brought in 30 more sick prisoners from Tayabas today. That camp continues to be a killer. One of the men was dead on arrival. We were told to expect 125 more in the next few days. That must be a hell of a road they are building. Reports coming in suggest that much of the suffering is the result of the ineptitude of their own American camp commanders. The cooks reportedly spend most of their time cooking for themselves. I understand that there are times when they have more food than we do. However, the fact remains that they live in a river bottom without shelter during the rainy season. There is practically no sanitation and the men bathe and drink from the same stream, while the Japanese water their horses higher up. There are no latrine facilities and dysentery, malaria and pneumonia run rampant. This camp incidentally is composed mainly of prisoners who requested to go there in order to escape the deplorable conditions at Camp O'Donnell. That's like swapping the devil for a witch.

Our friendly Japanese sergeant who tearfully left us recently, came back today to visit on his first liberty. He seems to have taken quite a fancy to Schweizer and Pfeiffer. The sergeant remarked, "I have been taught to hate Americans, but I find nothing wrong with them."

I looked over the medical wards with Clyde Welsh who is acting chief of medicine. He has been crying about his surgical cases. He only has four, and none of them in urgent need of attention. Same old Clyde—always a gripe. He wants to heal the world, but like all such helpful souls when you turn them loose, he only sits and complains. Clyde has quite a defeatist attitude and I have had to call him on the carpet several times about it. As I look down the line at chow time, I can see Welsh sitting by his bunk, fanning himself with a huge fan (where he got it, Lord only knows), naked to the waist and wearing glasses. He looks for all the world like some forlorn Buddha.

July 16, 1942

The Japs transferred a number of Filipinos out of here today, with prospects of more to go. Most of the O.R. gear has been moved into location. If I can only get enough pipe to connect up my sterilizing unit I would feel much better. As long as we have sterile goods we can actually work anywhere in an emergency.

The scuttlebutt tonight comes from "over the wall" telling about a naval battle underway south of Mindanao, but no details. The news from outside, if true, came via a hidden radio (station KGEI), many of which are still scattered around Manila. We have no way of evaluating such news. However, we have noticed that on days when we are favored by a lot of Japanese visitors, we generally hear of some war activity in our favor. Today we had quite a number of Japanese dropping by to chat. I have learned to listen to the news and forget it. I'll never lose hope, but I refuse to build my hopes on wishful thinking. I believe that ninety percent of the rumors are the figment of childlike uninformed minds. As of now, the facts of the past are brutally behind us, the present uncertain, and the future obscure. The real demands on our fortitude and courage are yet to come. However, we could stand a good hypo of worthwhile accomplishments to sustain us. There are those here who feel that we have been sacrificed. But if it has been for the common good and served for the ultimate victory, we don't mind. We have seen and suffered so much, that we are to be pardoned if we have doubts and find the need for reassurance that we have not been needlessly pawned. We hope our plight is one of necessity and not of neglect. If we lack faith we have reason, but every one of us still hopes for a faith restored.

More talk today from Kusumoto. He now says, "Soon you will be paid." That only means that we will be able to continue to supplement our rice diet with a few mongo beans, brown sugar, and maybe some native coffee. Our money is about all gone. Unless this Japanese "bayonet money" [occupation money] that the Japs are rolling off the presses is forthcoming, we are going to find ourselves too much the total guests of his Imperial Majesty.

July 17, 1942

It rained all night and the wind blew all day. We battened down our barred windows as best we could, but the roof continues to leak and the walls are damp. Our bedding and clothing are also soggy. However, we are still better off than the prisoners in the open cell blocks. They are now occupied by the Filipinos and Colonel Olympia's medical staff.

I didn't sleep worth a damn last night. All night long there was a constant moving about in the barracks. Then this morning, Colonel Duckworth missed his cigarettes and lighter. Silliphant claimed his wallet was gone and Lemire reported his trousers were rifled. And that wasn't all, two men from S.O.Q. came in to report losses from their end of the barracks.

I can't understand how any wholesale thievery could have taken place with so many men up during the night—unless everybody was involved. It's hard to believe that any officer here would do such a thing, but it's plainly an inside job. As far as I can determine, no Japs were in the barracks last night.

For the past two weeks items have been disappearing. Lieutenant George lost a wrist watch and Lieutenant Greenman lost his wallet on our first night here. I haven't missed anything yet. It seems that the Army officers are the most victimized.

I have been pondering over this situation. The most likely suspect is a certain individual who is broke and in debt to most of the crew. He has used his position to keep a hand in the operation of the store, and there is some question as to his manner of handling money entrusted to him. I thought this person would be concerned about last night, but he ignores the incident completely. I did notice him and his pal go in and out of the barracks several times during the night. I can't prove anything, but forewarned is forearmed.

Conditions are improving for the patients. Every man now has a bed and nobody is lying on the concrete floor. The wards are cleaner and better policed. Lieutenant S. W. Smith has been specially assigned to see that certain needy cases are given what little extra we can add to their diet. Most of the time this means soup between meals. Our corned beef, salvaged from Corregidor, is also mixed with rice and rationed to the patients. The profits from the store allow Smith to buy a few mongo beans and duck eggs.

Duckworth and his administrative officer, Lemire, were notified that they are to leave for Camp O'Donnell tomorrow. I'll feel much better with the Colonel gone from here. He's a very competent fellow in many respects, but has a well-known reputation for looking out for "Ducky." There is no doubt in my mind that he has had his eye on this command for some time. Lemire almost let the cat out of the bag in his efforts to have Kusumoto appoint Duckworth as liaison officer between the prison camps and the Japanese. It would have put Sartin in the awkward position of having to approve the appointment. The plan nearly worked. It seems that the less Army contact we have, the less intrigue we have to put up with.

As the day progressed, more cases of thievery were reported and Sartin called a conference with Joses and I. These robberies are evidently a desperate concerted action by one or more of our people. It must be stamped out and our dirty linen not aired to the Japanese.

It was decided that a continuous watch should be maintained during the night, and a light kept burning in the living spaces at all times. No one is to be allowed in or out of the barracks except on business, and then only at the discretion of the person on guard duty. All personnel were also warned to safeguard their valuables. These measures will help, but I don't think they are far-reaching enough to protect. My original suspicions still hold.

I made momentary contact with St. M. today. She has a plan for using my information and I'm satisfied that she will make it work. She also laid the groundwork for keeping in contact with me after she leaves Bilibid. However, I don't believe this will serve any useful purpose except to keep me informed as to what's going on. I don't think that it's worth the risk. She should be able to carry on and continue her activities with Leach. I thought of having her contact Trujilio, but I'm not sure of him. He still has many Japanese friends. I may be wrong about Trujilio, and I hope I am, but I couldn't discuss him with her as long as I had doubts in my mind. St. M. is bold—cold as ice and naturally disarming. I have no fear whatsoever that she can't take care of herself.

It has been raining incessantly. So far our drainage system has met the challenge, but I'm afraid that by tomorrow the whole compound will take on the appearance of a public anchorage—and the barracks a series of moored arks.

July 18, 1942

Duckworth left this morning for Camp O'Donnell. The reports from there are not good. There is no sanitation at all and the death rate is very high. Sikiguchi had talked to Duckworth about the transfer, and at one time (according to Duckworth) advised "Ducky" to go to Tarlac with the rest of the Colonels. The way I size up the story, Duckworth has played up to Sikiguchi and convinced him that he can straighten the camp out. "Siki" is anxious to have a good record and welcomed the help. After about two months, I fully expect Duckworth to leave O'Donnell and end up with a soft liaison job. He's a great schemer—for "Ducky."

Japs arriving from Cabanatuan report: "Their camp very bad—Bilibid number one." If that's the case, it must be bad. I understand that the men there have very little or no water—two canteens a day and a bath maybe once a week. One report says that the death rate is 35 a day.

I finally started having my first difficulties adjusting to the non-war regime here. Sartin has made a go of this place because he's a fine old man and everybody has been pitching for him. All this is great as long as his crowd can tell Sartin what to do, and Sartin doesn't tell them what to do. With the exception of Cecil Welch, Wanger and a few others, this Canacao outfit is a bunch of griping, argumentative, unmilitary group of "sitter downers"—who do little or nothing other than look after their own hides. They don't know how to take orders or give them. They haggle and complain and haven't an ounce of military sense. What they need is indoctrination, training, and discipline.

The officers who came with me have already assumed active places on the hospital staff. As far as my surgical responsibilities are concerned, my men will tick like a clock as long as I'm the boss.

A priest in town, just back from O'Donnell, reports that nearly twenty thousand Filipino prisoners have died there since the surrender. The priest is a German [Father Buddenbruch, also referred to as "B"]. He has formed an organization of rich women in town that are anxious to do war work. They call themselves "Chaplain's Aides." The padre wants us to submit a list of what we need, and to make the list a long one. The tough part is that we need food most of all, and that's the hardest item to come by. Medicines and medical supplies may be somewhat easier. The priest is trying to get permission to come to the prison tomorrow (Sunday) and hold services. I may be able to talk with him then. St. M. will have the dope on the priest by tomorrow morning. She is a very convenient Catholic.

I also learned that radio broadcasts in the States are now reporting the hellish condition of American prisoners in the Philippines, and how necessary it is to do something about it.

St. M. inveigled the guards into letting her use the phone to the outside. I can't understand how she got away with it—talking over the phone in Tagalog. The Japanese know that language fairly well. However, St. M. can also speak Chinese, Japanese, English, and Visayan. She will probably only be able to chance this a few times, but she has supplied me with important data that can be passed on to where it will do the most good.

July 19, 1942

Today is Sunday and the Manila priest will be coming. There were cloudbursts with much thunder and lightning all night. We are now completely flooded. The sewer lines are blocked and sewage from our dysentery cases flooded over the compound at knee depth—and it's still raining.

The small fires over which the men boil coffee or cook their mongo beans are now out. There are only two fires still going—the galley and the incinerator. Water stands knee-deep in the galley, and the water level is almost to the top of the rice tins. Contamination of the rice is inevitable. Welch and I decided to fry our rice from now on. That should kill the bugs.

Already this morning we have three bodies for burial and the graveyard is under three feet of water. Our barracks is leaking like a sieve. We are so cramped for space that it's impossible to dodge the rain. I have my bedding covered by a shelter half which helps to keep my mattress dry, but the fast growing tropical molds can't be prevented.

The roadways between the barracks resemble Venetian canals, but alas, we have no gondolas nor gondoliers. And gondoliers can't help us because we have no guitars—and no moonlight.

Several of the corpsmen were slow reporting down at the front gate to carry in provisions. They came in for a severe cuffing by the guards but nobody was seriously hurt. Our Japanese interpreter [Herri] is responsible. He's a vindictive low class of Jap who speaks very poor English, and almost as bad Japanese. His vocabulary is so limited that he keeps getting things mixed up and then protects himself by shifting the blame to the prisoners.

Our chow worked out very well today. I managed to grab a hunk of pork for grease and Cecil fried the rice in it. We even corralled a piece of garlic and seasoned up a mess of mongo beans. Regular "Sunday dinner down on the farm."

St. M. finally got word to me about the priest. I had arranged for her to send me a simple impersonal message by the boy who totes rice to their quarters. If the note was written in ink, I was to layoff, if in pencil, O.K. It was in pencil. As a result, I made contact with Santo Tomas and a stateside feeler message was started on its way.

St. M. said the priest reported that anti-Japanese feeling among the Filipinos is increasing daily. Every man, woman, and child has a hidden bolo knife. The Japanese are quite aware of this and continually search the people at all public gatherings. The padre is quite sure that he can get urgently needed medical supplies to us, but any food will have to be smuggled into the prison.

I carefully observed to see if there was any recognition between the priest and Olympia. I'm sure there was none, but the padre was under constant surveillance at all times. He didn't hear confessions and nobody talked alone with him. According to St. M., his contact at Santo Tomas is through Sister Clara. That almost guarantees him to me.

Kentner was just in. He said that it's impossible to bury our dead inside the prison. The Japanese are trying to arrange for a place outside. We began writing identification slips for the dead, sealing them in bottles, and placing the bottles inside crude coffins.

July 20, 1942

The water has fallen considerably and moving about is much easier. By accident rather than plan, I was able to talk with St. M. at length today. She managed to use the phone again and called Sister Clara (speaking in Visayan). St. M. spoke only a few words: "Father Cummings is at Bilibid." Sister Clara immediately arranged for "B" to be allowed into camp again. Cummings and "B" are from the same order. "B" is a German citizen but anti-Hitler, and at present, anti-Japanese. Not so, however, before the war. He apparently changed when he saw Japanese guards beating and bayoneting American prisoners on the march north from Bataan. The padre's plan is already underway. He has lined up about a hundred rich Filipino women to help us. Last night, Miss Lourdes Reyes, the town's leading debutante, had a dinner for a Japanese official in Manila. Miss Reyes is a mild naive little thing with great big eyes, and she knows how to turn on the heat. She worked on the Jap in behalf of our hospital. The ramifications of this meeting can be far-reaching. There is reason to believe that he will be able to contact the Apostolic Delegate in Manila—the direct representative of the Pope. The delegate enjoys diplomatic immunity and should be a great help to us.

This was a poor day for chow. The rice was thin and watery this morning, and like paper hanger's paste this afternoon. Tonight the rice was sour and smelled terrible. I couldn't stomach the stuff so I drew in the belt a little tighter. Pfeiffer tried to talk the guards into some good dry rice, but again it was our nemesis, the degenerate interpreter, that fouled things up and made us take what they gave us and like it. In my postwar revenge book, this guy heads the list. Our coffee also ran out today. It will be missed, however, the last pot was mainly ground up peanut shells, and didn't smell nor taste like coffee.

No rumors for several days. As a matter-of-fact, all bona fide war reports show everything quiet in the South Pacific. There are still a few of the "Home by Christmas Club" among us. I'm glad for them and the hopes they live with, but I'll be sorry for them when Christmas comes—and goes.

July 21, 1942

The Japanese are searching through our medical supplies. They are trying to determine what items they want to send to Cabanatuan. This robbing Peter to pay Paul has been a constant game with them. The Japs brought nothing into the islands whatsoever, and have drawn heavily on our supplies. They move the material around all over Luzon. For example, O'Donnell asks for supplies and they are taken from Corregidor. Then when we need something, it's taken from O'Donnell, and Cabanatuan's needs are filled from Bilibid. Some system!

The International Red Cross hasn't been able to function here at all, and the American Red Cross went out of business after the fall of Manila. The so-called Philippine Red Cross was then established (Japanese dominated of course) and nothing has been forthcoming from them.

I received word today that we are to have a new prison commander. The care of the prisoners will be turned over to a civilian group, part of the army of occupation. They are supposed to be specially trained and familiar with the Geneva Treaty—seeing is believing.

I choked down my rice tonight with the aid of watery soup and boiled grass. A little salt would have helped the taste, but we have to cut down on our sodium intake. All of us are developing too much ankle edema. Our metabolism is so shot to hell that it only takes some small factor to throw our bodies off balance.

Rumors are flying all over the place. A medical officer from Tayabas reports he was told that all prisoners would be sent to Ecuador in a couple of months. I guess I shouldn't get worked up over rumors, but I can't help thinking about it.

That bastard Herri slapped Schweizer across the face today. The Jap was drunk and in a nasty mood.

July 22, 1942

The rain has finally let up, but it's hot and sultry. One of the Filipino boys cut me a pair of wooden shoes from a two-by-four. They are more practical than leather in this climate.

A tunic, cut down from an Army shirt, and a khaki helmet constitutes the "uniform of the day" around here. The tunic serves to carry my rank and insignia, which is very important to the Japanese. Every time I meet a new guard, he never fails to examine my silver leaf very closely. The tunic makes for less laundry also. Which reminds me, tomorrow I must turn out an accumulated wash consisting of two towels, one shirt, a pair of shorts, and a sheet. The dirty clothes sure pile up.

Chow today was two sardines and a pan of rice—not a banquet, but it will sustain me. I can still remember my last good meal—Christmas Day on Bataan. We were camped at the headwaters of the Mariveles and Cabalog Rivers and had spent most of the day in foxholes. Enemy planes were constantly overhead. However, the Japanese aircraft were still based on Formosa, and after three o'clock in the afternoon they headed for home. After the bombing stopped, we climbed out of our holes to eat a delicious meal of ham, sweet potatoes, and lima beans. We didn't realize it at the time, but this was to be our last nourishing meal in the Philippines.

When food is denied, the sensation of hunger takes over. But this passes quickly. One adjusts readily to reduced quantities. However, when certain necessary elements are withheld, a craving of the most painful kind will persist. This is often interpreted as hunger, but it occurs even when the belly is full. This stage lasts a long time and some people never overcome the symptoms. Most often it's a craving for sweets—sugar is hard to do without. I have been through long sugar denials which were hellish, not only because my taste demanded it, but physiologically the old human machine was missing. Our blood sugar gets so low that we often fall asleep while eating or at work. It's during this phase of food denial that one becomes conscious of physical inefficiency, mental dullness, and the inability to concentrate. My memory becomes so bad at times that I can't recall the names of my friends, or read a page from a book and hold the continuity.

The men constantly talk about food—what they like—feasts they have attended—how food is cooked at home—menus of what they will order when they get back to the States.

Eventually the desire for food disappears, but one must eat in order to keep going. That is the cruelest punishment of all—hunger is to be preferred. I have lost all yearning for any particular food. I have forgotten desserts to a point where I no longer crave them. I can fill up my emptiness with rice, and my blunted gustatory senses are easily satisfied by the small quantities of supplementary items that we get occasionally.

We are, for the present, receiving enough sugar to keep us going. Our bodies have adjusted by now to a lower sugar level. Several men have developed starvation phobias and gorge themselves at every meal, doubtful of their next. They keep themselves so clogged up with rice that they are sick all the time. Food becomes an obsession with them.

The Japanese couldn't understand why we were in such a state of starvation and malnutrition at the time of the surrender, and yet there were tons of food stored on Corregidor. That's something we would all like to have explained to us. Someday we hope to hear what that bogged down quartermaster corps will have to say about it. There was no reason for stinted rations, nor was there any reason why the Bataan troops should not have had food up to the very last. There were field rations by the thousands, carabao and mule meat, bulk canned food-stuffs, all stored in tunnels. The Japanese had a right to wonder—even as we wonder.

The Filipino women were set free today and St. M. went with them. I made my last contact with her. She intends to continue her work and also arranged for further contacts with me. She didn't have time to explain her plan, but I expect she will most likely work through "B" if she can trust him. Her last words before she left were: "While you Americans sacrifice for my country, I will never let you down." I think there is an element of patriotic fervor that inspires her, but I also suspect the love of adventure and intrigue has a lot to do with it. She plans to be in Cavite tonight.

Sartin talked with Kusumoto this afternoon. He was told that Herri may be leaving when the new regime takes over. This news was greeted with much relief provided the son of a bitch doesn't get too far away. There are a few scores to be settled if I'm to return home with a satisfied mind.

Sartin asked Kusumoto if he was going back to Japan. The Commandant replied, "No—to Australia!" That's what he thinks. Kusumoto has always bemoaned the fact that in China he won many medals for bravery, but then was placed in charge of this prison. The more I see of him, the more I regard him as a big bag of wind. The Japanese have windbags just as we do. However, his comments reminded me of a Japanese major's remarks at Corregidor. It seems that the major received a letter from his family and they were very upset with him. The relatives at home couldn't boast of anyone in the family having been killed yet. They were mortified—losing face—something must be done about it. He should go south where the fighting is taking place and see about getting himself killed. I don't know whether he went or not. My recollection is no. I don't think he was that stupid.

Medical officers from Cabanatuan report there is nothing they can do to stop the dysentery deaths. No medicine is available, and they see nothing but the complete decimation of the camp from amoebic dysentery. The great numbers of Japanese killed on Bataan have already been exceeded by American deaths in prison camps since the surrender. There is a feeling that this is not coincidental, but according to plan.

The ration truck arrived today with pork and vegetables. The latter were so rotten that they had to be thrown away. We made pork soup tonight and fished out the fat to cook with our mongo beans tomorrow.

The Ecuador rumor assumed epidemic proportions. It became the topic of conversation throughout the prison. However, a working party returning from the outside reported they read in the Manila newspapers that the civilians at Santo Tomas would be the people going to Ecuador. Now that I can believe. A group has already been sent to Portuguese East Africa and further removal of civilians could be expected. As far as military personnel is concerned, I think we have a long time to wait.

July 23, 1942

Colonel Olympia was over for chow today. I apologized for our lack of pheasant. However, we did manage to cook up a pot of mongo beans, and along with rice and our famous pork soup, it was a filling if not elaborate meal. The pièce de résistance was the dessert—rice jumbles—small hunks of rice dough smeared with native plum jam. This delicacy was smuggled in from Santo Tomas yesterday. The Colonel enjoyed himself immensely—especially the rice jumbles.

More dysentery cases from Tayabas died today. I can hear the "bang-bang" and "knock-knock" of the boxmaker as he builds coffins for the waiting corpses. Even as he works, a guard comes in to report another death. We must box the bodies that we send outside for burial. Inside the compound, a canvas sack suffices. By tomorrow it should be dry enough to bury the dead in our own graveyard.

Schweizer reported that the Japanese have hurriedly cleared the harbor of ships and are setting up antiaircraft guns along Dewey Boulevard. Also, for the first time, Kusumoto asked for a night working party.

Schweizer is a competent mechanic, handles men well and is a valuable factor in this prison setup. Although he's Gooding's number two man, he manages the bastard job in a capable manner and with no fooling around. He also works on repairs and has contrived several ingenious devices, such as a self-flushing latrine. If Schweizer was in Gooding's place, it would certainly help.

July 24, 1942

Another busy morning as my surgical team swung into action. Schweizer hooked up my overhead light and began alterations that will eventually give me an O.R. of sorts. It's really coming along fine.

I didn't sleep well at all last night—tossed, dreamed, and such dreams. For example, I was elected mayor of Medford, New Jersey, and was instructed by the citizenry that my first duty was to put the local drugstore on a paying basis. Freud, or anyone else for that matter, would have a tough time explaining that one.

I annexed Major Wilson to my staff. He was moved down into the hospital compound and I asked for him. I haven't forgotten how he and Hagen were kind to me when the rest of the Army considered me like a case of smallpox.

I'm still continuing Hagen on the sick list. He doesn't look well and takes his illness and present dilemma badly. I remember while we were at Corregidor and under constant attack, he would always keep asking, "What's to become of us?" I tried to prepare him for the surrender and matter-of-factly told him, "You will be captured eventually, but only after they have softened us up. It won't necessarily be as bad as you might imagine." I was quite sure of the first part of the statement, but I couldn't even convince myself that the last part would be true.

Lieutenant Alfred Smith is still very sick. He never has recovered from his initial sickness after Corregidor. Smith joined me after the gunboats were evacuated. He hasn't been able to keep anything down for several days and vomited most of last night. Al is one of the unfortunate fellows who had served his full tour of duty and had signed orders to take the next ship home. However, before his orders could be delivered the war broke out.

A prisoner draft for Cabanatuan is supposed to leave here in the morning, therefore sick call is especially heavy tonight. This places our department in a difficult position. None of us like to see the boys leave here, but as long as the Japanese permit us to decide which of our own people are fit for work, we must play ball and be honest in our decision.

Wilson stopped in this evening and we talked over old times until lights out. I walked with him as far as his barracks. I wanted to stretch my legs a little and I enjoyed the walk under the high pale moon.

The air was cool and damp and very still—perfect weather for reminiscing. I think I'm becoming a little introverted, and losing control of my power to suppress thoughts that could be maddening. Nowadays I have much more time to fill artificially. Although I have had a great deal of experience in mastering loneliness—at one time loved it; I no longer accept life as something to live mostly alone. Two years ago when I went to sea, I knew that I would never again find happiness and complete adjustment to loneliness. Aboard the *Milwaukee,* I never did adjust.

I was a different man when I left Virginia two years ago. I had known happiness—real happiness. I had found the life I always wanted. But I knew when I left on this cruise that I was done, washed up as a happy wanderer. I felt that my present plight, or even death, was in the immediate future. My remark about eating "fish heads and rice" for the duration was not made in jest. I knew that never again would my hobbies of painting, writing, archaeology, tennis, and fishing; never again would they suffice for everything in my life. I realized that people and individuals as a whole had been pushed farther out of my life than ever before.

Times like these tend to produce comradeships of strong ties and deep feelings. It hasn't done so for me. The nearest thing to it has been my relationship with Bob Herthneck. I will always remember his courage, loyalty, and competency. It was a real blow to me when he was sent to Cabanatuan.

There are certain things in life so real that they defy substitution. If this results in loneliness—so be it. There are feelings that can't be turned on and off like a spigot. And such a loneliness, born of a true and sincere emotion, a real need that is denied, is to be preferred and endured. But one must survive, and under the present circumstances there can be something cruel in the picture of "a man and his dreams." To think, to dream, to wish, and to remember could be disastrous.

I was awakened from my masochistic reverie by the heavy tramp of trudging feet. I could see marching men filing past the guardhouse with barracks bags on their shoulders. They halted in the "sacred circle" and I edged closer to take a better look. There were a few hundred of them—American prisoners from Camp #3 at Cabanatuan. I learned that they were to be here overnight and then move out—destination unknown. The men looked in good shape. They hadn't been sent out on working parties and only had their own needs to take care of.

After a short time the ragged group was marched into the upper compound. That area is already crowded and not prepared to handle such a mob. It's going to be a rat race up there tonight.

July 25, 1942

I made my rounds through the prison compound with Wilson and then went down to the O.R. I stood by while the boys worked on an amputation case. It was our first job in the new operating room and everything went off without a hitch.

Sikiguchi is beginning to make a pest of himself. He showed up yesterday and laughingly asked Sartin if he could speak Japanese yet. "Siki" always manages to get that crack in. He then asked for a "three view" drawing of an American bedpan. He wanted to have them made in Japan. Johnson knocked out a mechanical drawing of a bedpan—three perspectives—along with specifications as to measurements and material. Sikiguchi returned today, looked at the drawings, and said we misunderstood him. He wanted drawings of "three kinds" of bedpans. Sartin explained that we only use one kind in the Navy, but there was an old-fashioned type around here somewhere. He would try to find it and have a sketch made. We offered to give "Siki" the genuine article, but no, he wanted drawings. I think this is just another way of Sikiguchi putting across the idea that since we can't speak Japanese, misunderstandings must be expected.

Johnson is back at work on technical drawings of the different bedpans. The old-fashioned kind is a monstrosity with a spout, sort of a combination bedpan and zither. I personally think this is Sikiguchi's idea of a hilarious joke—the sense of humor of a warped mind. I would feel better if "Siki" had urgent business elsewhere—like hell for example.

This bedpan episode reminds me of a story. It seems the Japanese established a bawdy house near one of their troop concentrations and imported 300 "beautiful" geisha girls from Japan. Those who saw the women reported that they looked like a bunch of sluts. A certain officer's first job as a prisoner was to dig a latrine for the ladies. He later remarked that when his youngsters ask him how he fought the war, he can sum it up in one sentence: "I dug a shithouse for a whorehouse!"

Another of Sikiguchi's "performances" is when he contrives to maneuver his sword in such a position that someone brushes against it. Whereupon "Siki" flares up and shrieks, "In Japan, to touch an officer's sword means death—cut off the head—but, of course, ignorant Americans, not knowing, excused this time."

We received word that the *Tai-sas* are getting along swell at Tarlac—taking Japanese language lessons and all that crap—those bastards would. The Japanese will treat the Colonels as important personages, and the Colonels will go back and tell how good the enemy treated them. The Japanese are wise as hell in this respect. Every civilized act of decency handed out to prisoners has an ulterior motive attached to it. The Colonels I know at Tarlac will fall for this garbage. They will forget the thousands who have died, the hunger, the beatings, the bayoneting, the sadistic mockery, and the insults we have suffered. The Japanese themselves have little respect for the *Tai-sas* and consider them useless—in retirement they call it. Regardless of whatever may be Duckworth's shortcomings, he was a colonel and rated Tarlac, but he insisted on staying with his command.

There is a general lack of respect for the *Tai-sas*. The feeling is that they are only concerned with their own safety and comfort. They have contributed nothing to the war effort and will never be respected by the commands they left. The Japanese admire Duckworth's attitude. Every Colonel at Tarlac could still be rendering service if they had the will to do so.

July 25, 1942

After the rain last night we have a cool and beautiful morning. The climate and weather, when good, are our greatest luxury. At *bango* this morning (Sunday), it was proclaimed by the "Field Marshal" (Gooding's new monicker) that besides Catholic Mass, Protestant services would be permitted in the upper compound. Kusumoto also advised us to keep our hot plates and other valuables out of sight for the first month after the new regime takes over—let them gradually get used to our "luxuries" or we might lose the little we have. I don't know if this is an act on Kusumoto's part to impress us on how considerate he's been, or whether he's actually sincere. I'll play it by ear until we find out.

I acquired a handful of raw peanuts last night and cooked them. I remember when I ate peanuts as a snack at ballgames, however, they are real food around here. We mix them with rice, cook them with sugar, boil them as a vegetable, and toss them in soup.

I talked with "B" this morning. We should know by Tuesday if our medical supplies will be delivered. The prospects seem favorable. The padre's organization of women is hard at work. Meetings are held in different homes to prevent detection by the Japanese, and supplies are collected at various locations.

The priest visited several prison camps this past week. Conditions continue bad and atrocities are committed daily. "B" is very much German, but his concern over the loss of Christian culture in the Philippines overshadows all other sentiments he may have. He reiterated the Japanese fear of a native uprising and revealed that over fifty prominent Manila citizens have been taken into custody. They are being held incommunicado at Fort Santiago. Anti-Japanese feeling continues to run high. The enemy has tried to enforce a harsh physical regime on the people and Filipino pride isn't taking it very well.

The padre told a story of six Filipinos who were made to dig a large hole and then told to lean over it while their heads were chopped off by a samurai sword. Six more natives were forced to bury the bodies.

The priest said that he would try and obtain a microscope for us within the next few days. We certainly could use the instrument for blood work. No word yet from St. M. However, she has only been on the outside for a few days. I expect to hear something later this week.

I understand there is a mistake concerning Sikiguchi's real name. We now learn it's Sakamoto. I think we can compromise on "son of a bitch" and everyone agrees.

The watery soup had a sewage smell tonight. I can't stomach dry rice, so poured the foul liquid over my food anyway. Later we managed to stir up a batter made from ground rice and cooked a batch of pancakes. They didn't taste very good. However, we poured a solution of raw sugar and water over the "delicacy." It wasn't maple syrup, but it served our purpose.

Rumor has it that the American Red Cross reported that they are satisfied with the Japanese treatment of war prisoners. The American Red Cross knows nothing whatever of how the prisoners are being treated. They are only allowed to operate at Santo Tomas, and Santo Tomas is not a prison camp. It's a concentration center for civilians, and there is a hell of a lot of difference. We know that at Santo Tomas the people eat well and live comfortably. In fact, there are those who prefer remaining there instead of living on the outside under the present conditions. As usual the Japanese are creating their own propaganda—making face at Santo Tomas, while the prisoners catch hell. I hope I'm wrong and the A.R.C. didn't make this statement. If so, they have become a malicious agent of the Japanese and should be wiped out.

This evening I was ordered to prepare a list of Filipino patients who would be benefited by immediate transfer to hospitals in Manila— patients who could be aided by treatment we are unable to give them. I submitted my list, but within twenty minutes I was informed that all the Filipinos were to go, and I had better include *all*. I objected vigorously. I felt that to throw up our hands and say that we are so damn helpless was the worst thing we can do. In spite of the conditions here, we have surgical cases that are not endangered by malnutrition, and we can offer more skill and experience than anything they have in Manila. For us to transfer all the Filipinos under guise of our inability to care for them is a bad move at this time. It's an admission that we really don't have a hospital. This will reduce our supplies in two ways—less will be given to us, and much that we have will be taken away. Our salvation lies in asserting ourselves and showing the Japanese that we can handle these cases. Of course, I lost the argument. I couldn't help thinking of "Will Bill" Cubbins, the Orthopod at Northwestern, when he would stand up before the class and shout: "We know we're crazy! But we get results! We are a voice crying in the wilderness!" In this case it sure as hell was a wilderness.

I made my rounds with Wilson. He has kept his sense of humor and I enjoy talking with him. We recalled the "speculum episode" on Corregidor. When the enemy took over, they established a whorehouse on the island and stocked it. The same day a Japanese doctor approached us and asked for a vaginal speculum. He was charged with examining the women and needed such an instrument—naturally. Well, we didn't have a vaginal speculum, but when the Japs say they want something, it's either produced or else. The situation was serious. We finally solved the problem by opening the veterinary case and giving him the nasal speculum for a horse. The Japanese doctor was delighted—perfectly satisfied—thrilled with his new toy.

We hope to have our galley moved back to the lower compound by tomorrow. During the flooded conditions, the kitchen was moved to keep our cooking above water. However, of all the stupid places, the Japanese moved the galley within 25 yards of the dysentery ward— in the midst of sewage and flies by the billions. I'll feel much better after we have our galley back where it belongs.

My smuggled copy of the Manila newspaper contained a long list of Filipinos who are to be released. The Japanese have been turning loose civilians and soldiers at regular intervals, but are not releasing the Filipino Scouts. Moreover, upon release, the Filipinos are required to sign an allegiance to the Emperor. This makes them eligible for military service in the Japanese Army. The Scouts will refuse to sign such a document and the Japanese know it.

According to the newspaper, the American Air Force in Australia has been wiped out and that country is entirely undefended by air. This all boils down to what the Japanese commander on Corregidor told Captain Hoeffel on the day they were discussing the Coral Sea reports: "I think both our governments are lying."

July 29, 1942

The new regime was supposed to take over, but the change has been postponed for a few days. However, during the afternoon a Brigadier General came through on an inspection tour. He had a medic with him whom I'm sure is the little guy we had with us near the end of our stay on Corregidor—a Lieutenant Nogi. I didn't have any contact with the inspection party, but I understand they were very cooperative and promised much—as usual. If Nogi is to be the head man around here, I believe we will be better off than at present.

Hagen is off the sick list and working with Joses at getting the patients in the upper compound properly organized. Sooner or later this hospital administration will realize that if we are to be responsible for all the sick, then we must have complete control over them. None of this wishy-washy halfway stuff will work. I have contended this ever since my arrival at Bilibid, but have been unable to sell the tight ship idea. However, as difficulties arise from the lack of a firm hand, they are slowly seeing the necessity for a close-knit organization. But in the meanwhile, for the sake of being good fellows, or because of a lack of military concept, we continue to make more trouble for ourselves than even the Japanese can think up.

Except for Hagen and Wilson, the rest of the Army still resides in the upper compound—unattached, doing nothing, completely out of the picture. Four Army officers (Craig, Adams, Manning, and Cagey) continue as invalids in the S.O.Q.—stuffing their guts, contributing nothing—not even good morale. With the exception of Craig and Adams, the others—horse manure.

Late yesterday we were notified that more than a hundred "heavy sick" were to arrive from Tayabas. Eight truckloads showed up this afternoon. They were the last of the camp and their medical officer came with them. Two men had died moments before they left and one was dead when we unloaded the trucks. Two more prisoners lasted long enough to be laid out on stretchers, where they immediately expired. Another dozen men, nearly dead, were placed on the ground until the Japanese released them to us. The others were horrible walking creatures, like living dead—dirty, bewhiskered, hollow chested—struggling to carry their few remaining belongings in small bundles.

It was a pitiful sight. As I stood in the prison yard and watched, suddenly all the bitterness and hate that had been building up in me over the past two months seemed to explode. At no other time in my life have I ever hated with the intensity of that moment. I vowed that never again would I be satisfied or content until every vestige of Japan was destroyed—until I have personally known the pleasure of running a bayonet through their guts, starving them, looting them of all they hold dear. Mine is not the feeling of a civilized nation. But the difference between my desire to punish, to torture, to kill, is to meet them with their own Oriental philosophy, and let them die by the philosophy under which they live.

This day couldn't end without another instance of defeatism and the "let George do it" policy cropping up. A prisoner was reported to me as having acute appendicitis. The administration wanted to send the boy to a Manila hospital for the operation. I was so damn mad I could have chewed nails. I offered to see the case and if the fellow needed the operation I would do it right here where it should be done. I didn't stop there either. I was too fed up with this "we can't do it" attitude and proceeded to lay down the law; that as far as our surgical service was concerned, this hospital was going to be a hospital in every sense of the word, and every man on the staff would do anything and everything that had to be done. I examined the boy and, after concluding surgery was necessary, operated on him immediately.

Kusumoto and several Japanese medical officers stopped by while we were in surgery. The operation was a complete success and Kusumoto informed me that he was glad we are able to do such things. He promised to have our sterilizers hooked up at once. I'm not going to hold my breath waiting, but I was very pleased. I still contend that if we act like a hospital, we will be treated as such by the Japanese. I'm also pushing to line up the Japanese surgical cases. Wade, Nelson, and Ferguson are with me, but I'm having a hard time swinging the "George" group over to my side.

I stay hungry most of the time now. The chow hasn't been as edible or plentiful of late and our extras have been held to a minimum. We managed to get a little raw sugar today, but mongo beans are scarce and that is cause for alarm. It's the lowly bean that keeps us going. If they are ever denied, we will find ourselves in dire straits.

The priest never showed up this afternoon. I was expecting him. Also no word from St. M. If this "B" and St. M. hookup is going to take place, it had better happen quickly. I have certain papers in my possession which I can't keep much longer. I must get rid of them. They are to go to St. M. via "B" after she establishes contact with the underground. If I hear from the padre and there is no evidence of a link with St. M., I will have to assume that it can't be done and make other arrangements. I can't afford to implicate myself in this matter.

In the meantime I found out that Trujilio managed to escape to Mindanao. When he was a contact man between the guerrillas and our armed forces he performed excellent service. The Japs had a price on his head—still have. Trujilio is familiar with the Moro people of the southern Philippines and has many friends among them.

Guerrilla activity is continuing throughout Luzon, but I don't know whether it's an organized force or only operates under local chiefs as undirected banditry. If there is organized guerrilla activity I doubt Trujilio will remain in Mindanao—price on his head or not. Trujilio is fearless, crafty, and loves the intrigue. To an ally he's invaluable. To an antagonist he can be bad medicine.

I remember a late afternoon about a week before the war. We sat on his veranda in the light of a flaming Philippine sunset and talked of what we knew was about to happen. Trujilio became emotional as he cried out against the coming invasion of his homeland. He fervently reviewed his blessings and the benefits America had bestowed upon his land and people. His patriotism seemed greater that day than the provincial blind enthusiasm for homeland so commonly expressed by the Filipino with much chest beating and alligator tears. I remember him now as I saw him then, silhouetted against the low red light of early dusk in the tropics. He was taller than most Filipinos and heavier—firmly muscled, broad chested, and slim of waist. His eyes were large and very black, with enormous capabilities for love or hate.

No matter what doubts I may have entertained in the days that followed, I have never doubted that Trujilio was ready and anxious to give his all for liberty and country. Unlike Olympia, Trujilio was not just Filipino—he was Filo-American. Whenever I did doubt him, it was my duty to doubt him. In this business I must doubt first and believe afterwards. I excuse myself on the grounds that the safety of many people depends on my being suspicious of everyone. I must rely on facts, actions, episodes, and instances—not motives nor reasons. I must take them as they occur—their meaning, their value, and their indications. I must learn to determine and evaluate. If experience has taught me to assume the worst, then it has well fitted me for the role I am destined to play behind the scenes in this "other life" of mine. As long as I can doubt men like Trujilio, I have not gone soft and will remain able to fulfill my tasks.

St. M. is the female counterpart of Trujilio, but they couldn't team

for long. They are both very human and sensual. They would clash—
then love. St. M. would fall for him like a ton of bricks. Trujilio would,
for awhile, be her slave. I know them both and it would be a waste to
pair them. They are at their best when working alone. Both are by
nature pursuers and pursued. Both hold a natural key to human
behavior.

I worked on my biographical sketches until late tonight. Little by
little they are taking shape. I would hate like hell to lose all this material after the work I have put into it. I'm taking every precaution
possible and still hope to sneak everything out of here intact.

As I sit on my bunk making these last notes, I look across the
barracks to where Erickson sits reading. He looks so much like Hitler
in appearance—it's striking as hell. But Erickson isn't Hitler by any
means. I could like him more, I believe, if he had a little of the Hitler
in him and less of the purring pussycat and effeminate "lavender and
old lace" complex.

July 30, 1942

Captain McClellan died today—dysentery. He was a nice little guy—
grandson of General McClellan. He had the same physique and manner as his grandfather. I recall the historical legend of how the General
was affectionately called "Little Bill" by his men. I can readily imagine
this "Bill" acquiring the same nickname. He was a fine curly-headed
fellow, mild mannered and quiet.

A desperate situation has arisen. Information from "over the
wall" indicates that food is becoming almost unobtainable. The little
available extras are priced well beyond any money that we have. The
natives refuse to farm the land and it's impossible to bring food into
Manila from the provinces. The local markets have collapsed completely. There is practically no meat on the island. The military has
control of all the rice flour and a family is allowed only one small sack
a week. Mongo beans are also in short supply and the little rice we
receive is brought from Saigon.

There isn't a chance in a million of a Red Cross relief ship steaming into Manila Bay. It's hard to conceive of Tokyo permitting this
sort of thing to occur. We have every reason to believe that our country
has scratched us off their list as a lost cause. Certainly, if they made

no attempt to help us while we were fighting, they surely won't consider it worthwhile now.

I have always felt that sooner or later the time would arrive when the idea of escape would come up for consideration. Tonight the thought presented itself and I have been mulling it over in my mind. The wall at the west end of the compound runs directly between the prison yard and the outside. A ladder and long rope are available. A dark rainy night would be ideal for my plan. I'm sure I can get over the wall, but staying outside will be the problem. It would be best to have a trustworthy contact, but if worst comes to worst, I might try to escape without help—we shall see.

II.

The Notebooks
August 1, 1942 to January 1, 1943

August 1, 1942

Rumors are rife again today. The Russians are reported turning over 200 submarines to us—the Japanese are suffering reverses in Mindanao—we are moving heavy tanks and motorized vehicles into Java—Kusumoto reportedly saying: "If the Japs don't watch out, they will lose Singapore." And so goes the stuff which the boys will dream about tonight.

I understand that back in February, rumors had MacArthur about to enter Manila. One of the departed Colonels, now at Tarlac, naively requested upon going to bed, "to be awakened when the street fighting started."

Olympia stopped by to see me tonight. He and his son will be leaving in the morning—free. We talked awhile and I made my last play at lining him up. He agreed to take a few messages out with him tomorrow—harmless notes, purely trial balloons. Their ultimate handling should tell me a great deal. In any event, it wouldn't be the first time that a semi-patriot served two masters. History is full of them.

August 2, 1942

There is quite a bit of dengue among my staff—always a few down with it at all times. Dysentery is also appearing with alarming frequency among our medical personnel and this is cause for serious concern. Orders were issued regarding the spread of the disease, but as usual no two-fisted directive has been published, hence no attention paid. In every instance where I have advocated strong central command, nothing is done. Sooner or later the need for authoritative decisions arise and everyone comes around to my way of thinking—but by then it's too late, the mischief has already been done.

No sign of "B" again today. I'm becoming a little concerned. In some respects he is so naive and clumsy that I'm afraid he won't survive the Japanese "gestapo" very long if caught. I realize that he's probably just a merciful old man, untrained in espionage, and all the wishing in the world will not make him a professional. Still nothing from St. M. but maybe it's just as well. I think her silence is good judgment. She evidently doesn't want to be allied too closely with "B" even if he means well. I expect her to make contact when and if it's safe. In the meantime I have to do something with these papers. It isn't good medicine for me to have self-incriminating material lying around. I must decide tonight what to do about it.

I acquired a coil of stout rope and hid it deep among the high grass in the upper compound. I worked the ladder along the wall until it's only 25 yards from where I can use it. Every day, I move the ladder a little closer to the corner of the wall. I'm still convinced I'll make use of it someday, and I still haven't given up hope for outside help.

A person can get used to anything eventually. Man is an adaptable creature, and a most interesting animal when the veneer rubs off. With the outer coat of civilization gone, he lays open his inner structure. There are those among us who have covered their crudities of thought and base concepts of life with a thin film of schooling and fine clothes. They have nothing but the shallow cloak of civilization to cover themselves and are sad, disgusting creatures indeed. The fine stock—how well they maintain their poise. Their nobility remains evident through ragged clothes and bewhiskered faces. No one can live among this group of half-starved derelicts and not appreciate the differences in humankind. One can also distinguish the stigmata of training and environment—good and bad. I have never experienced such a study of man reduced to the lowest common denominator. I will remember it, think of it, speak of it, and write of it all the rest of my life.

But even the most sympathetic harden to the horrible human wreckage about us. Ultimately we cease to see them as so dreadful after all. I wonder if we don't interpret this change of viewpoint as an improvement. To some degree I'm sure we do. Many of us consider ourselves healthy and all others sick. Those who claim to be well couldn't do a day's work if their lives depended on it. A good day's work would kill them. It's only our reduced activity that keeps us going. We all have nutritional edema to some extent. Our lips and conjunctiva are white—not red. God knows what our hemoglobin and red cells could be. Our eyes are bad, our teeth are yellow and soft. We can't concentrate for any length of time, but as long as there is somebody worse off than we are, we continue to call ourselves O.K.

There are several of the men who have martyr syndromes and they seem physically better off than the rest of us. Then there are those who are so inverted that they have spent their whole life taking care of themselves. They fought the entire war along these lines, but why shouldn't they. They lived their whole life doing the same damn thing—war only made them worse. It's the nature of the beast.

August 3, 1942

Kusumoto sent for Sartin today and told him to put on "something like civilian clothes" as they were going to town for lunch. Lt. George, who has been treating gonorrhea among the Japanese, was also taken along. This sort of thing has happened before. Kusumoto went to lunch with Duckworth on another occasion. If the Manila newspaper has anything in it deleterious to the Allied cause, Sartin will be allowed to bring a copy back to camp. We hope he may be able to bring back some fruit or a few eggs.

Late night—Sartin returned empty-handed. They had a Chinese dinner—only small talk at chow. Kusumoto felt very big-hearted for this concession. He asked Sartin that if the tables were turned, "would he take a Jap to lunch?" Togonata, Kusumoto's assistant, gave Sartin a brief resume of Kusumoto's war record. It seems Kusumoto received the highest award of the Japanese Army in China. He was called the "Fighting Demon." Same old crap—everybody Kusumoto takes to lunch hears the same speech. Togonata mentioned how the Japanese Army takes its whores right along with them. The men need relaxation after a long campaign. This is not unique—the Italians took "ladies" along with them to Ethiopia. Careful review of this subject reveals that America is about the only country which does not provide for this contingency. What interests me is that the custom does not seem to lessen the incidence of venereal disease. According to Togonata, the system works by rank and time of day—privates in the morning, noncoms in the afternoon, and officers at night. Prices and time limits also go up accordingly. I can see a hell of a lot of drawbacks to this system.

August 4, 1942

I began the day with an emergency operation and took the opportunity to prod Sartin again about being more forceful in having my sterilizer hooked up. I know damn well that the little piece of pipe I need is around here somewhere. There seems to be plenty of pipe for everything else. In the meantime I asked for an emergency request to have our operative packs sterilized in Manila.

More dengue among the staff each day. To some of the crew this disease is a suffering pestilence. Others seem to enjoy their ill health a little too much. As far as the Canacao crowd is concerned, having dengue doesn't change their routine one bit. They lie around in their bunks all day anyhow and always have an excuse for not attending *bango*—too weak or whatever. The only change in their routine I can see is that they now have physiotherapists come in daily to give them massages. What a gang! What a mess!

I'm not a stoic. I appreciate the good things in life as much as anybody. But all my life I have believed that there is a wholesome middle line along which a person can live. Overindulgence in self has made us a nation of inverts. We are neither rugged nor strong—physically or spiritually. Our concept of life lies within our physical being. I can hear the Devil in Kipling's poem: "I'm well o'er sick with Adam's breed"—and understand.

It would be hard for many, but the best thing in the world for the maintenance of our civilization would be if this war could affect all of our country—and I mean ALL. Our future lies in the return to a hardier, less indolent life, wherein living requires an effort. I am merciful and a humanitarian, but not to the degree where the lazy and incompetent set the pace of our life and standards. Such is the case in our nation today. There is no premium on real accomplishment. The premium is on monetary success with as little contribution as possible. The soul of our system is "to have"—not "to earn." Thus we have become soft, confusing our appetites with our rights, and each of us claiming much more as our natural prerogative than we deserve. We loll about on air-cushions of self-inflated ego—a little pinprick and down we go. We can't take it.

It's hot this evening with a low ceiling. The clouds seem to be pressing down upon the steamy tropical mud. Manila is built smack in the middle of a big marsh, and we are on the fringe of the city. The air is dead and heavy. There is no breeze. The thick blue smoke from my black cheroot almost tumbles and falls to the hot soggy ground. Everyone is sitting around half-naked—pouring sweat. The bugs are ferocious.

Early this evening a band of Filipino guerrillas and three Americans were brought into camp. They were captured down south a few days ago. I talked with the Americans. They were sent to Manila by boat and were fed well on the trip. According to the rules of war, and the declared intention of the enemy, guerrillas not surrendering at the time of capitulation have relinquished their rights as prisoners of war. It's hard to understand why they haven't been shot—of course, it's not too late. According to the men I talked with, these guerrillas haven't been very effective. They do little but live off the countryside and the rural civilians. Banditry in the name of patriotism. A good old Spanish custom.

Late tonight the Japanese brought in a prisoner from Pasay. He was caught throwing a note over the fence. Fortunately the note only asked for candy. The Japanese bruised him up pretty bad, breaking a couple of ribs. I questioned the fellow as to any news. It seems that he has been working at Nichols Field repairing the airstrip. He reported that small planes take off every day with bombs and return in a short time empty. I had heard that the Japanese are bombing guerrilla concentrations and chasing the Filipinos into the open. However, it's more probable that these planes are practicing bombing flights. During the day we see many small aircraft going through training tactics and towing target sleeves. This same man reported that there is heavy fighting in Mindanao and Java. Also, Japan has been bombed and the Japanese Navy is no more. The last is interesting because Tokyo reports that "the U.S. Navy is no more." To requote the Jap on Corregidor: "Both our countries are lying."

So now, after another impoverished and fruitless day, I will lay the body down. One last thought though, the day hasn't been a total waste. This practice of mine at being my own biographer may contribute to history. Even in confinement, as humble chronicler of this place, I too may serve. For an historical deed is not finished when it has merely been achieved, but only when an account of it has been handed down to posterity. What we term history does not represent the sum total of all conceivable things that have been done in time and space. "History comprises those small illuminated sections of world happenings which have had thrown upon them the light of practical or scientific description. The figures of the world's heroes would be shadows, and the deeds they did would have slipped into the infinite azure of the past, had it not been for the chronicler who preserves them in his story, or the artist who creatively reconstructs them." Thus sayeth Stefan Zweig in 1938.

August 5, 1942

I spent most of the morning teaching Spanish to Ed Nelson, which brings up a coincidence. I found that the best Spanish teaching system is the Cortina method. However, before I could begin I needed a Cortina book. I had seen a couple around the compound and finally located one. I opened it, and to my surprise, my handwriting was blazoned all over the damn pages. This was the same volume that Bill Grace and I had poured over while we were crossing the Pacific. I then recalled that Bill had given the book to Ken Lowman. Ken had asked for it at Hong Kong—Ken would. He wouldn't buy a copy if his life depended on it. Apparently, with the shuffle of personal effects in the hectic course of war, the book turned up here.

Major Jenson, our Marine paymaster with the 4th Regiment, now at Cabanatuan, came into camp last night with a work party. He had quite a lot to report, and if taken with a dose of salt, is worth repeating. The Japanese permit him to buy food for his camp—a privilege we have been unable to obtain. I told him of Sartin's letter of authority and Jenson seems to think we can arrange to have our supply officer do the buying for the prison. There should be a way to work it out. We still remain the poorest fed of any group of captives around.

Jenson also reported (as coming from the Japanese) that the Geneva Treaty is to be observed. All officers and noncombatants are to be paid, and the medical department eventually will not be considered as prisoners. Of course, everything has to go through Geneva—names, ranks, and organizations—probably sent by foot messenger, carrier pigeon, friendly porpoise, or whatever. Maybe after one or two years we should see results. All of which brings us back to the same old snag. It isn't going to do much good at that late date.

Of more importance, I believe, is the new change of command taking place today. Kusumoto is leaving and a medical officer is moving into the front office. This is the system we lived under on Corregidor. It worked out very well and I hope it will mean a change for the better around here.

Unless some sort of change does take place, we must do more than just wait. I have talked over the prospects of a breakout, but it can't be done without everybody suffering the consequences. However, with the cooperation of a couple of American Wardens, I'm sure I can get out one night, scrounge up some food, make a few contacts, and sneak back in the following night. My immediate compadres are all against approaching the Wardens on the subject. However, the time may come when we have to act. Eventually St. M. will contact me, but I can't wait until she finds it expedient. A monkey wrench must have been thrown into her plans. I have a hunch "B" is involved. Once outside, I know I can make other contacts and I'm sure I can get through the Tondo district at night. I acquired blue denims along with a native hat, and can walk in wooden shoes as well as the natives. I'm brown as any Filipino and browner than many. My one weakness is the scant knowledge of Tagalog, but I can speak Spanish. I could lie low at Garcia's place during the day and have him do the bargaining for me. If anyone can contact St. M., Garcia can.

However, I will need the consent of Sartin to go. I must be accounted for at *bango* and will need help sneaking back into camp— someone to toss me a rope over the wall. My associates are not ready to listen to my plan. Perhaps later, when our situation becomes more desperate, they will agree. But by then the plan may be more difficult to accomplish.

We did better at chow tonight. The soup was thicker and had a few vegetables floating in it. I was hungry and needed filling up. Cecil managed to obtain a few small fish from a Filipino working party. We fried them in deep fat and ate them—bones and all.

The latest rumor is that the Japanese lost 25 ships in the Aleutians and the islands are now in our hands. Also, our subs are taking a deadly toll of enemy shipping.

I tried to imagine what the people back home would say if they could see me now. Somewhere in my possessions I have a picture of myself when I was 18 years old, just after my return from the Mexican border. I was thin-faced, slender-legged, and had a 32 inch waist. Well, I'm right back there today. I certainly am a streamlined specimen. I'll bet that I could walk down the main street at home and not even my best friends would recognize me.

August 6, 1942

The new regime is beginning to make changes. Herri has nothing to do with the Americans anymore—only Filipinos. Time will never eradicate my vow to deal properly with that bastard. He must not get too far away. I don't want to hunt all over Asia for that animal.

This afternoon our new Japanese medical officer came by to introduce himself—it was Nogi. He wears a first lieutenant's insignia, but calls himself a "sergeant doctor." He's clinically minded, speaks a little English, and writes it quite well. Nogi was educated in Germany, but he's definitely Japanese—past master at promises and continually saying, "Yiss! Yiss! No! No! Yiss! Yiss!"—both words meaning the same thing to him. In all fairness to the little guy, he did what he could to help matters on Corregidor.

Jenson is going to take Bob's bedding roll up to him at Cabanatuan. I also gave the Major a note for Bob. I hope that Herthneck can be transferred back to Bilibid one of these days.

August 7, 1942

Our need for intravenous saline is critical, but there has been trouble getting it from the pharmacy. They have a distillery over there, and normal saline could be made if someone would get off their dead ass and make it. Finally it was decided that a fire could be started under the "still"—but only after I built a fire under the personnel first.

I'm not a morale builder. I haven't the factor in my makeup that makes people love me because of my pleasing manner and "good-hearted" personality. I'm of the other extreme, and have disturbed the peaceful coma that most of the men exist under around here. Everybody hides behind various excuses not to be doing their job. I find that in order to be satisfied and able to live with myself, I have to be a bastard all day long. But if that's what it takes to get the work done, then so be it.

The clang of the *bango* bell is now heard several times a day. The new regime is trying to get to know us better. As soon as I began to operate this morning—call for *bango*. I finally managed for Nelson and Wade to carry on and I stood formation. These interruptions will probably continue for another week.

Bango is the Japanese word for "a check by numbers." In the beginning we stood formation and went through the roll call entirely in Japanese. A few face slappings soon produced enough linguistic interest for the men to acquire a slight knowledge of Japanese, such as the words for: Attention! Right Dress! Front! At Ease! Count Off! Dismissed!

However, there was one problem, we had to count off in Japanese. We decided that instead of learning the numbers, it was easier to have each man line up in the same spot every *bango*. In that way a person only had to remember one number.

A typhoon blew in this afternoon with gale-force winds. We battened down the best we could, but nothing is tight or secure in these run-down old buildings. It's quite cold and the lighting is so poor that it's difficult to write. Word was just passed that we must remain inside the barracks for another recount. I wish these bastards would learn to count better. They are almost as bad at addition as I am, and I'm the world's worst adder upper.

I'm fed up with looking out these bars across the "sacred circle" to where the guards stand in their droopy pants, swaggering around like every kid does the first time he's allowed to hang around the fire engine house. But you have to hand it to them—and blush real red. They are great little soldiers. They smacked us all over the arena— hit us with everything but the water bucket.

I remember hearing people say that the Japanese were just a flash in the pan—what we were going to do to them—how they had stretched their supply lines too thin and had completely spent themselves. Now whenever I hear that crap, I remember the old story about the prizefighter staggering cut and bleeding back to his corner. His seconds and manager working away on him, telling him how great he's doing and what a sucker he's making out of his opponent. Then just as the fighter lumbers back into the ring for the next round, he turns to his manager and says, "Youse guys better hold that referee, 'cause there's someone out there beatin' the hell out of me!"

Yep! Those ugly, swaggering, smart aleck little yellow depravities with droopy pants, and two-thirds of them with gonorrhea, are beating the hell out of us.

Believe-it-or-not, I now have a bedfellow. A little lizard has adopted me. I don't know where he goes during the day, but as soon as I unfold my mosquito net for the night, he's right on top. I lie on my bunk and watch him scamper about catching bugs. At times he stays immobile above my head for over an hour. I reach up and tickle his belly with my fingers, round and round he races, up the net and back again. At first he was alarmed when I touched him, but he's used to it now. I don't think he understands what's happening, but he's learning that it's nothing to get excited over. Before this incarceration is over with, he may be holding up his hind leg and begging for his nightly belly rub. I have heard of prisoners developing a friendly intimacy with rats in their cells, but I don't know about lizards. However, friendliness even with a lizard is still friendliness.

August 8, 1942

Another day of *bango—bango—bango*! The count still doesn't come out correct. Somehow we are two men short. We stood in formation this afternoon for two hours in the rain, while guards scampered all over the compound looking for two "lost" Americans. My God, there are 15,000 lost Americans in the Philippines. Why don't they just reach out and grab a couple from another pile. That should settle the issue.

The last call for *bango* came as we were preparing for an emergency appendectomy of an American. He was brought to us by a Japanese doctor. The doctor and the boy's camp commander stayed for the operation. The Japanese Commandant was most solicitous for the lad's welfare and acted very fatherly toward him. After the two Japanese left, the boy told me that they were not in sympathy with the war.

I appreciate these Japanese examples of goodwill. The kindly attitude expressed by the boy's camp commander is typical of what we see throughout the prison camps. The treatment of individuals can be most considerate, but the group as a whole—horrid.

I'm reminded of the words a Japanese officer spoke to me a few days after the surrender: "You are unfortunate," he said, "in being prisoners of a country whose living standards are much lower than yours. You will often consider yourselves mistreated, while we will think of you as being treated well." This officer was a graduate of a large American university.

It's late night and the count goes on—two men still unaccounted for. However, I know that the Japanese had better find the missing prisoners or we are all in for a hard time. The old squeeze—much face slapping and chest beating has already begun. I can see by the latest turn of events just what my escape would mean to the rest of the men. But I think with a little cooperation that I could still get out for one night, unless the Japs pull a "sight" *bango*. The way my gut reaches back to embrace my backbone, I'm ready to try anything once.

Toothpaste is no longer a choice of flavor between Ipana, Squibb, Listerine, or Colgate. It's a case of taste between Fels Naptha, Ivory, or Dutch Cleanser. Soap is just about the only tooth washing material available. I made up a mixture of sodium perborate, sodium bicarbonate, sodium chloride, and soap. It doesn't taste nor smell as good as the highly advertised products, but my teeth feel clean.

We are now washing our used gauze and bandages. They are treated with creosol and then boiled. I remember the old days at St. Croix, where our gauze and bandages were used over and over. Of course, to the Japanese this is standard operating procedure. They never cease to remind us how wasteful we are, while they conserve.

August 9, 1942

"B" finally showed up today. After listening to him I'm convinced that he's practically useless to me. He's a simple minded fellow who means well, but is probably under surveillance by the "gestapo." The reason he gets around as much as he does is apparently because the Japanese appreciate his incompetency, and he's good bait if anyone should happen to fall in with him.

"B" admitted that he's unable to arrange for permission to send medical supplies into us. It's become evident that his Filipino "Chaplain's Aides" are pro-Filipino and not necessarily pro-American. Whatever help we receive from him will be incidental to Filipino help. The priest is a great little pawn being pushed around by his congregation. His unreliability for information became so obvious during our conversation that I'm inclined to ignore everything he reports. A senile recluse can inadvertently become a tool—sometimes useful, sometimes not. The only reason for his being with us at all lies in his papal fidelity, and the fact that under Japanese rule the Catholic Church is about to lose all their property in the Philippine Islands.

The padre still claims that about ninety percent of the Filipino aristocracy are for the Americans. I seriously doubt that. There is a large Spanish element in the islands who still remember that we took the Philippines from Spain in 1898, and they look upon the Japanese as liberators.

According to "B," the Japanese are losing no time in establishing their culture among the natives. School teachers are required to spend time learning the Japanese language and customs.

I also heard that all priests and nuns are under suspicion. That was no surprise to me. I did manage to send one message outside today. Incidentally, the punishment for having notes or messages in one's possession is to burn the note and have you drink the ashes. Not so bad if it isn't a twenty page letter.

General Tanaka has taken over command of the Japanese Army on Luzon. It's reported that he's not a strong military man. Ever since the surrender, the Japanese have continued to replace their elite fighting men with the "home guard" and reserves. Most of these soldiers are mere boys. It's apparent that they never expected any further military activity in this area.

The rumor mill has slowed down considerably. The progress of the "home team" has failed to manifest any further evidence of early liberation, or anything else. The rumor addicts admit they have been duped, but they will fall just as hard for the next batch of favorable news that comes along.

Colonel Adams, naive soul that he is, still expects MacArthur to arrive any day and liberate us. Poor old fellow, he lives in his dream world and that doesn't hurt him one bit. I also have hopes, but hopes should be based on logic, not on the fantastic fairyland miracles that these poor devils expect.

Speaking of Adams and his waiting to be rescued, reminds me of when we were taking our daily shellacking from the air, and being ripped to pieces by enemy artillery on the ground. Many of the men still looked seaward and listened constantly for relief ships. Then at night when we tuned in Manila radio, the station would always be playing "Waiting for Ships That Never Come In." This wasn't a co-incidence either. Copies of Manila newspapers reaching us would comment on this Japanese "theme song."

August 10, 1942

I dropped over to Ed Nelson's bunk before making my rounds this morning and was invited to come into "Lake Nelson." Ed has carefully placed his bunk with geometric precision directly under four leaks in the roof. He says that he's assured of constant high tide during the rainy season. The frustrating thing about the whole situation is that we have tar and material to repair the roof, but the Japanese refuse to let us on top of the building. They claim we can signal from there.

I stopped in S.O.Q. and outlined the future disposition for several cases. A few of these guys are beyond redemption. In every ward there are always a bunch of "goldbricks" of the very worst caliber. Most of them are mental derelicts to begin with. The war didn't cause their total absence of brains and guts—it only drew attention to the fact.

Art Barrett is laid up again—never physically strong. Al Smith is somewhat better but far from well. Ed Ritter is very jaundiced—looks like hell. Berley is back on his feet, but wobbly and down to skin and bones. LaVictoire is no sicker than usual, which means that he still sits and looks out the window or else lies on his bunk in a semi-cataleptic state. Clyde Welsh has dengue and is enjoying ill health. In a way this has been a blessing. It has helped to keep his mouth shut—which is appreciated by all.

We received orders today that 108 Filipino patients were to be released for hospitalization at local hospitals. While the sick were being loaded into trucks at the front gate, one of our corpsmen who is married to a Filipino girl was helping load the trucks. His wife is a nurse and "just happened" to be with the vehicles. The corpsman knew he was recently a father, but had never been able to learn if the baby was a boy or a girl. The guards kept a close watch to make sure that there was no contact between our men and the local medics. The corpsman was within speaking distance of his wife and there was nothing he could do about it. Finally the age-old prison system of communication came to his aid. Word was passed by whisper from one end of the long line to the other—it's a girl.

Our new interpreter [Yakasiji] believes that prison life will improve for us. We can use a whole lot of improvement. The observations of all who pass through this camp is that we are the poorest fed prisoners in the Philippines.

Dry rice was the menu this noon, but I couldn't stomach the stuff. Later in the day I acquired a bit of native cocoa and made a thin chocolate paste. At the evening meal I poured the sauce over my rice. A few days ago I mixed cottonseed oil with acetic acid and made my own "salad dressing."

August 12, 1942

I had been in my bunk for about an hour last night trying to fall asleep, when I suddenly heard someone in the shadow of the building next to mine whisper my name. I failed to recognize the voice and waited. Momentarily a man stepped out into the open. He was holding a small package. I eased out of my bunk and stood in the dark of the doorway. The parcel was pushed into my hands and the stranger disappeared in the darkness. I stowed the package under my bedding, then strolled quietly over to the barred window that looks out over the "sacred circle" and guardhouse. The sentries were seated around a table—nothing unusual astir.

I carried the box into the toilet and opened it under the light. It contained a sack of sweet smelling coffee and a small box of cigars. Not that the coffee wasn't welcome, but I decided to try the tobacco first. The Japanese drink coffee, but they don't smoke "stogies." I wasn't the only one who knew that. Underneath the cigars was a message (I can't write down how this contact was made, but will remember it). This was a dummy run that St. M. had tried and it worked to perfection. Her note mentioned that she doesn't intend to use this method again, but outlined other plans for contact after the first of September. She had reglued the seal of the cigar box and filled in the cracks with lipstick. The lipstick seal was unbroken, therefore I knew the box had not been tampered with. Another system she uses is to mark each cigar with dots and arrange them in order. If the line of dots is disturbed, then I know that the box has been searched.

St. M. reported she is busy and making progress. Her plans are excellent. I intend to send a message out to her tonight. I must warn her against making any unnecessary contact with me. I can be of no help and it's not worth the risk of detection.

Sartin received a letter from Nogi today. It was a reply to a request for medicine. Nogi's letter was significant. It was the first time that the Japanese ever answered one of our written requests. Its substance indicates a feeling of professional duty on the part of the writer. At the same time the letter contained only refusals. However, in all fairness to Nogi, the refusals have logical basis in circumstances beyond his control.

Late this afternoon a whole bevy of the damndest looking kids arrived in the compound. In our country they would probably pass as Boy Scouts. Crosseyed, nearsighted, and awkward, they look like a bunch of misfits who couldn't qualify for dogcatcher. The little fellows are semi-uniformed and run around in a fog. They remind me of the comic burlesque type of Jap such as found in the Charlie Chan stories. I understand that they are the "volunteer army" or armed civilian group who are to relieve the soldiers as our guards. What a gang! They don't know whether to salute us—make us salute them—run us through with a bayonet—or commit *hari-kari* for our benefit. They pry into everything like a pack of raccoons. Throughout the war I have managed to keep my only razor. One of the little bastards saw me shaving and he just had to shave also. It was apparent that the kid had never shaved before in his life—he had one hair on his lip. I foolishly let him experience the phenomenon, but then he took my razor over to the guardhouse so that all his buddies might enjoy the thrill. I thought I had lost the razor for good but he brought it back. All I lost was my last blade. I couldn't use it anymore.

Kusumoto supplied each of us with a parole form that we are required to sign, swearing not to attempt an escape under any circumstances. I guess if we break parole we lose our rights as prisoners of war, and in event of recapture we can be shot. We all signed the dumb thing. I could see no point in not signing the paper. As far as I'm concerned, I can put my name on anything and then interpret it according to my own national policy. I doubt if my conscience will keep me awake nights either.

A working party arriving back to camp tonight reported that the Filipinos were very generous to them. They continually ran up to the prisoners, giving the men cakes, candy, and ice cream—refusing to take money in payment. Several of the Japanese guards noticed the Filipinos holding up two fingers like a "V" and asked the prisoners what it meant. One of the wisecracking Americans replied, "Two dollars." It wasn't long before the guards were flashing the "Victory" sign. Someone's face is going to be red instead of yellow the first time a knowledgeable Japanese officer sees that.

This incident reminds me of a similar occurrence a few years back when Japanese made ladies pajamas were sold in the United States. The garments were embroidered with beautiful symbols which, of course, nobody could read or even thought of as meaning something. Finally a person cognizant of Japanese writing called attention to the fact that they were lewd and lascivious expressions. However, by that time the pajamas had been disseminated all over the country.

August 15, 1942

The latest news is that the road which cost so many lives at Tayabas ended up serving no useful purpose to the Japanese. Hardly a week after completion, guerrillas destroyed the bridge. They cut away the bridge uprights and the rain and floods washed the whole damn thing away. I also learned that the *Tai-sas* have been shipped to Formosa. I hope that their sailing was well advertised if there is any truth to the reports of American submarine activity in these waters.

An emergency meeting was called this afternoon. Word reached us that Gooding was making up a list of non-medical personnel to go to Japan with Kusumoto. Several of Gooding's pals are on the list and they don't want to go. They are appealing to us for help. This jump to Japan by the Field Marshal is not exactly surprising. He and Kusumoto are two of a kind—birds of a feather.

I prefer not to be a part of these conferences. My reaction to this affair is to let the whole damn bunch go to Japan. They threw in their lot with Gooding when it meant power for them over us. Now let them stew in their own juice and lie in the bed they made. This is war—in case we forgot. If it was a question of our neck or theirs, as far as I'm concerned, it would be ours. If we pull a shady act and place them on the sick list, and the Japs find out about it—which they will, then we have endangered the welfare of everybody for a questionably loyal few. To hell with them—let them sweat.

August 16, 1942

The priest showed up today and created a hell of a problem for us. Last Sunday we explained that we needed a microscope in the worst way, but we didn't want it sneaked into the prison. It would have to be delivered legitimately and reported to the Japanese for Nogi's approval. A microscope isn't something we can hide because it would be in continuous use.

So, wouldn't you know it, "B" shows up this morning with a microscope that he sneaked into the compound. We were naturally very grateful, but again tried to explain to him that doing it his way was a mistake. If the Japanese learned of this it would endanger our future chances of having anything else brought into camp.

Well, we finally decided to go see Nogi and find out how he felt about the padre giving us a microscope. When we reached the front office, only Kusumoto was there (he's apparently still boss until he ships out). "B" mentioned that he had a scope which he would like to lend our medical department. Kusumoto thought about the request for a few minutes, then instructed "B" to bring the instrument to his office. He, Kusumoto, would deliver the microscope to us.

This was rapidly becoming a comedy of errors and a cat-and-mouse game all in one. We had to hustle back to the hospital, repack the microscope, and let the padre sneak it back out the front gate.

This incident was just another case of the awkward spot that the poor guy puts us in with his efforts to do good. I can't help but feel that the "gestapo" is aware of every move "B" makes, but will let him operate as long as he's not endangering their position. They probably hope he will lead them to bigger game.

There is a new development in the Field Marshal's move to Japan. In the presence of Kusumoto, Gooding made a comment that "he would prefer to stay here with his unit that he has served with for so long." Kusumoto then suggested that Sartin speak to Nogi about the possibility of Gooding remaining at Bilibid. I think it's a cover-up for Gooding to be able to say that he wanted to stay, but had no choice in the matter.

Kusumoto told us that he's not leaving for Japan until October. That probably means that he will be out of here in a couple of days. It seems that in all my experience with the Japanese, they consider it prime duty to give false information, even in affairs of no consequence.

I understand that the prisoner list we made the other day was for the purpose of notifying the United States, through Geneva, that the names appearing thereon are alive and kicking. The Japanese expect the list to arrive in the States by the first of next year. There are actually a few men around here who believe that we will beat the list back. I would like to share their optimism, but I'm too much of a realist to place much stock in that daydream.

We had a disciplinary board meeting this afternoon. Most of the cases are the result of crooked dealings and the handling of money for food. Each case is judged on its individual merits. We have had a few drug problems, but that situation is clearing up slowly.

A rumor is circulating tonight that the ship carrying the Colonels to Japan was captured by an American submarine and the prisoners were taken aboard. I really had expected to hear that the ship had been torpedoed. Maybe that rumor will make the rounds tomorrow.

August 18, 1942

Last night I had an experience—the kind you read about in spy novels. I was sitting by my bunk knocking out a few lines of diary, when Gooding appeared and invited me over to his quarters on the other side of the compound. I had been "honored" on one or two other occasions by his visits, but each time he had an axe to grind, so I felt sure that I was in for another argument. However, when I arrived, the "Field Marshal" gave me a cigar and a drink. After a short conversation, he asked me if I would like to take a few pictures of the prison yard. This came about while he was showing me his expensive German camera.

In the meantime, Gooding was putting away quite a bit of booze and growing more and more friendly. I began to feel like a mouse in the lair of a cat. So far nothing had been said about the purpose of my visit. Finally, about an hour later, Gooding turned to me and delivered a proposition. "How would you like to take a run outside?" I knew I heard him correctly and that he wasn't fooling, but I thought he was going to accompany me. I knew that Gooding was allowed to make excursions outside occasionally, but I still wasn't sure what was transpiring or where I fit into the picture. Before I could answer, however, he added, "I'll get them to let you out and back in. You have to arrange your time with the guard."

I had to think fast. I realized that he intended to let me go outside alone. If I jumped at the idea, he would know I had a definite place in mind to head for. If I'm under suspicion it may not be wise to take him up on the offer. I answered that a trip outside for the novelty of it would be interesting, but I had no particular place to go—however it would be a break in the routine. All the while I was yacking away, I kept thinking just where the hell I would go, or should I go anywhere at all—was this some kind of a trick. I realized that I couldn't procrastinate all night. I figured that once outside the prison I could size up my possibilities and either carry on to an objective, or else return as I saw fit. I agreed to the journey.

Minutes later, my well-imbibed "friend" and I ambled over to the front gate where he jabbered in Japanese with the guard. The sentry soon got the idea and pointed to the clock, showing me that I had to be back by two o'clock when he went off duty. I asked Gooding what I should say if I was apprehended by a Japanese patrol while outside the prison. He told me not to say anything except that I had been sent on an errand and was trying to find my way back to Bilibid. That excuse didn't set too well with me, but I thought I could get to where I intended to go without being stopped.

Once outside the gate and into the street, I headed east along the dark boulevard. The entire city was in complete darkness, except where tiny slivers of light shown under the doorways of a few houses and closed stores. I had gone about two blocks when I heard the shuffling sound of approaching Japanese. I noticed a group of soldiers across an empty lot. They were marching in twos and trailing their rifles. I waited quietly until they had all passed, then I crossed the boulevard at a wide intersection. I saw no one else and soon reached the old Spanish building that houses the Sin Singan Clinic.

I don't feel it wise to continue in detail what transpired after that. Suffice to say, I made my way back to Bilibid safely. While on the outside I contacted St. M. and now know much more than I knew yesterday. I accomplished a great deal, and was able to help the underground in many respects. St. M. is doing a great job. I'm convinced more than ever that the Japanese will never subjugate these people.

I have been waiting all day for repercussions from my evening stroll. So far nothing—it will come. This was not just a drunken idea. It's face saving for something. I have a hunch, but nothing definite— time will tell.

August 19, 1942

Another contingent of Filipinos left today for O'Donnell. I heard the story of these boys—why they play sick and try to avoid that hellhole. If they are ill or invalids, they are sent to a hospital or home. The healthy men are sent to O'Donnell where they are put through a Japanese propaganda school. From there the Filipinos are sent out into the provinces and ordered to disseminate the "lies" among their own people. Others are trained as police units and sent out to round up guerrillas. The Filipinos don't want to take up arms against their own countrymen. They also know that if they start spreading propaganda, the guerrillas will make dead meat out of them. It's a tough spot to be in. That's why so many of the natives put on a sick and disabled act.

I saw by the Manila newspaper today that there has definitely been a battle down around the Solomon Islands. Washington is preparing the people for a casualty report that will floor them. It may be so. Landing operations are always costly, but that's the only way we are going to win this war. The Japanese have done it repeatedly. The question is—was the objective worth the cost? Losses are to be expected. The sooner we realize that fact, the better off we will be. I hate the idea as much as anybody else, but war is a bloody business and we have been too conservative as it is.

August 20, 1942

Another day—have managed to keep busy every minute—usual routine of ward rounds and consultations—more literary activity and time for Spanish lessons. But somehow this day hasn't been as productive as others. I measure the success of my days by how well I can forget, not how well I can remember. I try to erase from my conscious mind how sweet life can be, or else I will surely go mad.

A few of the people in this camp are masochistic. Clyde Welsh for example. Every day of his life, Clyde sits for hours, pouring over the same six letters he received from the States before the war even began. He has read and reread them so many times that he knows every comma and semicolon. He insists on reading certain passages aloud over and over again. It's no wonder he's pooped out all the time and lives a martyr's existence. Clyde is the world's most bromidic bromide. He shaves with an electric razor because it's the latest thing in razors. He plays golf because "one must play golf." Poor fellow!

I managed to do a little mending and tailoring tonight. I located a package of blue dye and will color my tunic, shirt, and two pair of shorts—my entire wardrobe. Mildew and poor laundry facilities raise hell with our clothes, especially since none of us had much to begin with. We look like tramps compared to some of the men who arrive in camp. But even they are eventually reduced to the bare essentials.

I have been on the run ever since the war started. I was bombed out of Cavite and barely escaped from Olongapo ahead of the enemy. I arrived at Mariveles in time for its first air raid, then on to Corregidor for the first air attacks there.

With each move I saw people part with their personal belongings and curse the emergency that made them do so. I'm glad I lost everything at the opening bell. Since then I have been cleaned out several times and replaced my essentials over and over again. A shirt from a dead soldier; a pair of shoes from a blasted supply dump; a discarded helmet from the roadside.

All of us at one time or another have found our belongings too heavy to carry and threw them away. But if a poor fellow comes along and benefits from what we have discarded, then our efforts haven't been in vain.

The razor I use was willed to me verbally by the owner before he died. The pen I write with belonged to an aviator—last seen as his PBY was losing altitude with smoke pouring from its belly. My canvas bedding roll belonged to an officer who was hog-tied one night by the Japanese and carted off from Corregidor. He was never heard from again.

I fled Cavite clad only in my bloody operating gown, khaki pants, shirt, shoes, steel helmet, and gas mask. I made a quick stop in Manila for two shirts, trousers, an extra pair of shoes, and a few toilet articles. However, I lost it all at Olongapo. I replaced my shirts, shoes and toilet gear at Corregidor. I also acquired a bar of soap, a mess kit, and a commander's hat. I arrived at Bilibid with a razor, comb, two shirts, two pair of shorts, an extra pair of shoes, steel helmet, and bedding roll.

In the past few months I have acquired a couple of towels, mosquito netting, a few handkerchiefs, and a raincoat. My greatest loss was the food that I looted from Corregidor and packed in with the medical supplies we brought to Bilibid.

So goes the war! I haven't had a damn thing since it started. Several times I watched men trying to save their dress clothes, fancy boots, and other valuables. It breaks their hearts to leave their possessions behind. I didn't have the opportunity to sort through my things. I was chased out, leaving everything.

I later discovered that my heavy boots turned up on the feet of a naval officer who spent the night in my bombed out quarters on Cavite. I also heard that one of my uniform caps is now in Australia and my binoculars in Cebu. War is very communistic—everybody's stuff belongs to everybody else—nobody owns anything—everybody has nothing.

August 21, 1942

St. M. smuggled a box of food into camp last night. As a result I actually ate a piece of fried chicken and a papaya. She was a lifesaver, and I don't mean perhaps. I only was able to talk with her for a few minutes. She's leaving for other parts and will be gone for a few weeks. St. M. didn't look well—showed signs of beriberi. I gave her a liberal supply of B-1.

I spent most of the afternoon investigating the case of a young Army fellow who apparently swindled over half the prison out of money, watches, food, and God knows what else. The more I looked into the accusations, the more I was inclined to punish the victims for contributing to the delinquency of a minor by putting temptation in the way of this nineteen-year-old mental defective who has the mentality of a ten-year-old. I'm having LaVictoire examine the youth to see if we can get him corralled into the status of institutional care— more for the safety of the rest of the morons than anything else.

August 22, 1942

These Japanese are unbelievable. Today they sent us a slab of ice, and frozen throughout its entire length were a bunch of little fish about the size of sardines. The only way we could use the fish was to put ice and all into an iron cauldron, boiling heads, tails, bones and guts. It made a stinking mess, but it was soup.

Cecil managed to locate a can of rice flour and a couple of eggs. We whipped up a bread-cake something or other. St. M. had given me a little garlic and a few hot peppers. I mixed them with acetic acid, salt, and mineral oil. We used the mixture as a dressing to pour over our rice. After that smelly fish soup, this was a banquet.

Nogi stopped by this afternoon. He said that our commissary officer will be allowed to go to town occasionally and buy for us. On the surface this sounds O.K., but what do we use for money? Not only are we down to our last peso, but the merchants are afraid of Japanese occupation money. Secondly, this still leaves the buying in the hands of Gooding and his tribe. They will get first crack at the goodies and we will end up dividing whatever is left. It's another case of the tail wagging the dog.

I talked with Sartin and suggested that he also go into town with the Wardens, or else send one of our men along. I'm afraid that I'm still a voice crying in the wilderness.

As a result of the latest buying trip there were four papayas available for the entire camp—after the Wardens had taken out their share. Everybody drew lots for the privilege of paying fifty cents for a ten cent papaya. This buying system could be more equitable under the right guidance, but as it is, nothing has changed. It's only another example of officer lethargy, incompetency, and the lack of ironhanded discipline at the top.

Pfeiffer was in town today and reported that the Filipinos are very resentful and arrogant toward the Japanese. The natives came right up to Pfeiffer as he walked with his guard and remarked, "He won't be with you long!" At the same time the Filipinos would point to the guard. The Jap understood, but nothing was said or done about the incident.

Kusumoto has served notice that traffic over the wall must stop. There has been an increasing amount of food being tossed into the compound by the Filipinos. It's bad business and can only end up hurting us.

August 23, 1942

It was one year ago today that I arrived in the Philippines. Much has transpired, but I can honestly say that I'm exactly in the situation I expected to be in at this time. "Fish heads and rice" was definitely my destiny. It was expected of me to come out here and be captured. All of a great plan. My contribution to the MacArthur political prestige. Swell plan. Great going F. D. R. However, it isn't all that simple when our death rate is so high that there won't be an American alive on these islands in another nine months. I guess that if I had it all to do over again, I would still be here. I'm just an incurable damn fool—without a doubt.

The guards beat Haase with an iron rod this morning and made him sit on his heels for hours. I witnessed the entire incident. One of the Japs entered Haase's quarters and engaged the corpsman in conversation. The guard remarked that the Ingersol watch Haase was wearing was no good. Haase replied that the Japanese stole his good one. The guard became angry and hauled Haase to the guardhouse where Haase was struck with the iron bar and forced to squat the torturous position. I have decided that these yellow-bellied bastards had better plant me under within the next few months, or I'll show them what amateurs they really are as sadistic specialists.

I managed to hear from Bob Herthneck, but under unusual circumstances. A Filipino girl by the name of Francesca has a boyfriend at Cabanatuan who knows Bob, and occasionally she hears from her friend. Francesca was sitting in a restaurant in Manila and overheard a person at a nearby table mention that he was able to sneak messages into Bilibid. Francesca scribbled a note on a scrap of paper, wrote my name on it, and addressed it to Bilibid. As she left the restaurant she dropped the note on the speaker's table and hurried out the door. I received the message the very next day. It said: "Bob Herthneck needs money—everything under control." I knew that note was genuine because of the remark "under control." It was one of Bob's favorite expressions. Due to this turn of events, I was able to send him a return message—but no money. I'm broke too.

Worked on my literary efforts today and Spanish class as usual. More stinking fish again—couldn't eat it. This was a day that might just as well not have been lived at all.

August 24, 1942

Late last night, a Lieutenant Isodoro of the Philippine Army showed up at the hospital looking for me. He was captured on Corregidor and recently brought to Bilibid from Fort Santiago. He has been placed in charge of the Filipinos in camp. Even as I write this, I'm still unable to explain last night's episode, but will learn of it eventually. One can't question too closely with their associations these days. Isodoro told me that the Japanese had permitted his wife and baby to visit him, and she brought certain items which "he wanted to share with the Commander." I tried to appear understanding and appreciative. As a result he handed me eight hen eggs, four bananas, two mangoes, and a package of rice cookies. That would be a week's ration, but of course I shared the food with the other men. After Isodoro left, I tried to figure out what all this meant as I knew no reason for his generosity.

Therefore, I made it a point today to see Isodoro and have a talk with him. I discovered that he knows Trujilio and they have worked together. He also knows Olympia, but I don't believe that he's had any contact with St. M. I'm sure the reason he saw me has something to do with people we both know. I'm inclined to think that more will develop with Isodoro later. He has more on his mind than just food sharing.

Lists! Lists! Lists and more lists! They are a habit with the Japanese. They continually want a list made out for this or that, whether it makes any sense or not. Late today they asked for a complete inventory of everything in the hospital, and they want it by morning. This may mean that the final turnover of command is about to take place—then again it may mean nothing.

Another problem arose tonight. We discovered that Gooding, in order to make his *bango* count come out correct, has forged a couple of death certificates. We learned about this by accident when the Japanese sent over a batch of the filled out forms for my signature. However, I recognized the forged names and refused to sign the false certificates. Since only the "Field Marshal" has been handling this task, I returned the forms to the Japanese. I also attached a note stating that the certificates can't be signed as the subject named people never died. Meanwhile, Gooding is on the sick list—supposedly dengue, but each time I see him he's just plain drunk. It will be interesting to see what happens now. There is a lot of truth to the old adage that if you give a person enough rope he will sure as hell hang himself.

This day has been no different than any other. It's very hot and the old barracks buildings simmer and sizzle like an oven. There is a sameness to every day that could be maddening and a few men do show occasional signs of slipping into a bomb-wacky state. On the whole, however, most of us are able to cope—especially the inverts among us who sit and do nothing. Someday when I look over these pages, I wonder if I will remember any of the days individually? Probably very few, but who wants to remember them anyway. I have my own list—things I will remember—things I will forget.

August 25, 1942

If we ever get back home, I think we should be locked up and gradually brought back to civilization. But just to shake us out of a tree and hustle us back into a world that has forgotten who we are—to put clothes on us and make us look like other people—to turn us loose on an unsuspecting public—hell, that wouldn't be fair to either of us. We can't even be trusted with a knife and fork after using our fingers and a spoon all this time.

To go for days and never have shoes on your feet—to gather around a rice bucket and dip your ration out with a wooden stick—to drink watery slop out of a hollowed out coconut shell—to squat around a fire with a half-dozen practically naked comrades and heat mongo beans, or boil a tenth run of coffee in a blackened tin can. You can't do these things day in and day out with nothing to look forward to except the mud, heat, flies, and the stink. You can't do this and then snap back into a world that can never comprehend what it's like—or even believe it could happen.

To sit for hours with a friend in utter silence and watch the sun go down behind the high white walls—to think and know he's thinking the same bitter thoughts you are—to know that he also sits and listens for the boom of guns and the wham of bombs that would mean the Yanks are coming. It's no wonder our minds become distorted—our concepts out of step with the world back home. It makes one wonder if we are missing that much—if we really want to go back to neckties, lambchops, and scotch and sodas.

To sit and remember how, through the hell of shell and bomb-torn months, we sat and waited for reinforcements. And then the news that everything must go to England—Churchill had seen F. D. R. again. Americans were arriving in Ireland. Someone had done a "wrong-way Corrigan" with our convoy. God, how that let our troops down.

Then to lie awake at night fighting mosquitoes and feeling un-comfortable, and wondering if our discomfort isn't just hunger. To feel we are forgotten—no longer a living part of the life back home. Of course, we are still a memory. It hasn't been that long. But by now our friends, relations, and even our creditors have come to realize what we should have realized long ago—just how little we matter in the scheme of things. We are gone!

The sun still rises in all its glory out of the eastern rim of Ches-apeake Bay. Old Tidewater Virginia still lies bathed beneath the bright benignant moon. Spring arrives with the dogwood, May flowers, and violets among the hills. Summer at the beach—golf, tennis, bright sunshine. The sports pages scream baseball, and there are new mu-sical hits for the season. Autumn—rich in golden crimson colors and the fragrance of dry burning leaves in the air.

Yes, life goes on very much the same. New names, new faces, and new customs take our place. To return to it we would be like ghosts—spirits of the dead revisiting the realm of our past. We are there but not a part of it. We are revered but beyond the pale.

As I lie on my bunk trying to sleep, I can hear the "knock-knock" of the carpenter as he works far into the night, making tiny crosses for the burial plot in the upper compound. A shadowlike figure ap-pears in the doorway and walks silently to a nearby desk, a sheet of paper in his hands—the report of another death.

There is enough fight left in most of us to justify it all "for the flag." But there are many of us who know we are here because of a foul system. That we have been sacrificed upon the altar of political prestige in behalf of a spurious ideal—a false premise. We are here because of ignorance, incompetency, bigotry, and selfishness. We are here because of our misconception of civilization. The ideals set forth for man are swell. But the first criterion of worthiness for such ideals is the ability to recognize that man at large is not yet ready for the life we insist upon for him. Basically man is still a beast.

No, I don't think we should suddenly be thrown back into a world that we no longer know, and which could never know, or be kind to us as we are.

This has been a miserable day and I have done nothing worth a damn. I think I must have dreamed a lot last night because I started out the day in a low frame of mind. I have been homesick as hell all day. I try to persuade myself that someday I will return and everything will be just like it was when I left. That there will be a life full of happiness and love. I have fought all day to try and believe that all is not over—that there is more to my existence. But with the cold heart of a realist I now come to the end of another day. And although sad about it, I remain convinced that all the good things in life must be forever in the memory of what has been. Only by living in my heart can they ever be known again. There are events which do not end when we consider them over. They live forever as a part of us. But although we are happy in having lived them, they hurt us because we realize that they are no more.

August 26, 1942

The day was born in a grey drab dawn. Another day of not knowing where night ended and day began. A typhoon blew in from the China Sea with gale force winds and torrential rain, and by afternoon we were storm bound again. I sloshed through my usual routine and spent most of the afternoon listening to disciplinary cases.

A sudden conference was called by the Japanese. We must declare all monies we have in our possession for deposit with their paymaster. The Japanese will then dole our money out to us a little at a time for buying purposes. Their justification for this decision is to save our money for us so that when we return home we will have a few dollars. They also say that they may even give us interest. This sounds good, but when I recall that it's exactly the same thing which happened on Corregidor, and we lost almost all the money we had, I'm a little hesitant. If we lose the cash we now have, it would mean only one thing—starvation. We can't survive on the rations that the Japanese provide and we seem to be faring worse each day. It's only the few items we have been able to buy that has sustained us. This situation is truly serious. Nogi assured me that the idea as presented is bona fide, but that isn't consoling. He said our money will be placed in Japanese banks in Manila and he thinks that we will be able to keep a certain amount.

Nogi also mentioned the Japanese intention to pay us, but he said, "I don't know how much you will be charged for food." This only means that we will have to buy our rice with the money they give us. That's O.K. if we can buy the rice with Japanese bayonet money—it won't be good for anything else.

Sartin and I held a conference late this afternoon with Joses and Welch. We knew that we couldn't advise anyone on what to do about declaring their finances. As for ourselves, we divided up our remaining money so that none of us had a preponderant amount—at the same time saving a portion for eventualities. Of course, this also places us at a disadvantage in that if we buy more than we have declared, the Japanese will know we held out on them. On the other hand, if we give them all our money, then we are certainly in desperate circumstances. It's a no-win situation any way you look at it.

Later this evening, I convinced Sartin to go to the Japanese and let them know that we are not a party to the falsification of the death certificates. He finally did tell Nogi of the irregularities. Nogi was very pleased and seemed glad that we mentioned the problem to him. It was also apparent that the Japanese were wise to the fact that something was wrong. The Field Marshal is out for no good and we can't afford to become involved in any deception.

I understand that the Japanese have prohibited the use of Spanish in the islands. Their cultural implantation program goes on. They are now running Japanese language lessons in the newspapers. A recent contest for a "national slogan" was won by a Japanese matron, which when translated literally means: "Let us further the coprosperity sphere in East Asia by learning the Japanese language."

For some reason I haven't been the least bit interested in learning the Japanese language. There is a psychological factor here of course. Eventually I will overcome it because I should. It would further my ability to actually oppose the Nippon influence. Their own language can also be used against them.

August 27, 1942

A Japanese officer came through camp this morning on a "visiting fireman" sort of tour. He talked quite a bit about the galley and our rations. They all do, but nothing is ever done about it.

Gooding is still hanging around the hospital. He's very quiet and behaving like a martyr—that's tough. I impressed upon Sartin the importance of making a note in our log about the forgery incident and holding action over the "Field Marshal's" head until after the war. Gooding would then be eligible for court-martial—and should get one.

August 28, 1942

This is my 114th day as a prisoner of war. During the hostilities, before Corregidor, I often wondered how it would feel to be awakened one morning to something besides the blasting of guns, the wham of bombs, and the smell of burnt powder. Well, I now know that one can waken to worse things. I can assure you that if I ever get out of here and have a chance to hang upon my wall a picture of our class (Bilibid, 194?), it will never arouse within me any desire to return to my old Alma Mater for any class reunions. I'm sure that if we ever did come back as an old alumni group, the Japanese would sure as hell serve us rice, water lily soup, and fish heads.

However, we are in a mess and must carry on—shrug our shoulders and try to rise above the humiliation of being smacked around. If we can't muster up any real remaining self-respect, we sure as hell can keep alive our spirit of hatred and vengeance. This feeling comes natural to some of us. I'm surprised how much it has come to predominate my thoughts. I have always been too cosmopolitan in spirit—too prone to allow for racial characteristics—too apt to see both sides. But not anymore. I now have definite views on life. I can hate like hell when I have to hate—and I do hate now. I could kill for 24 hours a day and still never feel satisfied enough to attain my old benevolent state toward mankind again.

Word from St. M. today. Major General Miramoto leaves by plane tomorrow for Davao. The Japanese have several "high ranking" American prisoners there, but she doesn't know their identity.

Sartin had another conference with Nogi this morning. Nogi says, "So solly—no meat." However, the Jap doctor insists that as soon as he gets better organized, the hospital will fare better. We have heard that story for so damn long that it doesn't even register anymore. Nogi is trying to increase our protein allotment, but if this war isn't over soon, there won't be enough of us left to worry about. Our rice and water lily diet isn't conducive to longevity. The water lilies are the stalks of a marsh plant that is about as big around as a green lead pencil—and almost as tough to chew. The native name for the plant is *kang-kong*. There's no taste to it whatsoever and I imagine that its food value is absolutely nil.

Rumors abound throughout the camp today. The Americans are supposed to have taken several islands down south and also the Marshall Islands. This latest flurry of news has an old familiar ring to it. I can even remember when Guam was supposed to have been recaptured. Maybe I shouldn't be such a skeptic, but after all, rumors are just that—rumors.

The Japanese indicate that they want no more said about the forging of death certificates. From where I sit, it looks to me that Kusumoto was also mixed up in the affair. He probably wanted the count to come out correct so that he could save face. In any event, Gooding is still in the Navy and forgery is a serious offense.

Lists and more lists! Every day the Japanese want a list of some sort. Their latest request is for a list of all patients who are "very strong." That list will be a short one. You can't stuff rice, suck on a *kang-kong* stalk, and develop muscle.

Wilson came down with dengue tonight, but most of the staff is up and back at work. Carey Smith can't seem to snap back. I think he belongs on the permanently disabled roll. Wade went under yesterday, but will be up and about soon. Al Smith looks better and has gained a little weight, but couldn't stand any rough going. Ed Ritter is still sick—fever again yesterday. He just can't seem to get well—looks like hell.

August 29, 1942

I visited Isodoro in the old stone building where the Filipinos are quartered. Several of the boys were squatting around a low table, half-naked, playing with a greasy worn-out deck of cards. It was raining hard and the building was damp and semi-dark. I marveled, as I always do, how these natives can squat for hours—actually sit on their heels in seemingly perfect comfort.

One of the guards from the front office stopped in with the news that "tomorrow all Filipinos go out." They had all finally managed to have themselves listed as "sick" with one diagnosis or another. The Filipinos will be sent to a hospital in Manila and then home. I wonder how I would feel if I knew that tomorrow I would be free? I'll graduate a few years from now, I hope. A finished product no doubt—accent on the "finished."

Today is a great one for rumors. The boys are buzzing over maps, locating islands, speculating on what could be—and just having a wonderful bull session getting us out of here in no time at all. It helps them for awhile, but then back to the thorns of reality. However, if they would raise their horizons beyond their noses and turn to a map of the war areas—then draw lines to indicate the Axis positions, I'm afraid their morale would hit a new low. We can still lose this damn war and prolong our stay in this reform school indefinitely.

Our rice ration has been cut. There is only a two month supply in the islands and no new crop is expected for several more months. Although we receive most of our rice from Saigon, there doesn't seem to be as much coming in as before. When the Japanese tell us that they are running out of water lilies, then we will have cause for worry.

Again to bed—which reminds me, I have had to change my brand of toothpaste from Cashmere Bouquet to Coconut Oil Castile. Ugh! It tastes lousy.

August 30, 1942

"Stone walls do not a prison make, nor iron bars a cage." The hell they don't, and don't let Oscar Wilde tell you any different either. I guess I have about as much soaring ability as the next guy when it comes to winging out of reality into where I ain't. But the futility of such mental wanderings has been painfully impressed upon me too many times. There are too many unhealed wounds in my heart to continually rub salt into them by spiritual aviation to the great outside. This spirit-aviation stuff would be O.K. if all the endings weren't crash landings. Nope, Oscar, that damn whitewashed wall over there and these barred windows cast a hideous shadow on this cold stone deck.

The bars stand out big as broomsticks against the moon. They sure as hell make the place look like a prison. And those little sons of bitches running around the yard in their droopy drawers, carrying short rifles with a foot of cold steel on the end—they aren't Hollywood extras either. They only add to the atmosphere and local color.

Rain! Rain! Rain! My mouth even tastes like mildew. The Japanese asked for an Army medical officer and three of our corpsmen for duty at the port area. I asked Major Breslin, the Army senior medical officer, to designate his man and I would take care of our personnel. Breslin is a smart aleck reserve officer. I remember him following at Bill Donovan's heels on Corregidor. Breslin always reminded me of a red cocker spaniel—only uglier and without as much sense.

More hot rumors today. Word comes from "over the wall" that Japanese casualties are being received in Manila hospitals with fresh shrapnel wounds. It was reported that a wounded Jap officer remarked that all Americans on Corregidor should have been massacred. Nice fellow! He's almost as bloodthirsty as I am. Maybe we could arrange a little personal get-together one of these days and "talk things over."

For our class flower (Bilibid, 194?), I vote for the *kang-kong*. Incidentally, the camp mascot is a rabid dog. How appropriate—even the dogs go stir-crazy.

The padre didn't show up again today. He has cooled off considerably—actually accomplished nothing. I think the "gestapo" has him pretty well circled—senile old gent—no business in the major leagues.

August 31, 1942

A break in the weather and the sun came out. The cases before the disciplinary board today were insignificant and never should have appeared in the first place—except for this prick "Prince Hede." Hede is Gooding's police chief and is a good example of a good-for-nothing who received an appointment to the Naval Academy. We whitewashed the cases completely. Hell, this is a man's world, not a kindergarten.

Nogi informed Sartin that our store has to be legalized or it must go. Sartin recommended that the Japanese put in a store of their own. I really think that would be the best idea. We would probably fare better if the Japs ran the store.

September 1, 1942

The last of the Filipinos left today. Isodoro stopped over to say farewell
and gave me a kilo of sugar. There are only Americans in Bilibid now
and I'm afraid we are in for a squeeze. In spite of all the talk and
· spoken intentions, the fact remains that we are still deep in the throes
of a food emergency and deaths occur daily.

Sartin asked the Japanese to relieve Gooding as Camp Warden
and recommended Schweizer for the job. Nogi reacted favorably and
will probably act on the matter—the sooner the better.

September 2, 1942

This morning a Japanese naval officer came through the hospital on
an inspection trip—another "visiting fireman." Then about an hour
later Nogi decided that he would like to see all the patients—and he
did, every one. I conversed at length with Nogi and discovered that
he did study in Germany. His education marks him as being better
trained than the average doctor from Japan. The Japanese medical
courses are very meager—much below our standards.

Nogi also said that while radios are prohibited in Manila, he is
allowed to have one. However, after listening to Japan, Germany, Lon-
don, and America, he doesn't know what to believe. The kid is more
honest than most of his pals. He stated that he didn't expect a war
until about last August, and even then only thought that relations
between our two countries seemed "a little strained." He has no idea
how long the war will last, but gave me some assurance that our store
would be legalized.

Our census tonight is 562 patients. Our maximum was 991. The
releasing of the Filipinos, deaths from dysentery, malaria, and beriberi
have reduced our numbers in spite of additional sick from Tayabas
and other outlying camps.

It's interesting to watch the tempo and general attitude among
the officers in our barracks. Community living comes natural to certain people and they learn how to successfully adjust to it. Others are
wholly unfitted for this kind of life. They will never learn how to cope
if they keep at it a hundred years. The men either love it, don't mind
it, or hate it—some won't survive it.

Men living under these conditions are more clannish than women.

I think women are more naturally community dwellers. The most serious conflicts that occur in the barracks are for example—who wants the lights out at nine, who wants to wake up at five, who wants to use the stove, or "my bunk is under a leak and his isn't." But even these insignificant arguments assume monumental proportions in the minds of this bunch of caged human animals. There is no general harmony whatsoever. Everyone is grouped in small cliques and keep very closely to themselves.

Cecil Welch in his philosophy has spoken terse words explaining much of their grievances. Says Cecil: "There are some people who have failed to observe the few basic principles which make the world go around, and failing of this cognizance continually stir an otherwise smoothly boiling kettle." This sounds like Cecil. There is a lot to what he says.

Cecil is moody—one of the moodiest people I have ever known. It's not noticeable to those who haven't lived with him, because he's not a euphoric person who grows quiet under moods or growls. He's a grumbler who suddenly becomes absolutely silent. In either mood he manages to think clearly and I like him. If I had to choose a personal comrade—just one for the rest of the war, I would choose Cecil. As I write this, he sits on his bunk studying Japanese. He hopes that when the occupation forces arrive they might give him preference for knowing something of the lingo. To date he has learned the Japanese expressions for "a cat has a beard" and "a fox catches chickens," neither of which has helped him much as yet.

September 3, 1942

Another day—usual routine. Let's hope we will still find life as we knew it a long time ago. There was a lot to be desired in our life back home before the war. But one is a fool to expect anything better after the conflict. I had an individual happiness before I came out here. I had found everything I ever needed or wanted. But I know from my knowledge of mankind, that if I do find life as I left it—it will certainly be different.

I made my rounds this morning, then stopped in at the O.R. and watched Ed do a bone plating job. I felt a glow of pride as I stood there watching the boys work. I'm proud that we have been able to establish this kind of surgical service. We are doing an excellent job of reconstruction on these cases, and not letting our prison time be completely wasted. Many of the patients will be rehabilitated by the time they go home, and others well on their way to complete recovery.

Lives are being saved in this dingy little room. It's a far cry from our white tiled clinics where the presence of a single fly would produce cries of horror. We are turning out a brand of work that compares favorably with the best anywhere.

Word was passed from the front office that the Japanese want 25 lieutenant commanders and commanders moved into the big building near the front gate. This is supposed to be a friendly gesture, but I'm leery of being in such close proximity to the guards. I would prefer to stay down here in the prison yard. Nogi is the person behind this move. The other night, Nogi stopped by our barracks and asked Sartin where he slept. Sartin pointed to his wooden bed. Then Nogi asked him if he would rather have a regular steel bed. Sartin is the type of person who would feel uncomfortable sleeping in a different bed than the rest of us. He told Nogi that his wooden bed was just fine.

A move to the big building would give us private rooms. However, I can't say that is any great inducement to me. As far as sleeping is concerned, give me ten minutes on the floor of a boiler factory and I'll be asleep. My main interest in a private room is that it will give me the freedom of movement without disturbing anyone else. Just when this change is to take effect we don't know. Sartin believes that it will be soon.

A prisoner draft from Corregidor arrived tonight, and among them was Sergeant Provo—the son of a bitch who went "Japanese" on the island. I understand Provo has gotten himself firmly ensconced in a job with the Japs at the front office. I was sure that he would. If I have anything to do with it, Provo will never reach the States alive. I heard he has done an about face of late, but no matter how much that Buddhist pervert about faces, he has American blood on his hands to answer for. He's a mutinous, disloyal, traitorous sergeant— un-American in spirit, and must be remembered by every one of us. Our lenient judicial system will not punish him for his crimes. It must be done by those of us who know him for the treacherous louse he is. To my way of thinking, he's worse than Herri. At least Herri was born Japanese. The Japs on Corregidor loathed Provo as a traitor, but they had him cook for them and used him as a servant.

I remember Provo only too well. Immediately after the surrender of Corregidor he became a Jap handyman and interpreter. He began to oppress the Americans and started preaching Japanese culture. An American officer [Thompson] reminded Provo that he was still an American sergeant and subject to court-martial. Provo then had Thompson hog-tied and hauled off to Bataan by the Japanese. Reliable reports say he was shot. Any American even associating with that son of a bitch should be court-martialed. To curry the favor of such a louse is a crime.

The Corregidor crowd brought plenty of radio news. It sounds good if any of it is true. Big naval victories down south—six Solomon Islands in our hands—Jap Navy on the run—Russia staging a comeback—Germany being bombed—largest convoy in history reaches England—Hitler tells people to expect worst winter of the war, tells Japan she has to do something.

Meanwhile, Manila newspapers report that either Admiral Togo or foreign minister Tojo has resigned. There is so much stuff flying fast and furious around camp tonight that everybody has taken a new lease on life. It seems as if "Yanks and tanks" are in the minds of all. The "myth-mill" sure hit the jackpot this time.

Our doctors and corpsmen continue to evoke praise from the Army. Two corpsmen with the Corregidor group brought letters from an Army officer testifying to the splendid work these young men have done among the sick. I endorsed all the letters with the recommendation that they be filed in their service jackets.

A young Army corporal reported to me that the senior Army officer on Corregidor was turning over classified information to the Japanese. I had a long talk with the lad and believe that personal grievances are at the base of his accusations. However, I know the officer. He's a little man, and like so many little men, has a "Napoleonic" complex. He's bombastic and quite puffed up with his self-importance. He has a personality which naturally makes every man on Corregidor hate his guts. This officer had already begun his pompous swaggering long before I left the island. But the information he allegedly gave to the Japanese turned out to be the location of the fuel and oil dumps. Under the circumstances it was better for the officer to reveal the hiding places. With all his faults, and as much as I and others dislike the man, I feel we have nothing to worry about as far as his loyalties are concerned.

In our present predicament, all is fish that comes into the net, and we must listen to many stories of no pertinent value in order to find one grain of useful information.

President Roosevelt made a speech today. He remarked that all fronts would be under control by the end of this month. He also stated that if the Japanese didn't start treating the American prisoners better, he would take reprisals out on the Japanese being held in the States. That sounds Rooseveltarian. He and Eleanor certainly do a lot of talking with their mouths. He should have learned the lesson by now that the Japs taught us at Pearl Harbor—bluffing doesn't work. And threats are one sure way of cutting our throats a little faster.

St. M. is back in Manila, but any contact for the time being is completely cut off. We must wait for a break. I have nothing of importance to pass along to her and I doubt if she has any news to give me. I knew of her return by a prearranged signal—a mark on the truck bringing wood into camp. I watched for the mark every day and today it was there.

September 6, 1942

Thanks for the memories! It was swell while it lasted. Memories of life that reeked of Old Spice, American cigarettes, Old Faithful [Tom's automobile], and love. Thanks for everything—for sunsets on the Nansemond after eighteen holes of golf—twilights along the York in summer—cold crisp nights under a steel blue moon over old Tidewater—dinners at Dan's Log House and Ma Smith's in Yorktown—the Skyline Drive in late summer—Carolina in the fall. Thanks for the memories! Thanks for everything!

September 7, 1942

Labor Day. There is only one Labor Day I remember—in Carolina several years ago. It was the day we tried to go fishing but the weather was against us. That was the day seventy year old "Pop" Beasley was bragging about his newborn child. I remember his deep blue eyes. I took a picture of him and later Jane sent him a copy.

Three weeks have passed and still no padre. I don't believe he will show up anymore. Now that all the Filipinos are gone, it's evident that his sympathy lay entirely with them. This is just as well. He was of little value to us and probably would have caused more harm than good.

I passed up soup today. It contained pieces of foul smelling meat, and stunk like Corregidor the day after the surrender. The stench of decaying flesh, human or otherwise, is still the same.

Nogi wanted to know the English names for all of our surgical instruments. I went over the entire lot with him. There really wasn't that much—but when you start out alphabetically, and try to explain to somebody who doesn't speak your language very well, and you don't speak theirs, it calls for a hell of a lot of pantomime.

There has been a considerable boost in morale since the Corregidor bunch arrived. There hasn't been any news since, but they brought in enough to last for quite awhile.

Tonight the Japanese brought in an American prisoner who had escaped from Corregidor in a small boat and made the China coast. He was picked up by the Japs and then brought here. The boy reported that two-thirds of the Japanese troops on Luzon are leaving tonight, going north, supposedly to "invade the United States via the Aleutian Islands." The story was so fantastic and farfetched that not only do I disbelieve ninety percent of his yarn, but I also consider this guy worth watching. I'm going to keep a careful check on him from now on.

Nogi came by this evening and we had an interesting conversation. He talked about the war and mentioned that he left Japan for the Philippines on November 20, and landed on the east coast of Luzon. The peace parley was still going great guns in Washington. According to Nogi's story, they met with some resistance. He spoke of being wounded during the landing, while several men near him were killed. They had left Japan expecting to lose half their force. That's a reasonable figure for an amphibious operation. But I don't believe they lost anybody landing on Luzon. I haven't heard of an instance where the Japanese met any actual resistance to their landings.

Moreover, Nogi was a Johnny-come-lately. We found diaries on dead Japanese killed on Bataan showing that their forces left for the Philippines months earlier than that. When I was making my prewar reconnaissance through Bataan, the Japs were already infiltrating the area.

Nogi began to reminisce a little while we were talking. He remarked that it's now autumn in Japan and the leaves are turning brown. I told him it was that way in America too. There was a long period of silence after that, but several moments later Nogi arose and quietly said, "I go now—Sank you—Goo-by." I knew he realized that we had both traveled far. Nogi from the island of Honshu and I, Tidewater—land of rum, romance, and rebellion—land of the Rappahannock and Potomac—my home.

My eyes are beginning to fail me perceptibly. I have worked under poor lighting conditions ever since the war started. And that, coupled with a prolonged absence of vitamin A in the diet, has seriously messed up my vision. Wilson found a box of spectacles and fitted me with a pair that helped considerably. However, our lights are so poor here, that to work at night or even late afternoon puts a terrific strain on the eyes. I suppose I could pull a "Nathan Hale" and say: "I'm glad I have more than one eye to give for my country."

"Carthage must be destroyed!" So stated our ex-ambassador to Japan, Joseph Grew, in reference to that country. What he really meant was that Japan could not be starved out—the idea of attrition wouldn't work. "Japan must be destroyed!" Mr. Roosevelt, General MacArthur, take note. However, it comes back to the old fable about who will bell the cat. Annihilation isn't an easy thing for us to accomplish. We have been militia minded, militia dependent, and militia expectant. It has been aptly and only too correctly stated in a book published in 1926: "In every American war the patriotic laity has revealed a cowardice and panic that are inevitable when rabbles of well meaning souls find themselves in the presence of an organized enemy. The nation has lost its tens of thousands of lives and risked its very existence again and again from its addiction to militia. If children were taught a little more of the truth and a little less of the flapdoodle, they would not be so easily victimized by the claptrap of politicians and the pious hosannas of the professional lovers of peace, which nobody loves better than men of higher and reasonable minds— but they realize that it takes strength to maintain it."

I have never wanted my son to have to take up arms, but I have always wanted him to know the fundamentals of war so that he might have a reasonable chance for survival—and at the same time contribute a service to his country.

I remember several years ago while at a formal dinner on the island of St. Thomas, having to rebuke my host very strongly. He was a professional lover of peace who had baited me all evening as one of the military. He was the type, that if still alive, would be yelling to annihilate the Japanese. Yes, thousands of us would bell the cat—if we had a bell. Years ago we should have annihilated such professional lovers of peace as my erstwhile host. We wouldn't have to bell any

"Japanese cat" today. However, as it stands, I agree—"Carthage must be destroyed!" It may take years, but it must be done.

More radio rumors today. Another commando raid on occupied France—German ships sunk with supplies for Rommel—Russians still hold Stalingrad—Americans and British bomb Holland. Another report states that the Americans will occupy the Philippines by November 15. I'm not packing my gear on the strength of that one.

I found out that Provo visited Hogshire today. I'll put a stop to that. Fraternizing with that traitor will not be condoned. Hogshire is a horse's ass anyway—always has been.

Paul Ashton, who came in with the gang from Tayabas, has been quite sick for a long time. We opened a rectal abscess for him tonight and he's more comfortable—fever down.

September 10, 1942

The outside working party was kept under close surveillance today, and not permitted any contact with the natives. As a result, the men returned to camp tonight minus their usual bit of papaya, cucumbers, eggs, etc. The Japanese are getting tough. Military reverses are producing a reprisal attitude in our captors.

The Japanese are now asking for a list of our sick who are permanently disabled, and those who will be disabled for the next two or three years. Immediately the "Home by Christmas Club" interpreted this as a return to the States. However, I'm afraid it's only another list that the Japs want for their innumerable grammar school variety of statistics.

This business of adhering to the Geneva Treaty and paying the men is just talk. The Japanese want us to be completely without funds and are apparently waiting us out. They know we have more money than we declared, and they aren't going to give us any of their bayonet money until they have all of our pesos. In spite of all the promises, our food rations are less and also poorer in quality. We are now living almost entirely on what we smuggle or buy ourselves. The squeeze is on and there is every evidence that it will continue.

September 11, 1942

This afternoon the Japanese reported that Ted Wallace, Lieutenant Reyes, and two sergeants will leave for Japan tomorrow. The reason behind this move is suspicious. Wallace is a radio broadcaster and one of the sergeants is a radio technician. It looks like a propaganda and publicity stunt of some sort.

When Wallace was first captured, he was worked over by the Japanese and kept in solitary confinement at Fort Santiago. He had been doing propaganda broadcasting for us and wasn't too flattering toward the enemy. Wallace didn't talk over the radio on Corregidor, but had a stooge broadcast for him while his whereabouts was kept secret. His real name is Ince, and as Captain Ince he fooled the Japanese for awhile. However, the "fifth column" had riddled us so completely it was inevitable that his true identity would be revealed.

An interesting development today. Sartin was approached by the Japanese concerning the physical condition of a one-legged patient named Sanchez. It seems that Sanchez was called to report to the front office for duty. Sanchez was a go-between for St. M. on various occasions and she had mentioned him to me previously. He's a Mexican and has lived in the islands for several years. I see this move as a front gate contact in progress. Exactly how St. M. is working her plan, I don't know. I will have to wait until she's organized and I am approached. I have an idea that St. M. made contact with Sanchez—and possibly Isodoro.

The Japanese are without a doubt bearing down to completely isolate us from the Filipinos and the outside world. There is a decided falling off of news and rumors—and "over the wall" traffic is now practically a death penalty.

While the working party was outside today, a guard noticed one of the prisoners moving toward a Filipino who was standing by a tree. The guard threw a cartridge into his rifle and would have fired, but the prisoner ducked among his fellow captives and lost himself in the group.

The little extras in the way of food brought in by the working parties is missed. More and more we are being thrown back on the issued ration of stinking soup filled with water liles and the usual moldy rice. The store receives practically nothing anymore. Donations from people outside are no longer allowed.

The new Japanese guards are entirely too "sharing." Ever since they arrived, their curiosity and habit of borrowing has worked overtime. They are natural born borrowers. They will borrow razors, pens, pencils, raincoats, caps, helmets, shoes, and anything else that they can get their hands on. They gaze over my shoulders as I type and marvel at the miraculous behavior of my typewriter. They are continually in and out of our barracks. Last night after lights out, two of the "raccoons" stomped into our galley and turned on the lights. They then proceeded to upset everything in their "bull in a china shop" attempt to start a fire in the stove. They made more noise trying to fry a couple of eggs than a regiment of skeletons on a tin roof.

Their clumsiness isn't appreciated by any of us, but this is hardly the time to lift them up by the seat of their pants and toss them into a trash can.

September 12, 1942

This morning the Japanese requested a list of all patients and their diagnosis. They have hundreds of such lists from which to obtain the data, but this particular list is for Sikiguchi. "Siki" arrived yesterday and gave Sartin the usual going over. Sartin in his quiet way told Sikiguchi that he had no intention of learning Japanese and that such conversations were unfair since he was a prisoner while "Siki" was the captor. And since this was the case, there were limitations on a prisoner's reply. I have an idea that Sikiguchi liked the retort, but he became very sarcastic and asked, "What do you need—food?" The last word was accentuated, followed by his heinous gutteral laughter.

Nogi came trundling in after Sikiguchi had left and wanted to know all about the visit. He had hoped that Sartin would cooperate with "Siki" since Sikiguchi was his boss. Nogi handed us two packs of Chesterfields to smooth things over.

In the building next to my barracks, Carey Smith is the news and rumor analyzer, commentator, and refurbisher par excellence to the amusement of the crowd. He can take a choice rumor and by the time he mulls it over and throws it back into circulation, man it's a honey. Of course, he isn't adverse to whipping up a little satire either. For example, recently a rumor was making the rounds that Port Morseby and Darwin had fallen to the Japanese, and MacArthur was enroute to New Zealand. Carey, in his best midwestern twang, broadcasted a speech imitating MacArthur's voice: "My friends will be glad to learn that I have established my headquarters in Little America, where for fifty thousand pesos a year I will train an army of penguins to ably defend the country."

Well, I don't know what to make of this new wrinkle. Nogi showed up again and mumbled something about seeing the Red Cross. He said we are going to get a volleyball, basketball, and softball. I wonder what they will taste like.

However, while we were at chow tonight, a guard brought in a large box. It contained nine toothbrushes, six cakes of soap, four towels, fifteen packs of cigarettes, five tubes of toothpaste, and a few items of clothing. All the gifts will go to the patients. Surprisingly, it's significant that anything arrived at all. The Japanese have previously denied us any communication with the Red Cross whatsoever. I'm inclined to think that this is a trial sample, and may mean the opening up of more contact with the Red Cross. On the other hand, very often these pitiful demonstrations of generosity by our captors is the salving of some severe denial or reprisal measure. One certainly is leery of "Japs bearing gifts."

September 13, 1942

A hot sultry day with low ceiling and thunderhead clouds. The rumors are becoming more outlandish every day. The latest scuttlebutt is that Rommel surrendered and Hitler is suing for peace. Of course, that last one crops up every now and then—it was about due. Roosevelt is rumored to be promising Japan a dose of bombing soon. That's when the Japanese will really put the screws to us. I feel like I have been living on a bull's-eye ever since this war began.

More kindergarten bickering in camp. These guys sound like a bunch of teenagers during their first six months at boarding school. Ordinarily a good gripe or growl is healthy and can be cured by a rough liberty or a three-day-pass. But this sophomore whining group wouldn't know what to do with a good liberty if they had one. They need to be turned across a knee and have their behinds paddled, or put to bed without their supper. My momma would tie me to a table leg whenever I needed dignified disciplining.

September 14, 1942

Last night about thirty prisoners from Cabanatuan arrived in camp. They don't know their ultimate destination, but believe they are en-route to Bataan as a working party. I heard that they are to be put to work excavating the destroyed tunnels and ammunition dumps over there. This sounds plausible—there is plenty of steel and metal of all kinds in the wreckage. The Japanese have stripped Manila of all metal and they are now probably after the scrap on Bataan.

Conditions have improved at Cabanatuan. Their death rate is down to seven a day. I was told that several of the civilian guards who arrived here recently are now on sentry duty up there. Quite a bit of strife has developed between them and the regular army boys. They can't seem to get along and a bayoneting is reported to have occurred during one of their fracases.

This little interpreter we now have [Yakasiji] has lived in the United States for most of his life. He told us today that he has dual citizenship—Japanese and American, and just happened to be caught in Japan when the war started. He still hopes and expects to return to the U.S. and live after the war is over. He seems quite unconcerned and feels that he will be able to return with impunity—as if nothing had happened. If he can and does, then I certainly don't want to fight any more wars for a country that adheres to such policies. This guy as an individual is O.K.—but he's still our enemy.

To top it all off, Yakasiji bemoans the fact of how much money he's losing in Seattle because of the war. Yakasiji got his start in America by traveling up and down the west coast, buying secondhand broken-down trucks and shipping them to Japan where they were reconditioned. He made a huge profit on every deal. Yakasiji also carried a first mortgage on a piece of property in Seattle and eventually foreclosed on it. From then on he was in the real estate game in a big way. He now owns blocks of property and is sitting on top of the world. His dual citizenship protects him in the States and he's in the civilian corps here—and not in the Japanese Army. He's also loaded down with American Defense Bonds—so he says.

Incidentally, Sartin asked Nogi why we are suddenly being held strictly incommunicado. Nogi replied that we are in a foreign country, and it's Japanese policy that American prisoners on foreign soil be confined in this manner. If we were in Japan, we would be allowed much more freedom. The reason for this is to reduce the American influence among the natives they are trying to indoctrinate. Looking at it from the Japanese point of view, it's a smart move and the right thing to do. We would do well to put a little absolutism into our policies for self-defense. We wouldn't be toasting our heels in prison camps and being slapped around all over the South Pacific if we did. The old expression "fighting fire with fire" is a well proven adage.

Speaking of fires, a couple of the "visiting firemen" came by this afternoon to look around. They asked Sartin if he was anxious to get back to America. Sartin replied, "Yes, after two years out here I'm ready to go." One of the Japs then answered, "Better chance." That was all he said. Now try and dope that statement out. I'll bet if I tossed that juicy morsel to the boys out there in the bullpen, they would have a ball. And by the time the rumor made its way back to me, I would have seventy different versions of it.

Experience has taught me that all Japanese assurances of an early return to the States is always predicated on their belief that we are about to fold up, and a Japanese victory is practically in the bag. They actually believe it too. The Japanese have a propaganda system that completely lulls their troops into the absolute belief of the invincibility of the Japanese Army and Navy.

I'm having mess kit troubles. I made the big mistake a few days ago of dipping my soup from the gasoline tin without smelling the soup first. The result is that even soap and boiling water hasn't eradicated the smell of a slaughterhouse from my canteen cup. I think I'll bury the cup in the ground for a few days and then boil it to kill the worms and bugs.

A group of prisoners arrived this afternoon from Mindanao. They included several high ranking officers. Old fathead General Seals was among them. I had heard that Mrs. Seals was in Davao, but I think that's wrong. I have definite information that the captured civilian women and Army nurses have already been brought to Santo Tomas.

Mrs. Seals had no more right to be out here than any other wife or dependent. She was underfoot and a nuisance from the beginning. She and the nurses were put aboard one of the evacuation planes going to Australia, but the plane cracked up. However, she wasn't the only civilian leaving the war zone. Whole families, servants, yes-men, and aides were all provided with space for evacuation. There wasn't any room left for military men with something to contribute to the war effort. We ended up sending a refugee camp to Australia rather than a fighting outfit.

The box of supplies we received recently which we understood was from the American Red Cross, we now learn came from a seventy year old Manila school teacher—Nancy Belle Norton. She has been very solicitous toward American prisoners ever since Manila fell to the Japanese.

The civilians and the Army and Navy nurses at Santo Tomas continue to do well. Naturally I'm glad to hear this, but I know it's only a face saving effort on the part of the enemy. Proof of this lies in the repeated requests by the Japanese for written testimonials from the Americans stating how well they are being treated. As one Japanese officer said, "I don't want the testimonials for publication, but only for myself." The Field Marshal wrote one such letter for Kusumoto. A United Press correspondent has been repeatedly solicited for an article, but told the Japanese that he can only write for his news service. So far he has gotten away with this excuse.

September 15, 1942

Today I received a few copies of the propaganda literature that the Japanese are using throughout the islands. These pamphlets are written in a manner which suggests high school compositions, or essays written in a school for imbeciles. They show a complete lack of understanding of the natives. The Philippines have a well informed population and the enemy's overplay of words lessens the value and force of their propaganda considerably. For example, the Japanese tell the Filipinos: "We are here for your good, not ours." They also extol the virtues, accomplishments, and capabilities of the Japanese people. It's the egotistical ranting of an inferiority complex. The opening lines of one of the pamphlets begins: "When on December 8, 1941, Japan completely destroyed the United States Navy. . . ." This quote I'm sure is enough to convince anyone of the pure rot of the rest. It's a giant wind balloon made of damn poor rubber and very thinly stretched.

The Generals and Colonels who arrived yesterday from Mindanao are to be shipped to Japan. Each of the officers is allowed to take along one orderly. There is a continuing practice among high ranking military figures to ask for officers as orderlies. This might be all right from the standpoint of requesting a friend, but it will lose us a hell of a lot of respect in the eyes of the Japanese. It also tends to lower their respect for our officers in general. This is a lousy practice and to my mind should be discouraged. It has always been my contention that our officers are only officers by the consent of Congress, and a little bit of gold on the sleeve. The consent of Congress doesn't necessarily make a man an officer and a leader of men. The lion is "King of the Forest" because he *is* a "King."

Provo has been expressing an ardent desire to go to Japan with the Mindanao draft. He remarked that he fully expects us to be liberated in a few months, and he feels that "he could be of greater value to the Americans in Japan." That pervert no doubt sees the handwriting on the wall. It must appear to him that the complete Japanese victories he expected, and hoped for, may fall short about 180 degrees. Mister Provo must be quite aware the betting odds are ten-to-one that he will never reach the States alive. But even if he should do so, there are plenty of people who have no intention of allowing the War Department to remain ignorant of his record. However, we all think it would be for the best to send him away from here, but it certainly galls the hell out of me to see him go clear to Japan. It will make it that much more difficult to get at him someday.

It was pouring rain this evening as we sat around having a bull session. Overhead we could hear the drone of a plane. The aircraft didn't seem to be following any particular course, and then suddenly its motor began missing badly. Moments later we heard the motor stop and an explosion in the distance. Within minutes we could hear the scream of sirens as ambulances passed the prison heading in the direction of Santo Tomas. We can only surmise what happened—pilot caught in a sudden heavy squall—lost his direction—motor acting up—dropped his bomb in the bay—forced landing necessary—crashed. I hope so.

More than 400 Filipinos arrived tonight. They are to leave for Bataan in the morning on a work party. The rumor is that the Japanese have discovered many of their own dead in Bataan and these Filipinos are going over there on a burial party. This is plausible—they were all over the peninsula at one time. In fact, dead Japanese soldiers were hanging so thick on our barbed wire that they made a complete curtain along the entire front—and did they stink after about two days of "curing" under the hot broiling sun.

September 16, 1942

Another list request today. We have been directed to submit a list of all those covered under the terms of the Geneva Convention. The

Japanese will then decide as to their status. We broke out our copy of the treaty and have listed our staff accordingly—medical and nonmedical. This may have some significance, but I have gone through the same thing several times before. I have discovered that it's only a cover-up for a squeeze in which we get less food, fewer privileges, and fewer comforts. The softer the Japanese talk, the harder they bear down. It's an old Oriental custom.

Our concerted efforts to get Provo on the draft to Japan has hit a snag. The Mindanao crowd doesn't want the bastard either. However, I still hope we can unload him. Also, the brass hats continue to insist on having officers as flunkies. Nobody listens to me. I guess they will just have to learn the hard way.

We managed to get ahold of several giant cucumbers and calamondin today—fresh stuff and man was it good. We ate the cucumbers like apples and made juice from the calamondin.

Nelson has recovered from dengue. Joses is up and about, but he looks a little wild-eyed and has a peculiar mental attitude. There were several days when I thought he was going to have a relapse into his manic-psychosis—a repeat of the Shanghai episode for which he was brought to Canacao just prior to the war. It was his going balmy that landed me with the job as Regimental Surgeon for the 4th Marines.

Joses is a funny duck anyway—a pituitary type with gigantism. He's tall with a huge build, heavy facial contours, and wild-eyed with thick lips and jowls.

September 17, 1942

One hell of a day! We received word early that there would be an inspection of our compound this afternoon by a senior medical officer of the Japanese Army. Then the following Sunday we would be privileged with an inspection by General Tanaka.

At two o'clock, Sartin, Joses, and I strolled up to the front office to greet the visiting dignitary. However, instead of a medical officer, Major General Miramoto stepped out of the car. There was the usual saluting, etc. We then stood at attention for about an hour while the General made himself comfortable in Nogi's office—drinking tea and ordering the furniture moved about. He rearranged the entire interior of the room, while at the same time making the guards stand at attention and recite their ritual and creed. But that wasn't all. Next there was a drill for us as to the correct manner of saluting and bowing to the Japanese.

About an hour later, Nogi and the missing medical officer finally showed up and the inspection began. During the walk through the wards, everyone was admonished as to the proper manner of greeting a general of the Japanese Army—the call to attention—the salute— the bow. But the one thing that the General objected to most strenuously was the fact that no one faced toward him. That's very important to these boys.

Later in the afternoon we learned that this was only a dummy run for the big inspection on Sunday. My impression of the whole affair is that our Army and Navy aren't the only services which have generals and admirals who find it necessary to find fault at inspections, and manufacture their own importance by overwhelming themselves in piddling unimportant details while exhibiting a total lack of sense of values.

The most amazing thing about the whole episode is that immediately after the inspection a rumor ran rampant through the camp that a German officer had accompanied the inspection party. However, since I had been along on the tour, I knew that this just couldn't be. But later I learned the origin of the rumor. The only clean clothes I had to wear were my dyed blue shirt and shorts. All the other officers were dressed in khaki. I guess that with my blue uniform and jodhpurs I did look like a Prussian officer. Anyway, I was the German man in blue.

Once back at quarters, Sartin decided that we should hold some sort of drill and instruction so that our men could properly render military courtesy. This gave me an opportunity to ram home what I have preached ever since I have been in the Navy—discipline. I voiced my opinion that I was strongly against instructing and demanding our men to give military respect to Japanese officers, unless the Japanese were required to render equal respect to our American officers. I reminded Sartin that he and his staff must be accorded equal military courtesy with the Japanese, or else lose all the respect of his men (as a matter-of-fact it's already lost).

I have demanded the courtesy prerogatives of my rank. I don't want to give the impression that I'm "rank-happy" or snobbish, but it's only through strict ironbound discipline which acknowledges rank, that proper execution of military function can be attained. And I certainly can't agree to any system whereby American troops are taught obedience and respect to Japanese authority, and neglect the issue in regard to American officers. It's just another instance of our appearing sloppy, inefficient, unmilitary, and unsystematized as compared to the enemy. Under proper training and policy, good discipline will not break down—even among prisoners of war. Of course, as usual, I found myself telling Sartin that the fault lay at his own door—and it does. I explained to Sartin, that unless he insists on salute and proper respect, the rest of us can't expect it unless we demand it, and then we end up being sons of bitches.

Our American Navy personnel are glad to pay respect and courtesy to their officers. But when the Navy is belittled by officers who don't appreciate the essentials of leadership, and who don't act like officers, you can't blame the men. You can't expect the men to properly evaluate the basic principles of military command if the officer doesn't set the example.

I don't believe there is any officer more interested in the welfare of the men of our Navy than I am. And I would be the last person to place undue harshness and unreasonable demands on them. However, the military service is not a democratic machine—its basic principle is class distinction, and "command and obedience" makes it go. Unless this discipline begins with small things, it will not endure through the big things.

The military is for war. You can't put on a uniform and play soldier. Severe military courtesy and discipline is not playing soldier—it's training for war. Our lack of discipline has contributed greatly to our being kicked around in the Philippines—before and after the surrender. But we never learn—we aren't a military people.

This afternoon the Japanese posted the front page of a Manila newspaper. It told of a Red Cross ship underway with relief supplies for American prisoners in the South Pacific. The story read well and we can certainly use the gifts. I will take a toothbrush, toothpaste, and a pack of American cigarettes. No knitted socks or sweaters need apply. From the article it would seem that there are also individual boxes for the prisoners. All this sounds great, but I have experienced so many promises that end with disappointment that I'm afraid to build my hopes up.

September 18, 1942

Word was passed this morning that General Tanaka will hold his inspection tomorrow [Saturday] instead of Sunday. A dummy run was held in the wards for two hours regarding what honors to give the General upon his arrival. After a series of conflicting instructions, it all boiled down to doing exactly what we have done in the Navy for years—the senior officer calls attention, salutes and that's that. There are a couple of formalities peculiar to the Japanese that must be observed. Each man must keep his eye on Tanaka at all times and hold his salute until the General passes. There is nothing complicated about the ritual—except for the fact that everybody has made a big deal out of it.

Our daily rations have been very thin lately. The water lilies are neither tasty nor sustaining. The little fish they send in are about the size of my little finger, and when you deduct the head and tail, there isn't much left but bones. We still manage to obtain a few extras, but not enough to do us much good.

September 19, 1942

Soon after I turned in last night there was a lot of commotion outside in the yard. About 400 prisoners from Cabanatuan had just arrived in camp. The "Field Marshal" was in charge of getting the men settled down for the night. Gooding was drunk and abusive to everyone.

This group is a mixture of Army, Navy, Marines, and most of the crew from the *Canopus*. The men believe that they are on their way to Japan. These Cabanatuan boys looked in good shape. Their camp conditions have improved, and the death rate has dropped considerably. The men receive a prize of three cigarettes for every can of flies that they kill. They also have a baseball diamond and volleyball court. The tension in that camp has eased quite a bit. However, three prisoners were shot trying to escape. They were taken to a prominent hill where they were executed in full view of the rest of the camp.

General Tanaka arrived at exactly ten o'clock for his inspection. We were lined up to receive him and gave the General his usual honors. Tanaka then proceeded to a desk where he heard Nogi's report on the hospital. Next a whirlwind tour through three wards- then off he went. The General is an elderly man with coal black hair and a handlebar mustache. He acted very quiet and dignified. Tanaka is reputed to have been a military attaché in Washington at one time, and the Manila newspapers report him as being a "humanitarian and poet." All of which may or may not be true. The General speaks excellent English as was manifested on several occasions when he asked questions. The only comment Nogi had about Tanaka's visit was that the General remarked, "We are kind to the sick." I wonder how he guessed that?

Kusumoto showed up this afternoon to tell several of his buddies good-by. He leaves tomorrow for Japan, but judging from his manner, I don't think he likes the idea very much.

A Japanese intelligence outfit also came through camp today. I recognized the group and learned that they were on their way back to Japan. The Japanese seem to have rapid promotion rackets in their services the same as we do. The Colonel of the group was a major when I last saw him two months ago. If my memory serves me, he was a captain shortly before the war began. Incidentally, I recognized one officer among Tanaka's staff who has been in the Philippines for several years in a civilian capacity. He was known to us before the war, but as usual, nothing was ever done about it. These islands were taken by the Japanese long before the first bomb fell. The Philippines were so riddled with "fifth column" that we couldn't have held the islands with a hundred thousand tanks and planes.

September 20, 1942

The day began like one of those clear sunny days at the seashore, and ended in a young typhoon of wind and rain. I still fight to keep busy and fill every moment so I won't have time to think about home and those who are dear to me. I must bury such thoughts. There is still a long, long time ahead that I must fight loneliness, worry, and concern.

The Japan draft left late this afternoon—with Provo. Tonight we received word from the port area that a Jap cruiser and several destroyers were in the harbor, and fifteen transports were busy loading thousands of Japanese soldiers and civilians. As soon as this news knifed through the compound, the "Christmas Club" had it all doped out that the Japanese were evacuating the Philippines.

A work detail arriving back from town had been serving as bus drivers. They reported that the Japanese discontinued the bus service because there are no longer enough Japs to haul around. They also had more radio reports but the news was so ludicrous that one wonders if any of it is true at all. For example, Roosevelt is to resign if the American prisoners aren't free by the first of the year. There were other similar stories—each one more fantastic than the other.

A certain amount of reliable news did arrive. The Japanese newspapers are admitting that New Guinea has been evacuated by their forces for "strategic purposes." I also learned from authoritative sources that there are two organized guerrilla bands operating in Negros. The Japs have a garrison force of about 200 soldiers on the island and can only travel about in armored trucks.

Cebu continues to be a hellhole. The Japanese have always resented our burning the island before their occupation forces arrived. They are holding sixty of our Navy personnel in dungeon cells. The men are being starved to death and the wounded receive no medical attention whatsoever.

Of course, when this war is over, there will be the old soft-soap and whitewash act. The politicians will come out of the woodwork. It will be hands across the sea and all is forgiven.

September 23, 1942

I woke up this morning with a nasty headache. I'm afraid my eyes are being overtaxed. The lighting has been very bad and the lack of vitamin A hasn't helped either. The glasses that Wilson found for me help a little, but they certainly weren't made for my eyes. I have done practically nothing all afternoon but lie on my bunk.

Nogi stopped in today and personally saw every patient that we had reported as permanently disabled. With this sudden policy of transferring prisoners to Japan, I'm inclined to think that's where we are all going with the exception of the disabled. The wishful thinkers can already see a Red Cross ship tied up at the pier to take them home. They are also talking about expecting big things "on the wane of the moon." I have heard that wane of the moon story ever since I have been here. It doesn't seem that I will ever be able to convince these "children" that war has its principles—if not its rules. The rumor of the day is that Formosa has fallen and Hirohito asked Roosevelt to allow Tokyo to be an open city.

September 24, 1942

I felt better today. I guess I needed a day of rest. I made my rounds this morning, saw the cases in S.O.Q., worked on my biographies, and studied Spanish with Wilson.

The outstanding event of the day was the financial affair. The Japanese sent over a paymaster and returned all the money they took from us on Corregidor. Every dime of it was returned to the rightful owners.

The "Christmas Club" immediately jumped to the conclusion that the Japanese see the handwriting on the wall and are making face. These American stir-wacky boys have been hit with so many rumors that they are hanging on the ropes and groping for the referee's suspenders for support. They don't know Japanese psychology if they believe that the Japs are moved by any feeling of a need for face saving at this time. After all, the enemy still holds most of East Asia and doesn't have to make any friendly gestures at this stage of the game.

One of the refunding episodes is typical of what goes on in this prison. Greenman received a refund of over a thousand dollars. He came to me tonight and asked what I thought of the idea of him lending out some of his money to the boys in camp "at a fixed rate of interest—all business like and above board." It didn't take me long to tell him what I thought of his suggestion. The son of a bitch! With his shipmates fighting like hell to eke out an existence, and this bastard wants to lend them money at interest! An American Navy officer with pawnbroker propensities. If that's the crap we commission as an officer and a gentleman, they can have my suit anytime.

A few weeks ago I mentioned hearing a plane, then an explosion in the air and ambulance sirens. Well, we now learn that two Japanese planes crashed in the rain squall with the loss of their crews.

September 25, 1942

"Ali Baba and his Forty Thieves" are back! When I awoke this morning and looked out the barred window I saw the changing of the guard. Our meddlesome, prying, "help yourself" raccoons are taking up the guard again today. Word was quickly passed to batten down everything. Anything you want to keep, get it out of sight. This particular gang is a mess—just like a bunch of hoodlums. They are into everything and want anything they see.

The rainy season has apparently broken. The middays are hot, but for the most part less humid and quite comfortable. The Japanese are now offering us two bottles of beer for every can of dead flies.

My "over the wall" contact brought me the latest information concerning Japanese infiltration of Philippine life. As I mentioned before, when the conquering army moves in, their civilian colonizing group comes along with them. They are called the "civilian military" and includes interpreters, teachers, lawyers, bankers, and tradesmen. There is also the propaganda corps and secret police. The Philippine puppet government is so infiltrated with Japanese that it runs like a player piano.

The latest innovation reported to me is the intermarriage order. The Japanese have learned that the Filipinos are family oriented and hang close together according to blood ties. The Japanese can see that one way to induce a true sympathetic relationship with the Filipinos is to marry into their families. Moreover, intermarriage with the native women will spread out the ever increasing population of Japan. It's a measure which insures a Japanese conquest of these islands—to some degree anyway.

The directive is out from Tokyo for Japanese soldiers and civilians to marry Filipino women—and plenty of them. It won't matter whose hand the referee holds up when this fracas is over.

Shortly after dark tonight, several of our inmates strolled over to the front wall and could hear the radio playing in the Japanese headquarters building. It was a KGEI broadcast. The latest news coming over the station revealed that Mr. Knox is reputed to have said that our control of the Pacific could be expected in November, and that our shipbuilding has doubled. He also stated that we have 8,000 planes in Australia and 5,000 planes in China. After that last announcement the Japanese switched to a music program.

It's a cool night but I'm not sleepy. As I write under a faint shaded light in the toilet, I can hear the men tossing in their bunks trying to sleep. Everybody is restless tonight. There's an uneasiness and it's contagious. Zookeepers have noted this kind of behavior among their animals. An unexplained restlessness for no apparent reason. It starts with a few and runs through the entire population. I have a feeling that I'm not going to do well myself tonight.

September 26, 1942

Sooner or later I knew this would happen. An Army private who had been on a working detail took "French leave" [escaped] last night. The late night *bango* at ten o'clock showed him missing, but the short count wasn't reported until this morning. The whole day has been filled with nothing but *bango,* visits by Japanese headquarters officers, and our continuous trips to the front office as corrective measures are ordered by the Japanese.

Reprisals have been threatened and that can be serious. Retaliatory measures at other camps have been to line up a half-dozen other prisoners and shoot them. This hasn't been an easy day, and I'm expecting curtailment of what few privileges we now have.

The escape route was easy. Anybody can escape from this place, but then one's troubles are just beginning. It's our responsibility to discourage such escapes. To sneak out and back on missions of value and importance is one thing, but to take "French leave" at the expense of the rest of the camp is dangerous.

When our present *bango* system was instituted, I pointed out that since the Japanese had turned the policing over to us, it was our job to make it thorough enough so that the Japs would keep their hands off. The system required that every ward officer be responsible for his own patients. I recommended a directive be issued that our medical staff officers conduct every *bango,* and not relegate the count to a corpsman. I never could convince Sartin to be that explicit. He only required that a medical officer had to sign the count and assume it had been done correctly. I can't understand the reluctance of officers to issue implicit orders. I'm not asking for favors in this game, but somebody has to run the show—and I mean "run it."

Last night was a bad night all-around. I was awake most of the time—restless with eyes wide open. Everyone in the barracks was tossing or talking in their sleep. Several men would get up periodically and have a smoke. The raccoons also had our galley going most of the night, and they can clatter, rattle, and bang tin cans to make more disturbance than anybody I know.

September 27, 1942

In the shade of a mango tree on the roadway that leads to the upper compound, through a line of high stone walls, we held Sunday services this morning. The maimed, the amputated, and the weak sat or lay upon the narrow grassy strip along the wall. The Chaplain, like the rest of us, wore a loose tunic with bare feet shoved under the canvas strap of his wooden shoes. A young officer played a violin—his music nailed to the trunk of the mango tree. His back was to us as he played "Ave Maria." And we could see the long deep gash that marked the back of one leg, and the scars on the other—still red from recent surgery.

I gazed down the road where papaya and plum trees lined the wall on the opposite side. The hot glaring sun was at its zenith. And as I watched the Chaplain under the cool shade of the mango, surrounded by his few gaunt bewhiskered listeners, I was reminded of Sidney Lanier's beautiful poem: "Ballad of the Trees and Master." I remembered the scattered lines:

> Into the woods my Master went,
> Clean forspent, clean forspent,
>
> And the great green trees had a mind for Him,
> And the little green leaves were kind to Him.

Then it came to me—Sidney Lanier had also been a prisoner of war. He had been captured while serving in the Confederate Navy.

September 28, 1942

After days of short rations, the Japanese sent in several sheep carcasses and we had mutton soup tonight. I understand that there is enough meat to last for a few days.

About a hundred prisoners from O'Donnell arrived in camp today. They are on their way south to Davao where they are to be put to work on plantations and clearing the jungle. Probably another mass murder project. There's a lot of malaria in that part of the country. Shades of the days of the Tripoli pirates, Moslems and Turks, when our seamen rotted and died in Oriental prisons. The white man is sure as hell serving in bondage today.

I managed to talk with a few of this group. They have been in northern Luzon on working parties and the death rate has been high. They mentioned that guerrillas are very active in the north and are led by Colonel Cushing.

Doctors Andrew Rader and Charles Osborne were also with the O'Donnell draft and told me that at least 25,000 Filipinos and 1,500 Americans have died at that camp since the surrender. Duckworth is still there, but it's rumored that he's going to Japan. Apparently "Ducky" ducked the Davao detail and sent his boys Rader and Osborne in his stead.

My talk with Rader was enough to convince anyone that all these rumors are a bunch of hooey. He has had constant radio access and practically all his information comes from reliable sources. He told me that Germany is being bombed heavily, but there's no reason to believe she will fold up this year—New Guinea and Guam are still in Japanese hands and no new Allied front is intended at the present time. I guess the boys will have to join me and settle down to the realization that we will be here for another year or more. It's a hellish long haul, but I can't see any brighter prospects. Of all the men in this prison camp, there isn't a damn soul more homesick than I am. That's why I never mention it much. I'm not masochistic.

I can't properly appraise the Japanese attitude toward the Geneva Treaty. They have worked the American prisoners in handling ammunition and repairing airfields. They have given reprisal punishments. They have treated our medical units with greater severity in many instances than that dished out to combat prisoners. They have stolen our personal property, held us incommunicado, subjected us to indignities, and have not observed our coincidental rank. Any officer is subject to a Japanese private's least whim. We have eaten garbage and are kept on rations insufficient to sustain life. We only survive because we have a little money and have been able to buy a few extras on the outside.

However, it's wrong to assert that the Japanese pay no attention to the Geneva Treaty. They pay a lot of attention. They study it constantly to find loopholes and build alibis for their violations. Their best stunt is to obviously comply with a small stipulation and then violate a provision that hurts. Any demonstration indicating compliance with one part of the treaty is a sure sign that they will break another.

September 29, 1942

A late season typhoon blew into camp last night and has been growing in intensity all day. Solid sheets of rain are falling. The noise is the worst part. The constant din of rain on our metal roof makes conversation and sleep almost impossible.

Nogi showed up this morning. He had been up to O'Donnell and confirmed the fact that Duckworth is slated for Japan. Nogi also mentioned that "things won't be so pleasant for our hospital if any more escapes occur."

This afternoon the Japanese brought in a couple of boxes of clothing to be distributed to the sick. They turned out to be odds and ends that the Japs couldn't use—thirty-nine socks that don't match and several officer dress shirts and overcoats.

LeComte recognized a few of his things in the donated clothes. All of it is recognizable by name markings. I heard that the Japanese broke open all the officer's gear at the Army and Navy Club, and now clothes are scattered all over the islands. Vandalism and barbarity—what a combination!

These "kindhearted" sons of bitches have lived off loot and theft for so long that they think it's the normal thing to do. I heard that after a conquest, the Japanese give their soldiers a reward—eight days of uninterrupted looting.

Morale is poor today. The rumors that the men created as a mental refuge have all been washed away. They all now know how little we have accomplished in this war to date. I still say that it's wrong to foster false beliefs—the letdown is too great. With the facts of life along with the rain suddenly dumped on them, I guess happy and contented faces would be too much to ask.

September 30, 1942

The O'Donnell draft for Davao left early this morning in the driving rain, but had to return. The weather was so bad that their ship couldn't sail. There was no need for the Japanese to send the prisoners out in weather like this—pure cussedness.

There is general unrest everywhere in the camp. Ever since the escape here and the attempts at Cabanatuan, there has been an undercurrent of uneasiness among the Japanese and our routine has been somewhat upset. There have been many parleys at Nogi's office and one of our staff officers takes *bango* early every morning in the wards.

Details concerning the executions at Cabanatuan have finally come to light. Two Army colonels and a Navy supply officer by the name of Gilbert were caught while attempting to escape. They were shot after several days of torture and beatings. As a retaliatory measure, the Japanese divided the prisoners into groups of ten. If one man from a group escapes, the other nine will be executed. Americans are placed as sentries around the compound and forced to act as guards over their own comrades.

Tonight we managed to get hold of a hunk of tough beef from the outside, and the ration of mutton was liberal because it was beginning to spoil. My God, but meat tastes good! This was my first good meal since I left Bataan. My teeth and stomach were both surprised at having food to chew. I gorged—everybody did.

October 2, 1942

We are animals in a cage—fed out of a bucket, rice and garbage. The "visiting firemen" arrive to view us like monkeys in a zoo. Even a zookeeper is more solicitous of his animals' comfort and health than the Japanese are toward us. This Nipponese coprosperity sphere is based on sadism, ignorance, degeneracy, and the lowest standards of animal life. Mass murder of the white man is the order of the day. Until we learn to hate like they can, we can't win this war. But our people back home can't hate that way. They have no conception of this beastliness. And because they can't hate, we who are rotting in these prisons must pay the penalty.

I had a talk with Nogi today. He had gone to lunch with General Miramoto. Nogi isn't the best informed guy on the war. He only knows what he reads in the newspapers or hears over the radio. Miramoto told Nogi that it's going to be a long war and they shouldn't expect to get home for two or three years. Well, neither do I—so what. Miramoto figures that it's going to take a long time to defeat us, but ultimate victory for Japan is firmly believed by everyone. To the Japanese this is a foregone conclusion. They are convinced that they are going to win. There is no reason for them to believe otherwise. They are masters of the situation in every respect.

Nogi reported that Java is peaceful and everything is running smoothly—plenty of good oil, but few ships to bring it out. Japan is richer in resources now than ever before in her history. All things considered, it's going to be a long war.

October 4, 1942

Excitement all over the camp today. Nogi announced that several top Japanese officials will visit the camp tomorrow to attend a ceremony for our war dead. The Japanese, with their ancestor worship, have a great reverence for the dead—friend or enemy. The ceremony will be held at our graveyard under the north prison wall. As usual, I'm a little leery of this memorial service. I fully expect the Japanese to bring cameras and take movies. I wonder what atrocities we will hear about that will offset this act of human kindness. Anyhow, tomorrow's the day—it will probably rain.

October 5, 1942

It rained most of the night, but the memorial service wasn't canceled. I dressed quite differently this morning. Usually I put on a pair of ragged shorts, my wooden shoes, and I'm ready to meet whatever the day has to offer. Today, however, I wore a long-sleeved khaki shirt, khaki trousers, jodhpurs, and my cap with the scrambled eggs. I felt awkward as hell. I hadn't really dressed up in so long that I didn't know whether I was comfortable or uncomfortable.

We marched across the compound to the front office where we met with Nogi and the Japanese guests. Then all of us proceeded to the burial plot in the upper compound. Everyone lined up in columns on the four sides of the graveyard. Chaplain Cummings opened the service, and we all stood uncovered as Chaplain Wilcox rendered prayers for the dead. It started to rain about this time, but slacked off as the services progressed.

Two large floral wreaths had been sent by the Japanese. One was from General Miramoto and the other from the prison staff. Nogi and a lieutenant from the General's office placed the wreaths on the graves.

Later in the morning, the Japanese distributed candy, cakes, and bananas to the patients. Nogi called the occasion a "festival." The little guy really means well.

October 6, 1942

Early this afternoon, Nogi sent for me. He had decided that I should go with him to the port area and examine a prisoner who he had seen, but was undecided whether the man had appendicitis or not.

As we traveled through the streets, I turned the conversation to subjects that I knew interested him—poetry, flowers, and books. All the while I was observing the city and its people. I was given a knowing look and a word now and then by the Filipinos, but on the whole there was every evidence that the Japanese have rapidly indoctrinated the native life. The people were going about their everyday business in a very easy manner. They all seemed well nourished, clean, and neatly dressed. Even the streets have been renamed in Japanese. Japanese symbols are everywhere—streetcars, traffic signs, and notices. I watched a few hundred Filipino schoolboys being drilled in the "goose step." They were smartly uniformed in khaki shorts and lined up by size. They drilled with a precision that was beautiful to watch—and they enjoyed it. This is the standard youth movement of the totalitarian nations. The Japanese have lost no time in indoctrinating these islands. No matter how the war goes, the enemy can't lose for winning.

After we finished our business in the port area, Nogi took me for a walk along the piers. There were several ships in the harbor including two destroyers and a cruiser. Nogi mentioned the shortage of gasoline in Manila, and pointed to a couple of small vessels which he called "gasoline ships."

The port area was completely littered and every inch of space was covered with prisoner drafts on their way to Japan. The men were a miserable lot—a horrible mass of human wreckage.

After our walk, Nogi treated me to dinner at a little place off the Luneta. We had soup, bread, sauerkraut, roast pork, yams, ice cream, and tea. I didn't enjoy the meal. The food stuck in my throat. After witnessing all the misery and starvation of the men waiting to board ships, how could I eat. Granted I was hungry, and I have been hungry for so long that I don't know when I last felt gastronomically happy. But the best food in the world wouldn't taste good under these circumstances.

It was dark when we left the restaurant and was beginning to rain. Nogi said that he had to hurry back to the port area as "many prisoners were arriving." He sent me back to Bilibid accompanied by a soldier. As we drove through the night, I noticed that the dance halls and night spots were still operating, and the movie houses were open. However, none of them seemed very busy. There were no American movies advertised and the big neon signs were dark.

A local newspaper reports the first graduating class of the Japanese Navy Auxiliary—women navy officers in noncombatant jobs. I remember when we would joke about that ever happening.

October 8, 1942

Activity is the word of the day. Another draft left for Japan and a new group of men arrived for further transfer. The Japanese are evidently covering their troop movements with prisoners of war. The prison ships are unmarked—an open violation of international agreements. It's rumored that a ship carrying almost two thousand prisoners bound for Japan was torpedoed and sunk.

"Wild Bill" Harrington arrived from Cebu this afternoon—he had been in jail down there. Harry is a funny guy—he went completely nuts at Mariveles. Harry is the original "Major Hoople." All he needs is a pool hall to make him a living cartoon. However, with all his faults, he has a lot of good in him. He's kindhearted by nature and is fond of children. I remember how he took fatherly care of a little Chinese girl on our ship all the way across the Pacific.

Harry was very affable today, but he could still explode. I gave him my last cigar. He always chewed cigars and hadn't had one recently. He was very thankful.

October 9, 1942

The whole damn compound smells to high heaven. The Japanese hauled about three tons of tiny fish into camp. Extra cooking pots were set up, and the entire galley crew was kept busy frying fish by the thousands to feed the prisoners passing through the port area on their way to Japan. The entire prison is saturated with the fetid odor of half-rotten fish.

One of the Japanese guards said that we would all be in Japan by Christmas. He may be right—we aren't out of this mess by a damn sight. However, there is the possibility that the medical department would still be the last to go.

Late in the afternoon, Sartin, Joses, Welch, and I were invited up to the front building to have supper with Nogi. The meal wasn't anything to write home about—a tiny piece of meat about the size of a half-dollar, a hard piece of *camote* [yam] and tea that tasted like medicine. However, we knew the fellow was doing his best and we sat around and talked.

After a short while Nogi said, "I have ordered another dinner." Then in came five steaks with potatoes, tomatoes, and a bowl of spaghetti. The steak may have been thin and hard, but it wasn't rotten— and it was meat. There was more talk and then a glass of hot canned milk. We later learned that Nogi sent one of his men out to buy the food and Nogi paid for it out of his own pocket. That amounted to a big hunk out of his pay.

Nogi is hard to figure out. He mentioned during our conversation that he was glad we could sit and talk. He enjoyed the company. We talked of damn near everything and asked a million questions: "Do you hunt in Japan? Do you grow apples, corn, grapes? Where in Japan is it hot? Where is it cold?"

We also talked about the Japanese language and its three sets of characters. There was mention of Tolstoy, Ibsen, Gorki, and Karl Marx. Nogi has read them all.

It was after midnight when we arrived back at the barracks. Nogi generously gave us the use of the big room in the front building for a medical library. There are a couple of tables and chairs in the room and the lighting is good.

October 12, 1942

It has poured most of the day, both rain and more problems. One of the older ladies in town, who has been successfully bringing in food for the patients, was caught in a lie by the Japanese. She was attempting to smuggle us money. This will probably end her good work. If only she would have contacted one of the underground. I had a professional agent in touch with her and she should have entrusted the job to him. These amateurs mean well but they continually mess up because they don't pay attention to details. "B" is completely washed up for the same reason. He's not even permitted to speak to Americans.

It's the same old story. So few people are willing to stay behind the scenes and leave the actual work to the pros. The Catholic sisters have been allowed to send in small boxes of medicine, but they were refused today. It was probably a good thing too. I understand they hid 5,000 pesos in one of the packages—clumsily done and easily caught. It was lucky for them that they were turned away at the gate and the boxes not searched. St. M. reported long ago that the nuns are watched very closely. My contact with her at present is practically nil. We are completely isolated—for the time being anyway.

Weird sounds from the front building tonight. One of the guards is singing. There is nothing more eerie, doleful, or sadistic. The singer is really suffering—so is everybody else. Maybe that is why the Japanese are great artists—they can't sing.

October 17, 1942

It's been several days since I have entered any notes in my diary. Paper is becoming very scarce and difficult to obtain. There has been no departure from the dull routine of prison life and nothing of any importance to record.

Up before daybreak each morning, and the first crimson streaks of light reveal the round red ball in the center of a white field—the flag of Japan. I had never noticed flags much before. But I have come to learn their importance and the value of their symbolism in the lives of a people. A flag is a tangible object. It can be offered to the masses for them to revere and respect. A flag can give a people purpose when they fumble such abstract things as ideals, ways of life, national character, and integrity. We can begin beating our way back to a strong nationalism by emphasizing our flag.

Major Houghton arrived today from Cabanatuan on a temporary mission of sorts. He looked pretty good, except that he's rice-fat and his head's practically shaved. He certainly appeared different in his dirty undershirt and khaki pants. He didn't look at all like the "out of the bandbox" Houghton that I knew on Corregidor.

I finally convinced Sartin that regular weekly inspections would help a lot toward keeping this place clean. The result is interesting. Yesterday I made my inspection and the improvement was amazing. Not only was the equipment clean, but the buildings and toilets were spotless. Even the patients looked decent and the corpsmen were neat and respectable looking. The men were as proud of the place as I was and hospital morale received a much needed boost.

October 18, 1942

The Japs delivered a dog carcass for our meat ration today. Consequently we ate burned rice. Lord knows what they will think of next.

Nogi showed up this afternoon. He has orders to send a draft of medical officers and corpsmen to Davao. However, he would like to keep our hospital unit intact and ship out the Army group that's loafing around in the upper compound. Nogi asked Major Breslin if he would like to take the assignment, but Breslin pulled out of it fast. He told Nogi that he would make a list of Army personnel available but, as for himself, he wants to stay at Bilibid.

I already have enough Navy volunteers for the job, but you will never get an Army volunteer out of that gang. This Army crowd should be happy for a chance to do something constructive for a change.

October 24, 1942

Nearly a week since my last entry, and it has been one hell of a seven days. The problems began when the Japanese asked for a medical detail to go to Davao and set up a hospital. Nogi and Sartin decided that this was a splendid opportunity for the Army medics to step out and really accomplish something. Major Breslin made his selections, but carefully excluded himself. Breslin isn't worth a damn and never has been. I knew him from Bataan and Corregidor and he's a complete loss any way you look at it.

In the meantime, the Army boys are growling like hell about going to Davao on this detail. Enough Navy personnel volunteered for the assignment but, as Sartin pointed out to Nogi, Army and Navy wouldn't mix well in this kind of arrangement.

The attitude of the Army on matters of this kind is hard to understand. As a group they haven't acted like officers and doctors. I recall the days immediately before the surrender and remember how every damn one of their medical stations were deserted while the Navy remained to the last with our troops.

After the surrender, when the Army morale broke, the Navy carried on in the Army's hospital in all key positions and handled the load. And now, at this late date, with a splendid opportunity to do some good, they welsh on the deal and consider themselves martyrs and discriminated against. Just a bunch of no good politicians.

The situation went from bad to worse in a hurry. It so happened that Nogi went out of town for a few days and left Kito, his four-eyed Japanese sergeant, in charge of the camp. Well, with the top honcho away, it didn't take long for a few of the Army boys to get the ear of Yakasiji and the sergeant. Sartin was immediately called to the front office and ordered to substitute Navy names for the Army men that the Japanese had checked on the draft list. Sartin refused on the grounds that Nogi had already made his decision. Old "four-eyes" was mad as hell. This was "Mutiny on the Bounty" all over again. Rumors began flying fast and furious. The "myth-mill" had Sartin on his way to another camp and an Army Colonel was to be the new hospital Commandant.

Our medical staff called a hurry-up conference. We didn't know if the sergeant had enough power to make this decision. On the other hand, would Nogi back up Sartin or his own man? Plus the fact, we didn't know how much "last word" authority Nogi was permitted.

Reprisals for our disobedience was to be expected—probably by breaking up our tight organization. It began to look as though all the goodwill we had built up over the past many months had been wrecked by two Japs and that ratty Army outfit.

The following morning, Kito sent down the draft list and he substituted two Navy names for two of the Army men. Then to make it official, "four-eyes" rushed the list over to headquarters for the "seal of approval." In the meantime, the Japanese in the front office refused to talk to us about the situation. There was nothing we could do but wait and hope that Nogi returned before the draft shipped out.

Nogi arrived back in camp the next morning—just in time, and the fur flew all over the place. Much to our surprise and relief, Nogi backed up Sartin completely. It has taken a while, but there has been a gradual lessening of tension since the incident.

Nancy Norton should be honored by our government for her unceasing efforts to help American prisoners. Her persistent and sincere wholehearted attempts are worthy of eternal memory. She has sent in baskets of papayas, clothing, and toilet articles. Then this past week about eighty pounds of carabao bones. Also, in spite of the Japanese isolation campaign, we have managed to get a little money smuggled into camp, and that greatly relieved the food problem.

Camp morale received another boost from the "myth-mill." The

Americans are now supposed to have taken all the islands to the south (for the ninth time), and there was a big sea victory for our side. Everybody's on the crest of the wave again, but that wave like all the others is going to hit the rocky beach one of these days and sink into the sand. And so goes the cycle from week to week. These guys are children, not soldiers. Romanticists, not realists. Escape artists—mentally.

A new recipe for coffee was invented the other day. It's really a coffee substitute made from banana skins. We bake the skins very dry, then crumble them in boiling water. The resulting drink is dark and sweet, not bad to taste, but it's not coffee and has no kick to it.

Copies of the Manila newspapers mysteriously show up in camp whenever the news benefits the Japanese. I noticed a long list of names in the latest issue—people tried and convicted for various crimes. Their heinous crimes were listening to foreign propaganda; uttering or disseminating foreign propaganda; failing to salute a sentry; and other such nonsense. The punishments ran the gamut of beheadings, hangings, shootings, and long prison terms. This coprosperity sphere is getting serious and "Nippon Go" is in earnest—in their own way.

Reports from the port area tell of Japanese troops and war material traveling in vessels marked as hospital ships. A real neat violation of a treaty that was meant as a boon to mankind. Soon we will hear Sikiguchi raising hell again about Americans sinking Japanese hospital ships.

Within a few days if all works well, we should be receiving a large sum of money from "over the wall." I have been appointed to handle the fund when it arrives and to see that it goes where it will do the most good.

Nogi came by this afternoon to visit. We sat and talked awhile, and then he gave me a pack of Camels when he left. Just like dumping a carload of ice cream cones in "Little Henry's" lap.

October 26, 1942

I was busy up at the front building today where we have fixed up a reading room. A few medical books that we managed to salvage are available and the Japanese also brought in a bunch of old magazines and books of various kinds—including the usual propaganda material.

Wada, one of the Japs that speaks English well, reported to me that American prisoners in Japan work in the sugar beet fields. However, they are treated good—much better than in Bilibid. He also said that American civilians interned in Japan are living in first-rate hotels. He expects that we will be allowed to send a censored mailing card by the end of the month. The little guy is certainly propaganda saturated.

The Japanese regular army soldiers have been completely relieved of guard duty and the young civilian boys have taken over the job. When the youngsters left here a few months ago they were raw high school kids. They have been under intensive training at O'Donnell and arrived back here looking fitter and more like soldiers. However, they are plainly not the physical best of the Japanese troops. They have been issued American Enfield rifles, American cartridge belts, and American ammunition. I understand that old "four-eyes" will be in charge of the gang.

The Japanese have placed American prisoners at every probable military objective on Luzon. The Japs also report that Americans in Japan are working in factories, and are well cared for and happy in Japanese homes. A very clever way of advertising the fact that we will be bombing our own people whenever we bomb Japan. A nice touch!

October 31, 1942

We had been using the Bilibid execution chamber building as a hospital ward, but the Japanese ordered us to vacate it a few days ago. Then today 200 prisoners from Cabanatuan arrived enroute to Japan. Among the group were nine Americans caught trying to escape. The unlucky fellows were tossed into the small building and locked up in solitary confinement. Other American prisoners were given the guard duty responsibilities. The orders demanded that there be five guards on duty at all times. If anyone escapes, the men on duty at that time will be executed in place of the prisoners in solitary.

Barnbrook, the lad who escaped from here recently, was not among the nine men brought here from Cabanatuan. However, the front office has taken pains to insist that he was apprehended and is now undergoing a period of beatings. This may be true. On the other hand, it would be just like the Japs to save face by stopping us from asking the question: "Where is Barnbrook?"

November 2, 1942

Three days ago we were suddenly notified that 2,000 Filipinos would arrive the next morning and would occupy the entire upper compound. That meant we had to make room in our buildings for the men already in that compound, and also a prisoner draft waiting to go to Japan. We had to double up on the ward space. Patients were placed on the concrete decks, under beds, between beds, and in the aisles. It was a job, but we finally managed to pack them all in before the Filipinos arrived.

This group of Filipinos are Visayans from down south and they are on their way to O'Donnell. We are told that they are to be trained for constabulary work. It's chiefly a matter of indoctrinating and propagandizing them. Most of the Philippine Scouts were Visayans. They are good fighters and have a distinct language. The men looked sturdy and strong. They have been apparently well fed.

The nine men in the execution building continue in solitary confinement. We finally did get permission for a doctor to visit them once a day, and are trying to get consent to have the men deloused. All the lads are eaten up by body lice. Their condition is fair but they are allowed nothing to eat except dry rice.

November 7, 1942

Since my last entry there has been a general movement of prisoners from Cabanatuan to Japan via Bilibid. Groups arrive at all hours, leave at all hours, and from them we annex the very sick.

A few days ago a group of Filipinos arrived under heavy Japanese guard. The men were either recently captured guerrillas or else had been escorted through heavily infested guerrilla country. I'm inclined to believe the latter because they show every evidence of Japanese indoctrination. Their discipline was very strict and they were unmistakably Oriental trained, even down to the face slapping. I think they might have been a graduating class from the indoctrination and propaganda school at O'Donnell.

In the meantime the Japanese squeeze gets tighter. We are now forbidden to cook our mongo beans over small outside fires—hobo style. This started when one of the guards spotted a prisoner making a cooking pot out of a five gallon gasoline tin. The gas cans are as sacred to these bastards as they are to a West Indian native who would pawn his soul for one.

Sartin talked to Nogi a few days ago about the prisoners in solitary and told him that the men were being fed only rice. Today Sartin went up to the front office again to complain. Nogi stated that he had left orders for the prisoners to be fed a full ration, but "four-eyes" neglected to do anything about it.

Nogi also mentioned that Barnbrook is confined in Fort Santiago. Nogi doesn't know what the authorities plan to do with the boy. Santiago has an unsavory reputation among all the prisoners. Everyone there has either been beaten, shot, or both.

The latest scuttlebutt is that there has been a big sea battle down south and our fleet has been destroyed (again). The Japs are claiming that we don't need ships—only Admirals.

November 13, 1942

No entries for a few days. The paper shortage is becoming very acute. The routine of prison life is not very conducive to daily recapitulation. One lives it and that seems adequate. To relive a day by writing about it doesn't seem to bring any satisfaction.

The prisoners in solitary were taken to "gestapo" headquarters the other day and they haven't been heard from since.

We did manage to get a few of the outside fire spaces back. However, today our little "hospital soldier" discovered the hot plates. He ripped them out by the roots and now all hot plates are ordered turned in. This is just another method of throwing us back on regular chow. I had expected that something like this would happen. Yesterday I overheard the Japanese talking about increasing our food ration—give one favor and take another away. Just an old Oriental custom.

Incidentally, another Japanese medical officer came through on an inspection tour which as usual amounted to nothing. From the very beginning of our association with Japanese doctors, it has seemed to me that we have contributed to their medical education. Most of our third year medical students would be able to answer their questions. Anything we mention of common advanced knowledge, the Japanese greet with awe and astonishment as though it was something brand new.

We are continually receiving more and more patients from other camps and are still considered "the hospital" by the Japanese. And yet our food continues the worst of any area. A few days ago we received a ration of rotten fish—so rotten in fact the eyes were gone. We just ate rice.

November 16, 1942

Last night, despite a downpour, the prisoners put on a variety show. We managed to locate a few musical instruments and a survey of the camp population revealed a surprising assortment of talent. Musicians, magicians, singers, and comedians appeared from nowhere. The production was very entertaining and the preparations for the show occupied the interest and minds of the men. The morale factor was excellent and I hope that this evening can be repeated.

The Japanese recently sent twenty of our malaria cases to one of their hospitals for study and treatment. The men returned yesterday. One prisoner had died, but the others looked to be in great shape. The men reported that in addition to their medicine they were fed very well. They were given plenty of meat, fruits, and vegetables and also milk between meals. A ward next to theirs was filled with Japanese malaria cases and whenever the American prisoners walked by, the Japanese patients handed our men gifts of cigarettes and anything else they might want. The Americans were also taken for a walk in the park every day. It's no wonder they improved. They received decent treatment.

This morning we were honored by a visit from the Japanese "gestapo." They were in civilian clothes rather than their usual military police uniforms. They always ask the same question: "Where were these men wounded?" The usual answer: "Bataan and Corregidor." Sartin was notified that tomorrow we are "to talk to several people about a lot of things." I have no idea what this means. We will have to wait and see.

November 19, 1942

Several members of the Japanese press paid us a visit this morning and toured our establishment. One of the reporters spoke excellent

English and was very familiar with the west coast of the United States. This newsman stated that he always liked the Americans, but can't say as much for the British. He recently interviewed the British Commanding Generals of Hong Kong and Singapore and found them "very snobbish." He also remarked that, knowing American people as he does, he couldn't understand reports by returning Japanese that they had been mistreated by the Americans. We couldn't understand that story either.

The reporter also boasted that the Japanese had scored another big naval victory down south. One gets the impression that there are Japanese naval victories practically every day. I don't know where these ships are coming from that they claim to be sinking, but according to my tabulations we were out of warships months ago.

He then began to brag about big German victories in North Africa. Under any other circumstances I may have been obliged to remark, "That ain't the way we heard it, Charlie." Our latest reliable information seems to put the African situation entirely in our hands.

I think the logical assumption after our conversation this morning is that the Japanese propaganda bureau was completely devoid of anything that could be embellished. A dearth of material for twisting.

I have seen our own propaganda departments labor under the same conditions. It's certainly a sad situation. I don't believe there is anything sorrier than a balloon with no air in it. That's one thing about propaganda, when you haven't got something to develop convincingly, it's better to say nothing. Poor propaganda is worse than no propaganda.

However, the Japanese reporters did their best for the cause. They told us that Dewey had been elected Governor of New York and the Republicans gained half the seats in Congress during the recent elections. The Japanese have been playing up this election as evidence of America's disapproval of the present "war party." They don't grasp our political setup at all. They attach attributes to our "two party" system which are comparable to "parties" in other countries. Therefore they evaluate our elections all out of proportion.

The English speaking reporter told us that Dewey will be the next President. When I asked him about Willkie, he replied that Willkie is "in the doghouse" with Roosevelt. The Jap was probably referring to Willkie's recent remark about the administration talking too much about our production and not doing enough about shipping war material to where it will do the most good. The reporter's further comment was to the effect that Willkie wasn't a politician, but only a "business man."

The members of this press group were the people that Sartin was to "tell a lot of things to." However, Sartin isn't a talker and the interview was unproductive to the Japanese. Before they left, the Japanese reporters permitted Sartin and Joses to send messages home. The Japs expected the messages to be commendatory but such was not the case.

While on the subject of news, if only half the European information now reaching us is correct, it is encouraging. I also believe that many of the "diehards" in camp are now willing to admit that their future lies with the fortunes of war in Europe and not in the Pacific. They are finally beginning to realize what a small part of the general war the Philippine Islands really are.

The other afternoon, Nogi made a dummy inspection run in preparation for the real thing the following morning. That evening he had dinner with us. The pesos I recently acquired permitted me to buy a little meat from a merchant who is allowed into camp occasionally. It was a good meal and since Nogi has fed us a few times, I didn't mind reciprocating. Nogi acts under orders, but I'm convinced he offers understanding up to his limits.

Our big inspection was conducted by Colonel Ishi, a rather tall man for a Japanese. Sikiguchi also tagged along, but he was outranked and out of the picture on this tour.

Following the inspection, Nogi reported that Ishi was satisfied with conditions in the camp. However, he did increase the meat allowance for the sickest patients, but not by enough to do any good. The Japanese don't seem to have any conception as to the necessary amounts and quality of food. There seems to be a general unfamiliarity with the commonest facets of medicine and life as we know it. Our standards will never be approached. "East is East and West is West" is not a line of poetry. It's a sociological fact and the sooner we realize it the better.

While I was standing by the front building waiting for the inspection party to arrive, I looked across the street at a small gathering of Filipinos. They waved and made other gestures of goodwill. I also noted the new installation of electrical wiring around the entire compound. After the Japanese finished stringing the line, they ran regular current through it, but there wasn't enough power to harm an ant. Then they got the bright idea of cutting the real heavy stuff into the line. The electricians in camp doubt if the wire will take the load.

We attempted to keep three of the corpsmen who arrived recently with the Corregidor draft, but the Japanese insisted that they be sent to Cabanatuan. Before the men shipped out this morning, I had a chance to talk to them. They reported finding the remains of a Marine sergeant on top of a water tower in the east sector of the island. I happen to know the story about that incident. The sergeant's name is Sweeney. He and another sergeant were on the water tower observing and directing fire during the battle. They were discovered and blasted by an enemy machine gun nest. Sweeney was killed, but his companion jumped down into the nest and cleaned it out, dying in the fight.

The latest report from "over the wall" tells of a Japanese destroyer anchoring in the port area with about a hundred dripping wet Japs on deck. They were dressed only in their skivvies and swords. The Japanese wouldn't dream of going overboard without their swords. It's believed that they are survivors of a sinking in nearby waters.

Spanish classes continue in a big way. I hold two classes daily with eight men attending regularly. Progress is satisfactory, but the greatest difficulty in teaching Americans a foreign language is teaching them English first. It always astonishes me how little English is known by the average college graduate.

November 22, 1942

The Japanese are preparing to pay us. Last Friday I was issued my "chop." The chop is a wooden stamp with my initials carved on it. The Japanese take the first two letters of your last and first name, provided the second letter isn't a consonant. If it happens to be a consonant, the Japanese replace the letter with any vowel and that's how they write your name. My chop reads *He Tu* and is pronounced *Hay Two*. The entire stamp is shaped like a lipstick and there is a notch in the wood to show the top of the stamp. This is important because Japanese characters are read vertically, not horizontally. We will use the chop to sign for our pay. We were also told that the money "we don't get" will be put in Japanese postal savings and in order to get our money out someday we will need the stamp, so "don't lose the chop." Just another souvenir as I see it.

Another problem arose today and I decided to write a letter to the Japanese. After all this talk about paying us, the Japs now issued orders forbidding outside fires and hot plates. It's like filling the galley with all kinds of food and no way to cook the stuff.

In my letter I explained how these little outside fires served to cook our mongo beans which are important in the prevention of food deficiency diseases. I also pointed out that we economized on wood and that it was impossible to cook anything additional in the galley.

Nogi arrived about noon and I gave him the letter to read. After listening to my comments, he stated that there were three reasons why the extra fires could not be allowed. They were against the Japanese regulations, not enough firewood available, and there was danger of setting fire to the camp.

Realizing that I was losing the argument, I asked Nogi to take the letter, read it over, and think about it before taking any action— he agreed.

November 24, 1942

Yesterday, Nogi gave us permission to light our fires in safe designated places. He assured me he would give orders to that effect to his four eyed assitant [Kito]. Today, however, Kito threw a monkey wrench into the machinery. It so happens that Kito was told to look over the designated areas before we would be allowed to start the fires. But "four-eyes" was "too busy to do any looking over." I went direct to Nogi and we were allowed to light one fire tonight. I hope to have permission to light the rest of them by tomorrow.

Among the latest news reaching me is the report of the torpedoing of a ship outside Manila Bay with the loss of over 1,500 Japanese. That explains the hundred or so survivors who were brought into port on a destroyer last week. No large ships have left the harbor since.

There's an American civilian in the upper compound who is supposed to be a United Press correspondent. He's known by the nickname of "U.P." His real name is Weisblatt and he was already at Bilibid when I arrived. Weisblatt has a healed femur fracture and still walks with a decided limp. I was asked to look at him, and while the fracture hadn't healed properly, it certainly didn't require the "crutch and limp" act.

Weisblatt broke his leg in a fall and the Japanese sent him to their hospital where he was given every attention. He was uncooperative and his present state is the result of his bullheadedness. He's anti-everybody, an ignorant bastard. I refused to do anything with his leg in spite of his insistence on an operation. There was no emergency and it's not as disabling as he pretends. However, he does need a hernia operation. Regardless of how I feel about the man, Aesculapius would operate and so would I.

I have found it necessary to discipline Weisblatt on several occasions. He repeatedly gets the idea that he's above disciplining and is a great user of such expressions as, "They can't do that to me" or "I'll take it to the American people."

This character has a fine little wife. I ran across her at Fort Mills and Bataan. She was a hospital dietician and carried on splendidly during the entire campaign. I understand that she married Weisblatt in Shanghai. Just how that brave woman could tolerate her husband is difficult for anyone in the camp to understand. They are both originally from Pennsylvania.

Last night the boys gave their second show of the season. It was very funny and the crowd enjoyed the performance. Nogi and several officers from his staff showed up for the entertainment. The show lasted about an hour, most of it in a light rain which turned into a downpour by the end of the performance.

November 28, 1942

Funny thing about nostalgia. A whiff of a stray breeze, a remembered fragrance, a colorful sunset, a haunting melody, and suddenly you realize with a strange tug at your heartstrings that you are missing something or someone. And that speaks volumes on this late sultry afternoon in old Bilibid. We won't talk about that anymore!

A few days have passed since my last entry and we have had our usual round of problems. We finally received permission to set up our cooking fires in the designated areas, but then the Japs cut off our wood supply. After several conferences with Nogi, it was decided that we could have our fires as long as the scrap wood around the compound held out, but we could not use the Japanese woodpile. Of course, this means that before long the men will be tearing the damn buildings apart and chopping down the few scattered trees.

Following the escape from camp awhile back, the Japanese weren't satisfied with the outdoor assembly *bango*. They just couldn't make the count come out correctly. Then somebody had the bright idea of counting heads inside the barracks and wards. An armed guard along with one of the Camp Wardens did the counting every morning and night. This system was carried out expeditiously and accurately. However, during the past week, somebody up at Japanese headquarters put out a book on how everything is to be done. And now, here we are back at the old system with everybody milling around in the yard before daylight in the morning and after dark at night— 1,500 of us and the Japs trying to come up with an accurate count. They can never arrive at the correct figure and we are continually being counted and recounted. God, what a frustrating mess!

Payday happened to be this week and one had to laugh a little in spite of the tragic confusion. We stood in line all day and it was a slow endless procedure. The Japanese paid us with the "bayonet money" that they have been turning out on a printing press. The paper bills have no serial numbers and represent nothing in the way of government backing. According to international agreement I drew the pay of an officer of corresponding rank in the Japanese Navy—220 pesos ($110). I was allowed to keep 25 pesos and the rest I had to give back to the Japs to be placed in postal savings—minus 60 pesos that I'm charged for "room and board." Momota, our Japanese paymaster, says "I will get my money back when I go home."

Lord knows, this paper has no value and when you stop to consider how the paying is done, it's plain to see how the Japs can take 700 pesos and pay the entire prison.

A man gets in line number one to draw his pay, then steps over to line number two where he deposits all his money except 25 pesos. Desk number two hands the money over to desk number one and the process begins all over again. The sad part about the whole affair is that prices are so high that there is very little we can buy for only 25 pesos.

Everyone who drew money is giving ten percent to a fund for the sick and needy. This is necessary to save lives. The very ill prisoners can't get well on the little money they are receiving from the Japanese. They need additional food and the extra pesos will be used for that purpose.

Nogi returned from Cabanatuan with the news that he's sending Warren Wilson up there to work on the eye cases which are becoming more prevalent. I hate like hell to see Wilson go. I have been through the entire war with Warren and our association has been most pleasant. He's a good worker and to my mind was the outstanding doctor on Corregidor. He's one of the few contacts I have made in this war that I hope to maintain when the conflict is over.

Nogi reported that there is an outbreak of diphtheria at Cabanatuan and the death rate will probably rise this month. We are diagnosing an occasional case of diphtheria here also, but I isolate the men as soon as any suspicious signs of the disease appear. Diphtheria in this hellhole would decimate the camp in less time than it would take to tell about it.

Ever since I have been at Bilibid our galley cooks have been Chinese prisoners. They are to be released soon and the American Army and Navy cooks are now running the kitchen. The Chinese were a lousy crowd ever since the surrender. Immediately after the fall of Corregidor, they became arrogant and rebellious. They were plainly in open revolt against the whites. The one fact that characterizes this war is the everyday evidence that it's a "race war." An interracial conflict. Consequently it has the ferociousness, cruelty, hatred, and fanaticism of a religious war.

December 2, 1942

After six months of living practically naked, I'm still not used to flies crawling on my back. They continually annoy me. I should think that after this length of time I would become oblivious to the mere matter of a half-dozen flies scrambling around on my dorsum. Apparently I still retain some vestige of exquisite sensitivity to external impulses. As a further example of this condition existing among us, Sartin always takes off his glasses when he eats. He says that this way he can't see the worms in his rice. Not seeing them is the whole solution—you can't dodge them all.

Today our four-eyed friend Kito sent more of our corpsmen off to Cabanatuan. It has always been interesting to me, not to mention disturbing, how much clout these Japanese Army non-coms have over their superior officers. At times Nogi seems to be only a figurehead. We can depend on Kito or that hunchback dwarf Wada to keep us in constant difficulty.

Following our first payday, the "share the wealth" plan was put into effect. I collected a total of 258 pesos for the indigent fund. The American Wardens held out and contributed nothing. They prefer to handle their own money since this is a voluntary donation. The sick and indigent will be materially benefited by this additional support. These men will not receive any actual money, but extra food and necessities will be bought for them from the merchant and the store. To dole out cash would be futile. The men would buy what they want, not what they need.

Captain John Haines [Army] who has been imprisoned at Fort McKinley arrived in camp today. He reported that the food was poor, but it's the same chow that the Japanese are eating except the Japs get a ration of beer. He did relate one interesting incident. A Japanese guard threw a knife at him one night and fortunately missed. Haines reported the incident to Jap headquarters by bluffing an interpreter. He told the interpreter that he had been instructed to report any mistreatment of prisoners. The interpreter then delivered the complaint to headquarters. Haines was called on the carpet and was reminded that Japanese soldiers always spoke the truth and the knife most likely fell off a ledge and landed near Haines, etc.

Gooding left this morning with a draft going to Fort McKinley. His departure was really a shanghaing by the front office. He hasn't been on the Japanese favored list for some time. Kito said that Gooding wasn't doing his job. No matter what anyone may say in his favor, Gooding was crooked, untrustworthy, characterless, and dumb. The Japs have done for us what I tried to do the first two months after my arrival at Bilibid. The most disgusting and unforgettable fact associated with Gooding's regime is the toadying, backslapping, handshaking, and condoning of his acts which has marked the conduct of so many of our officers. They feared him and hoped to feather their nests by playing up to the bastard.

The latest reliable information tells of the arrival of a Swedish Red Cross ship which was unloaded by the Philippine Red Cross and the cartons hauled to a storehouse in Manila. According to reports, the boxes were marked for American war prisoners and are supposed to contain clothes and other supplies. Whether we will see any of it is questionable. I heard that the Japanese soldiers steal truckloads of food from their own warehouses and sell the items to the Filipinos.

The mosquito pestilence grows worse with the advent of dry weather. As the occasional rain showers come and go, the insects breed like hell. They are very annoying at the present time, but there is nothing we can do about the situation. Besides the mosquitoes, we have ants in our beds, cooties in our clothes, and flies on our backs.

Ho hum, never a dull moment. Even the bedbugs lend a hand keeping us busy, if not amused.

December 6, 1942

I thought we were given full authority for our cooking fires, but once again Kito and Wada squashed the privilege. I cornered Nogi again about the situation and he finally said that we can have our fires if we buy the wood. I agreed to do this and allocated part of the indigent fund for the purchase of wood.

I recently found out that the Japanese have retained over 32,000 pesos of our money, less the 60 pesos per person for "room and board." We tried to itemize how much they are actually spending on us and arrived at a figure of about four pesos a month per person. What a racket. Just an old Oriental custom.

The disciplinary board met recently concerning the case of a corpsman who assaulted an officer because he believed that the officer had reported him for sleeping on watch and neglect of duty. The accused is a nasty bulldozing type of individual, but is the favorite of one of the chaplains. The chaplain went to bat for the corpsman and influenced Sartin to try and convince the board of the man's innocence. In spite of the damning evidence brought out against the corpsman, he was completely exonerated and given no punishment whatsoever. I immediately recommended that Sartin disband the disciplinary board as it was serving no useful function under the present circumstances. As for myself, I asked for my release from the board. I told Sartin that I considered myself totally unable to support or carry out any policy of such a namby-pamby nature. As might be expected, I received no reply to my request, but I know one thing for sure. I will never sit on another board meeting in this outfit. My mind is made up.

I received a note from Bob Herthneck. He's still at Cabanatuan, but hopes to return to Bilibid in a few days. I also learned that Commander Brookes and Colonel Hamilton are conducting an investigation at the Cabanatuan hospital. They are checking into reports that certain Army officers are selling medicines. The accused Army officers are offering the defense that since there was no medicine available, they had bought the medicines themselves and were only trying to get their money back. I will leave that case to the jury.

Several weeks ago, Captain Zeblen [Army] left us to go on a working detail operating out of Fort McKinley. He returned the other day with about 80 of the very sick from McKinley. Zeblen told me that he was supplied with absolutely no medicines whatsoever and was unable to do anything for the men.

Zeblen is a real character. He's from Charleston, South Carolina, and I first met him on Corregidor. He was one of the few medics over there who actually worked under fire, continually in the front lines. He was pretty well shell-shocked by the time the surrender took place.

Captain Zeblen is a mental case to begin with. He's a typical schizophrenic praecox. He claims that both his mother and father died in an insane asylum. However, in spite of his schizophrenia, he is brave, willing, kind, and pleasant. I have come to admire the guy and like him, but feel sorry for him at the same time.

If my memory serves me, Zeblen was awarded the Silver Star for gallantry in action on December 29, and he really deserved it. I remember talking with him at the mouth of the Malinta Tunnel on Corregidor that night just before he left to go topside. I was adjusting the chin strap on his helmet as we stood under a tree at the mouth of the tunnel. "Naturally," he said. "I hate like the devil to go up there again, but it's sure as hell my duty so let's get it over with even if I come back a corpse." Then off he went into the darkness.

The next time I saw Zeblen was at the end of a five day bombardment. I was at my casualty station as the dead and wounded began to arrive. Suddenly, leading a group of bloody, weary gladiators, Zeblen stumbled in. He was drooling, covered with dirt, and his clothes in tatters. After a few days in bed, he reported himself ready to go again. He's an O.K. guy, even if he is a little nuts.

During the time that our forces on Corregidor became starving creatures at the hands of our own quartermaster corps, and even to the present day, one topic of conversation is practically nonexistent— women. Instead, all you hear is food, menus, and recipes. Consequently I was a little surprised recently to hear our two Swedes, Olson and Johnson, discussing the most pleasant way to die. Olson led off with a prayer that he would like to be trampled to death on the runway of Minsky's Burlesque. Johnson parried with a wish to be suffocated by a boatload of female movie stars.

A new draft arrived this afternoon from Pasay, a work camp for Nichols Field. The men hobbled into camp more dead than alive. They are on their way to Cabanatuan and a group from Cabanatuan will take their place. This Pasay gang has been worked out—nothing left in them. The camp itself has a bad reputation. It's run by the Japanese Navy and Marines—tough taskmasters. From reports I have received, these Pasay prisoners have been worked harder and cared for less than any group in the work camps. Most of this Pasay draft will end up on the sick list by tomorrow. The number of Americans surviving this mess is going to be very damn few.

December 10, 1942

This is the anniversary of the day we were bombed out of Cavite and the beginning of our long "Dunkirk" which took us to Bataan and then Corregidor where we made our last stand. It has been a tough year, with much of it lived as a helpless target. The outlook was always hopeless. We had the hell kicked out of us day after day and week after week. And then the surrender with all of its chaos. Officers and men becoming animal derelicts with only the crude law of the jungle as the order of the day—the primal urge to survive. The veneer of civilization, thinly spread to begin with, was wiped off like chalk from a slate. There was not one leader big enough to meet the issue as a whole. Although, here and there through the pandemonium and graveyard of decent human behavior, an occasional self-disciplined courageous personality would emerge. But their numbers were so small that they cast only the feeble light of a tiny candle throughout the black and crumbled world.

Today, however, as I write, the world situation has certainly improved in our favor. And while we must view it from the darkest center, it's encouraging to know that we are at last fighting back and there is reason to believe that Nippon can't take it as well as she can dish it out.

The Japanese declared a holiday on the anniversary of their attack on Pearl Harbor. Their propaganda was to the effect that on this date Japan began her war to "free the Philippines." Large multicolored posters are plastered all over Manila with wording that says "Watch the Philippines grow." Toy balloons were sent aloft with messages in Tagalog that read "Happiness is one" or "United in happiness." Other posters tell us that "Wherever the Japanese Army is, there is peace." Of course, Bilibid is also blanketed with posters.

I had barely closed my entry for the day and put away my notes, when I heard a hubbub in the prison yard. A new draft had arrived from Cabanatuan, and among the men returning to Bilibid were Herthneck and Strangman.

I hurried to the upper compound where the draft was to spend the night. Bob was a sight for sore eyes. He's rice-fat but otherwise in good shape. Bob and I went through the entire campaign together. His loyalty and diligence left nothing to be desired. We shared everything, even the toilet paper. He was sent to Cabanatuan when that camp was at its worst and carried on despite bouts with jaundice and beriberi. Every Cabanatuan draft that passed through here had nothing but praise for Bob and the work he was accomplishing there. He carried a letter with him from the American camp commander recommending him for an award in recognition of his splendid work among the prisoners.

Bob reported that the food at Cabanatuan has greatly improved in the past month with more carabao meat being allowed. Maybe that's where our meat ration is going. The last couple of meat deliveries we received were barrels of pickled beef that stunk to high heaven. It reminded me of the ancient seagoing ration of beef in barrels of brine. Shades of Magellan!

December 15, 1942

Warren Wilson left for Cabanatuan today. Sartin asked me to write a commendatory letter for him. I wrote the letter at once and have arranged for its ultimate delivery to the War Department. Cagey also went up there, but he didn't rate any letter. I still have a score to settle with him over an incident that occurred on Corregidor. Cagey attempted to convince the departmental surgeon that the Navy contingent was planning to have Colonel Cooper replaced by Olympia. It was absurd and I spiked the rumor in no uncertain terms—but I won't forget it. When the going got tough after the surrender, Cagey took to his bed with tuberculosis (?) and arrived at Bilibid as such. It was his own diagnosis pure and simple. I yanked Cagey off the sick list as "no disease" and he considers the Navy a hell of a gang as a result. There are times I wonder if Cagey isn't a little bit nuts. Some of his Army associates think the same way.

That yellow son of a bitch Manning is just as bad. He still remains on the sick list because nobody has the guts to handle him as he should be. Just another instance of this pampering attitude with which I am wholly out of sympathy and which nauseates me daily.

December 20, 1942

Four more shopping days till Christmas. Best not to think about it. Just like it doesn't do any good to listen when the gang gathers around the firelight at night to sing the old songs that open doors to treasure houses filled with memories, sweet unto the point of pain.

The weather has turned nice. The rains have gone. The early mornings are quite chilly, but the days heat up if you are in the sun. Best season of the year around here.

The Japs managed to finish my O.R. this week. After five months of haggling they finally got around to it. If I had waited for them before opening shop, we would be exactly 700 operations behind and any number of emergencies lost.

December 23, 1942

A year ago today I was camped in the jungle east of Olongapo. I ran into Berley and Langdon and met Marion Wade for the first time. He was acting Regimental Surgeon for the 4th Marines ever since Joses had been sent down to Canacao as a mental patient.

That reminds me of another interesting story. I saw Joses upon his arrival at the Canacao hospital and he didn't impress me as sick, physically or mentally. He was perfectly oriented around the place and when war broke out he was attached to the hospital staff. However, when the time came for Joses to return to his outfit, he was suddenly unfit for the job. Davis and Lowman were afraid he might break down again. I had been Chief of Surgery at Canacao, but in order to make room for Joses, I was transferred to the 4th Marines as Regimental Surgeon and Joses was given my position. Apparently any nut could do my job.

The truth is, Joses has never done enough surgery or anything else to warrant the title. He's just a big hulk of disgusting laziness, no damn good for anything. He foxed his way out of Shanghai when he saw trouble brewing and then slid out from under when he should have returned to the Regiment. I'm not sorry I drew the assignment with the 4th Marines, but I have to sit alongside that skunk Joses every day—and I hate it.

Everybody wondered why I didn't try and get back to the Canacao outfit immediately after the surrender. Well, it's because that gang is full of tripe and disgusting people like Joses. Physical cowards with no guts and ignorant of the first principles of command. Mindful only of their own comforts and useless as the pope's balls. They have been nothing but a demoralizing influence ever since the war began.

Anyhow, to get back to a year ago. Wade and I, along with Crews, spent the night near a camouflaged hospital site. I outlined my plans for three battalion aid stations and a regimental aid station.

I had a good bath in the cool waters of a river which flowed nearby and bedded down with my blanket under the bamboo brush. Natives from one of the villages came near us several times but passed on by. They were apparently hunting wild chickens as they carried their long-bow arrows like spears.

I left at daybreak with Wilson and Herthneck for Bataan. We planned to organize our battalion medical facilities and establish a line of evacuation for the wounded. Our forward defense lines were already falling back and I knew it was only a matter of time before we would be forced to retreat to our final line of defense on the Bataan Peninsula.

As we drove east from Olongapo, I looked for our troops which the day before had filled the rice paddies and bamboo jungle. The area was deserted. We stopped at a camouflaged medical station and talked to a couple of Army medics from the 41st Division. They were all packed up awaiting orders to pull out and fall back along the Hermosa Road to Bataan. I knew damn well that if the 41st moved out, the 4th Regiment wouldn't be able to hold the position alone and would be driven back into Bataan before another day passed.

We drove on hard and didn't stop till we reached Balanga. We "borrowed" a barber shop and washed off the heavy yellow dust, shaved, filled our canteens, sweated out an air raid, and then headed south again.

Everywhere I looked there was evidence of our forces retreating into Bataan. The roads were jammed with trucks, tanks, and soldiers as they poured through the bottleneck at Hermosa.

I was never to see Balanga again. It was destined to be blown to pieces by our artillery in a futile effort to stop the enemy advance. We finally reached Limay where the Army had set up a hospital. I met Colonel Duckworth there and learned that the Japs were already pushing in on Manila from the south. The Colonel told me that the city was being evacuated of all military personnel and supplies. It was evident that our lines were being rolled up at a fast clip. I made arrangements with Duckworth to receive our wounded as I knew that adequate ambulance roads were available from Mariveles, either direct or over the Bagac Road.

We had driven only a few miles south of Limay, when a Japanese air raid forced us to take cover in a shallow ditch behind a hill. The Japs were dropping bombs in the valley below and in an area directly behind us on the hill. After the raid I discovered that the Army had built an airstrip there and we had inadvertently taken refuge directly on the target. I also learned during that air attack just how large a foxhole is required to reasonably protect a 160 pound guy.

We arrived at Mariveles about noon. I contacted the battalion commanders and saw Lieutenant Bookman. Before the war began, I had arranged with Bookman what procedures to take in establishing an aid station and sent field medical equipment to him at Mariveles. Bookman had his field hospital already set up in a river valley behind Camp Dewey.

Shortly after we arrived, the enemy launched a heavy air attack. The entire harbor area was blasted. Our new field medical unit certainly justified its existence on that day. It was inspiring to watch the cool competency and willingness of the doctors and corpsmen, many of whom were having their first taste of enemy fire. They behaved splendidly. I have been proud of them ever since and have repeatedly reported their gallantry.

Early the next morning, Christmas Day, we went into the hills and joined the troops moving into bivouac. I heard that the 4th Regiment was evacuating Olongapo and the Naval Station was completely demolished and abandoned.

Our bivouac area was in the hills behind Mariveles in a dense bamboo jungle. The enemy was continually overhead and we spent most of Christmas Day in foxholes. During the afternoon, contingents from the 4th Regiment straggled into the bivouac area from Olongapo. It was a "Dunkirk" Christmas, but we managed to keep our organization intact and discipline was well maintained.

All during the day, aviation units from Nichols Field kept arriving. They were strung out for miles along the dusty road that led north to the high ground and protected areas. Enemy strafing operations during that time would have been disastrous, but as far as I can learn, the Japanese didn't attempt any strafing sorties.

About five o'clock, Ken Lowman arrived from Manila. I was surprised to see him. Admiral Hart had already left for Australia aboard a submarine and Lowman was supposed to be on the Admiral's staff.

Ken was without orders and was apparently not attached to any organization—just a refugee. He talked about working with Bookman at the field hospital, but planned to return to Manila if the town was declared an open city.

Later that night, Dan Boone and a medical unit arrived by truck. They had been sent by the District Medical Command with orders to "render whatever service was required." They were dispatched with no supplies, no orders for attachment to any specified unit—no directives whatsoever. They arrived in the capacity comparable to a bunch of guerrillas—to live off the countryside about them. This action was typical of our District Medical Command, and the record of our first week of war is full of such asinine instances.

Boone reported to Lowman since Ken was the senior medical officer. However, Lowman decided that Dan wasn't needed and sent him back to Manila—Ken also went with him. The rest of the medical group stayed and were absorbed into our organization.

Early the next morning, the 4th Marine Regiment was ordered to proceed by echelons to Corregidor and take up the beach defense of the island. I sent Crews and Tyler with the first echelon while I joined the 27th Regimental Headquarters at the headwaters of the Mariveles River. Enemy planes were overhead for the next two days, but dropped nothing in our vicinity.

On the afternoon of December 28, I received orders to proceed to Corregidor. Bob Herthneck and I sneaked out of the hills just before dark. On our way down to the beach area we stopped at a small building off the Bagac Road. It was a combination bar, nightclub, and whorehouse. We bought a bottle of warm beer and a can of beans. We also cleaned the dust and dirt out of our ears. The beer was putrid, but it was safer than drinking the water. We also wanted to conserve our canteens as much as possible.

All the foregoing is in retrospect, just as Bob and I have sat through the last few days and reminisced. One incident we both remembered happened the night we were bivouacked in the jungle. I always wore a rabbit's foot on my belt. It was one my prized possessions and meant a hell of a lot to me. Before rolling up in a blanket I loosened the khaki belt on my trousers. I awoke sometime during the night and realized my belt was awry. The first thought that entered my head was of my rabbit's foot. It was gone. I searched everywhere with a flashlight and the next morning continued the hunt, but to no avail. I felt it in my bones that I could expect some sort of catastrophe and all through this mess I have been ever mindful of my missing rabbit's foot.

December 25, 1942

Christmas Day at Bilibid. Very little to say about it. For the previous week the Japs have been unloading a Red Cross ship at the port area. The cargo is supposed to contain American medical supplies, cigarettes, food boxes, and clothing. All we have seen so far are several cartons packaged in England and marked "Prisoner's parcel from the British Red Cross and the Order of St. John War Organization."

This shipment was from the International Red Cross. Each box contained canned meat, soap, sugar, apple pudding, and jam. This additional food helped our Christmas dinner considerably. Otherwise, the usual diet of water lily soup and rice would have been the menu of the day.

We never received any of the American boxes that were aboard the ship. The Japs took them. We know for a fact that entire cases were grabbed by the guards at the pier. And, of course, everyone else handling the cartons also got their cut. What eventually reaches us is anybody's guess.

Reports tell of huge quantities of everything imaginable. Even the Japanese are astounded at the amount. They have never been used to big league numbers. They can't understand or appreciate our standard of living. It's beyond their grasp. They can't visualize how our country can afford to expend so much on such a small handful of prisoners. Unfortunately we are to see very little of it.

Christmas Eve, I crawled under my net early in order to avoid the great droves of mosquitoes. Ed Nelson and his choral group marched about the prison yard singing Christmas carols. They did very well too.

The next morning I received a package from "over the wall." It contained a cooked chicken, corned beef, crackers, preserves, soap, and a toothbrush. I also found a note in the chicken stuffing telling me where a few pesos were hidden. Feast or famine has been the story of 1942. The money will certainly help as 25 pesos doesn't buy very much. Our friends at Santo Tomas were permitted to send a few items into camp. Bob received a box of cigars and shared them with me.

Sick prisoners continue to be brought to us from Pasay and other outlying camps. All are in hellish shape—starved, beaten, and miserable. We received two cases from Palawan with broken arms from warding off blows from an iron bar. One man was brought in from Pasay, dead and already boxed. We were not allowed to open the coffin, just bury it. This is a gruesome business.

A few days ago the Japanese finally delivered our mailing cards. We completed them according to instructions, but they are still sitting in the front office. Very few of us have any faith in the delivery of these messages. All of us hope to beat them home.

After two paydays, the money collected for the indigent fund has helped provide additional food for the sick, but not really enough. As a matter-of-fact, our greatest single expenditure is for firewood.

It was concerning our pay allotment that my latest battle with the establishment occurred. I let go with both barrels and our relationship is now visibly strained.

Sartin called me into his office for a conference. He had heard that about twelve Navy nurses in Santo Tomas were not being paid and he thought it would be an excellent idea if the fund would allocate enough money to give each of the nurses 25 pesos. I agreed to the idea, but pointed out that there were a hell of a lot of Army nurses at Santo Tomas who were equally deserving. And since the Army boys also contributed to the indigent fund, then we should be fair about distributing the money. I strongly advised him against allowing this to be exclusively a Navy affair and insisted that the Army nurses should receive aid also.

Sartin assured me that the Army would be taken care of. A few days later, without my knowledge, a list was circulated among several of the Navy personnel for contributions to the nurses relief fund. When I found out about it I asked if I could give to the collection. I was told that the list was closed and had already been submitted. I asked if the Army was included. It developed that once the Navy nurses had been allotted to, no more was done. It was an out and out partisan job. Frankly, I was disappointed with Sartin. In fact, I was so damn mad I could have cleaned out the whole hospital. I buttonholed Sartin and openly charged him with deliberately sliding this nurses relief effort through without bringing it to my attention because he knew my sentiments on the subject. Sartin tried to convince me that the Army nurses were not left off the list intentionally, but the facts were too obvious. I refused to mince words and insisted that he do something to remedy the situation, and pretty damn quick. I told him that it was for the good of the service and the morale. I demanded that this group distinction be stopped at once.

All of our previous arguments have been devoid of any real bitterness on my part. For no matter how disgusted I may have been at times with his policies, I have always given Sartin credit for being honest and sincere.

Our talk ended with my refusal to retract my remarks or my belief that he had deliberately engineered and condoned the whole affair. In good conscience I couldn't forget the Army nurses who were with me on Corregidor and helped so many of us there.

The following day, Sartin changed his mind and all the Navy and Army boys donated to swell the fund for the gang of nurses held in Santo Tomas.

This original Canacao crowd have played the Navy clique business too close to the vest. I can see the logic in maintaining an intact organization, but not at the expense of others in the service. I personally have more reason to feel bitter toward the Army than any person in this outfit, but as much as I dislike them as a group, I hope I never allow my personal convictions to make me act unjustly toward them.

War certainly does strip the veneer from the rotten wood, whether they be labeled Army, Navy, or Marines. Man can be wrought only by fire and forge and shining brush into that which the basic material permits. God help the poor potentialities of us all.

January 1, 1943

I awoke when the *bango* bell rang. I noticed Charlie LeComte crawling out from under his net and wished him a Happy New Year. "I wish I could say the same for you," says Charles. Just a good old American custom.

I haven't been feeling too well lately. I tire easily and am mentally sluggish. My memory for recent events is poor. I can't remember when we last had meat—only water lilies, rice, and an occasional ration of fish. I can honestly state that if we had been obliged to live entirely on the food furnished by the Japanese, hardly any of us would be alive today.

It was seven months ago that I was marched as a prisoner through the hills of Corregidor. Starved, hungry, weak, and sick with beriberi, I was loaded into the hot stinking hold of the *Lima Maru* to be brought to Manila. I had only eaten a half can of salmon in over 24 hours and the stink of fish was still on my scraggly beard.

The next day I lay on the sweltering deck, hot as an oven under my back and with the hot tropical sun stabbing at my eyeballs. A Filipino nurse passed by and knelt beside me. She gave me a stale piece of bread and a drink of weak tea. As I drank, she whispered in my ear, "My name is Santa Maria. You will have food tonight. I will find you."

The hard roll was moldy and sour, but I ate it. Don't let anybody tell you that a starving man can't find sweetness in garbage, sawdust, or shoe leather. You can swallow it, you can stomach it, you can even digest it—but you can't like it or want it. I ate to live that day. God, it seems a long, long time ago.

Thomas Hayes in full dress uniform with cap at a characteristic jaunty angle, 1939. He inscribed this photo to an unknown recipient, "Just a Country Boy."

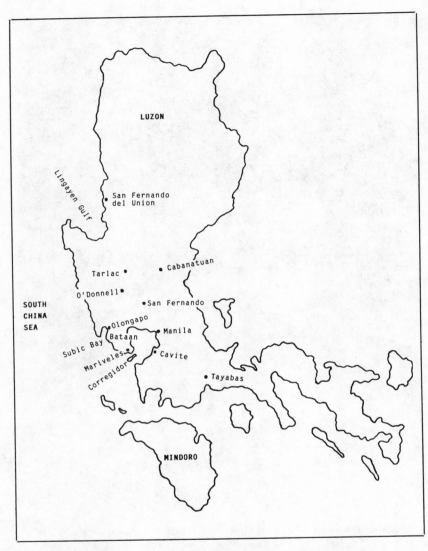

A map of Luzon, main island in the Philippines, shows locations of prison camps established by the Japanese. Bilibid, in Manila, was the clearinghouse for prisoners moving from camp to camp.

Cavite Navy Yard after bombing by the Japanese. Wreckage of a naval launch is in foreground. Photo taken 17 December 1941. Courtesy National Archives.

Japanese General Homma landing at Lingayen Gulf on the island of Luzon, 24 December 1941. Japanese photo.

Bataan Death March. Japan photo.

l view of Bilibid Prison showing barracks and round guardhouse. Courtesy National
ves.

Bilibid Prison showing barracks and round guard tower with dividing wall. Courtesy
nal Archives.

Circular Japanese guardhouse that divided the upper and lower compound at Bilibid Prison. Courtesy Dr. Paul Ashton.

Vegetable garden under cultivation at Bilibid Prison. Execution chamber can be seen in background. Courtesy Dr. Paul Ashton.

Bilibid Prison Hospital photographed by Captain Kusumoto, Imperial Japanese Army, in August 1942. The doctors and corpsmen here were identified by Mr. Jan Herman of the U.S. Naval Medical Command in Washington, D.C., and Dr. Paul Ashton.

1. Nelson 2. Welsh 3. Boone 4. Erickson 5. Silliphant 6. Hayes 7. Wade 8. Sartin 9. Zundell 10. Joses 11. Cross 12. Rogers 13. Berley 14. Haase 15. Percival 16. Hunt 17. Bray 18. Kornbloom 19. Schwiech 20. Klumker 21. Kentner 22. Compton 23. Novak 24. Gooding 25. McCurry 26. Schweizer 27. Byers.

THE BILIBID HOSPITAL.
FOR MILITARY PRISON CAMPS OF P. I.

December 25, 1943.

Captain M. Nogi, Imperial Japanese Army,
Manila, Philippines.

Dear Sir:

The moving picture show given on December 23rd
was greatly enjoyed by us all.

Again we thank the Japanese Authorities for
their kindness in providing this wholesome recreation for
American Prisoners of War.

We sincerely appreciate being permitted to
enjoy these entertainments made possible by the Imperial
Japanese Army.

Respectfully,

T. H. HAYES,
Commander, Medical Corps, U.S. Navy,
Senior Medical Officer

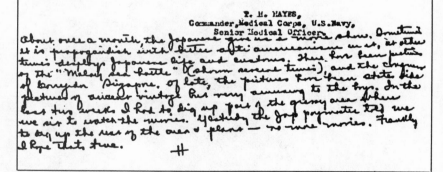

This "Christmas letter" written by Hayes is typical of the polite face he showed to his captors. The annotation at bottom gives a somewhat more honest reaction: "Sometimes [the movie] is propagandish with bitter anti-Americanism in it, at other times displays Japanese life and customs. . . . Of late, the pictures have been state side pictures of ancient vintage but very amusing to the boys. . . . Yesterday the Jap paymaster told me. . . . no more movies. Frankly I hope that's true." Courtesy U.S. Naval Medical Command.

THE BILIBID HOSPITAL
FOR MILITARY PRISON CAMPS OF P.I.

July 1, 1944.

MEMORANDUM FOR COMMANDER THOMAS H. HAYES,MC,USN:-

Subject: Approval of Punishment.

    1.   Punishment in the case of the below named men
is approved as indicated.

NAME	RANK & ORG.	OFFENSE	PUNISHMENT AWARDED
SHAW, Ted.	S.Sgt.USA	Drinking alcohol on duty	Confined for a period of five(5)days.
ALDERETE,Melcor	Pfc, USA	Drinking alcohol on duty.	Confined for a period of five(5)days.

N. NOGI,
Captain,Imperial Japanese Army.

This case was unducted & tried by Japanese. Hence no report sheet from our side. This was Shaw's second offense. He was given a warning the first time; for that reason. He was bringing alcohol into the compound and dispensary as to men already in close confinement for use of alcohol; see attached sheet.

Hayes.

This copy of a punishment memo is annotated by Hayes as well, but it is not the second offense of Sargeant Shaw that alarms—it is Hayes's enlarged handwriting, caused by the deterioration of his eyesight. On 17 September 1944 his diary ends, "Writing paper and my eyes are both about gone." Courtesy U.S. Naval Medical Command.

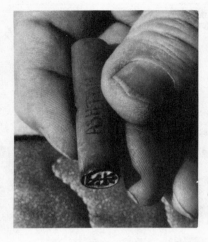

Signature stamp or "chop" typical of those issued to the American prisoners at Bilibid. Courtesy Dr. Paul Ashton.

Hayes devised this letter in October 1943 as a model for POWs to follow as the Japanese had agreed to broadcast ten such messages daily. In his instructions to the men the complexity of Hayes's position was clear: "Subjects to be avoided are . . . maltreatment or monotonous diet and other rigors of war" but "it is not necessary to express undue appreciation for this privilege." Courtesy U.S. Naval Medical Command.

MODEL

I am John Doe, Lieutenant, United States Army. My next of kin (friend) (family) is Mrs. John Doe, #16 Cedar Street, Omaha, Nebraska. Anyone hearing this please write her (him, them).

I am well (sick, better, comfortable, under treatment and happy to be able to greet you now.

If you need money, sell the car. Send John to some school as always. See Jones about insurance. Do not worry (any paternal or brotherly advice).

All my love (best wishes, greetings, remembrances etc) to Mary, Uncle Joe, etc. (Other love and endearment do not be bashful).

This is only a guide. Do not make your messages stereotype on the above, except the introduction which is in parenth Limit it to 100 words.

THE BILIBID HOSPITAL
FOR MILITARY PRISON CAMPS OF P. I.

March 27, 1944.

MEMORANDUM TO CAMP:

Subject: /   Care of Library Books.

1.   This Camp is very fortunate in that an excellent
assortment of good books were received recently, from the American
Red Cross, for library use. In order to permit reading by the largest
possible number of persons, serious attention must be given to the
care of these books. The following rules, if observed by all wards,
will be helpful:

    a. Keep books clean by not handling with wet or soiled hands.
        Do not use them to carry hot utensils or dishes.
    b. Open new books carefully. Do not fold covers backwardly.
    c. Use a thin book mark, not a pencil or large object.
        Do not place open book face down instead of using a book mark.
    d. Do not deface book by turning down corners of pages, writing
        in margins or fly leaves, underlining words, or removing pages.

2.   Improper usage of books will result in suspension
of library privileges.

3.   Officers in Charge of Buildings and Wards shall
publish this information to all persons under their jurisdiction
and post a copy of this memorandum on the bulletin board.

                                    T. H. HAYES,
                        Commander, Medical Corps, U. S. Navy,
                                Senior Medical Officer.

1   2 DKL   3 HR   4 AN   5 CVC   6 pro   7 al
10   13   14-15   16 B   17   18

For information:
                    Chief of Surgery
                    Chief of Medicine
                    Mr. Schweizer
                    Mr. Weissblatt

The sort of memo Hayes wrote could easily result in his reputation for
nit-picking among enlisted men. This one admonishes library users to
"keep books clean. . . . Do not use them to carry hot utensils or dishes."
Hayes kept his sanity through such use of irony, but this was not always
appreciated—or understood—by his colleagues. Courtesy U.S. Naval
Medical Command.

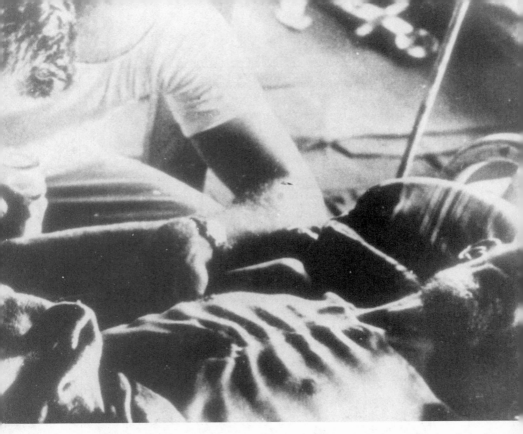

American POW being treated at Bilibid Hospital for beriberi. Courtesy National Archives.

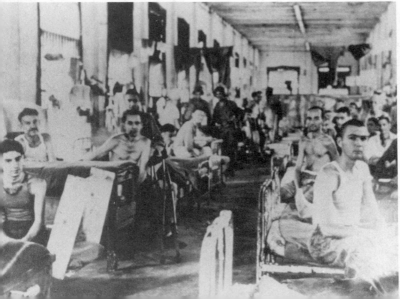

Bilibid Prison hospital ward. Courtesy National Archives.

...erican POWs from Bilibid about to embark on a ship bound for Japan. Courtesy National ...hives.

...e S.S. *Oryoku Maru* ... Olangapo Naval ...tion on ...cember 15, 1944. ...mbed and sunk by ...e planes the next ...y, this was the first ...many "hell ships" ...ere POWs bound ...o Japan were packed ...o airless holds. ...ves was among ...m. Courtesy Naval ...torical Center, ...shington, D.C.

POWs from the *Oryoku Maru* floundered ashore at Olangapo where Japanese machine gun held them at bay against a seawall. This newspaper illustration shows the path to the tenn court where men were eventually herded and where Hayes operated with razor blades in makeshift sickbay. Courtesy Scripps Howard Foundation.

Survivors spent six days in the tennis court, broiling by day and freezing by night. A single hydrant served some 1,300 men who waited an average of eighteen hours for one drink of water. Courtesy Scripps Howard Foundation.

III.

The Notebooks
October 1, 1943 to September 17, 1944

The portions of Commander Hayes' diary from the period of January 2, 1943 to October 1, 1943 are missing, and so far as is known, they have never been recovered.

On September 25, 1943, all officers of the camp were ordered to report to Nogi's office. They were notified that Commander Hayes would relieve Sartin as the senior medical officer of the Bilibid hospital.

Hayes was instructed to prepare a new organizational list consisting of 177 medical personnel and submit it to Nogi the following day. All remaining medical people not on the list were to be transferred to Cabanatuan.

October 1, 1943

I assumed my duties as Senior Medical Officer this date. I have all the responsibilities of command, but without the full prerogatives of command. The Japanese retain much of that.

For the past six months we have been in the doghouse with the Japs. Nogi's revelation that I was to be placed in charge of the hospital came as a surprise to me. I was directed to submit a draft list of men to be transferred to Cabanatuan and was told in no uncertain terms that Sartin and Joses were to be on the list.

Out of respect for Sartin, I asked to retain him, but the Japanese wouldn't hear of it. I chose Wade as my executive officer and we immediately went to work on the list of men we wanted to keep and those who were to be transferred.

My reorganization plan was accepted by the Japanese and we began to ease our personnel into their respective new jobs. There were plenty of good officers that I hated to let go. However, my selections were based coldly on our needs at the moment. Loyalty, competency, and physical condition were also considered.

My new regime got off to a flying start when one of the Americans was found in possession of stolen sugar and several corpsmen were caught giving medicine away without authorization. Luckily these incidents occurred before I had completely assumed command and the Japanese didn't hold me responsible.

It seems that we have as much trouble with our own people as we do with the Japanese. This has been the experience of every American who has been in charge of a group of prisoners. It's a constant fight against personal selfishness. A continual battle against individuals who would sacrifice their comrades for personal gain.

My policy will always be "the best of a bad bargain for the greatest number." Our mission in this war is to bring back alive as many of our fellow Americans as we can.

The final outcome of the Japanese investigation into the sugar and medicine incidents resulted in one man [Graham] going to the brig for ten days and warnings in the other cases. In this instance the punishment was limited to the offender and the rest of the camp didn't suffer.

October 2, 1943

I instituted drug conservation measures on all wards today and also a system for the equitable distribution of food among the sick. We are beginning to function with no perceptible break in routine.

This afternoon I had my first conference with Nogi and Yakasiji. Their directives are very clear. This is to be a 600 bed hospital and will serve the prison work camps of the Manila area. As soon as the patients are convalescent they are to be transferred to Cabanatuan. Any medical personnel now on the sick list are to be transferred when recovered.

Sartin left for Cabanatuan this evening. My last words to him were, "I want you to always feel that we are running this place for you. It's still your command. If you can manage to get back here someday, we stand ready to turn the hospital over to you."

I also told Joses to use his influence to have Sartin returned to Bilibid. Wade and I both mean that. This outfit belongs to the "old man." It has been his war-baby from the beginning.

October 4, 1943

The galley is functioning efficiently and a big improvement has been noted. I assigned Art Barrett the job of keeping a current classification of all patients as to their mobility, stretcher cases and walkers. I want to be able to move this outfit at a moment's notice. You never can tell when the "Yanks and tanks" will show up. I also reclassified all patients as to their degree of illness—heavy sick, light sick, convalescent, and well cripples.

October 5, 1943

We received a soap issue today—one bar per person. This was our first soap allotment since August. I was also given a new toothbrush and toothpowder. The toothbrush will come in handy. For the past two months I have been using a piece of gauze on my finger to brush my teeth. I sent a letter of appreciation to the Japanese.

Our hospital laundry consists of one small, home washing machine (G.E.), but wood is so scarce that we have very little hot water. The washing machine has an interesting history. We had two of them on Corregidor. During the last weeks of intensive shelling, the machines were running constantly—standing on the side of a hill with shells crashing all around them. They were pierced several times by shrapnel, but kept right on working—one of them still is.

The store opened today for the first time in a few months and I was able to buy a small cup of sugar, a banana, and several peanuts. Peanuts have been the single greatest addition to our diet, but they are in short supply.

We are up to our ears this afternoon formulating a system of reporting our census and classification of the sick to the Japanese. We were also ordered to have another Cabanatuan transfer list ready by tomorrow. I'm already being assailed by those who want off the draft. In order to maintain control of choosing who is to go and thus prevent the arbitrary moving of the very sick, it's my duty to railroad the recovered patients and those better able to travel. Let the chips fall where they may. This is a cold-blooded business, but I feel equal to the task. I'm not a politician and neither is Wade. An honest judgment of patients will be made.

I heard tonight that the Japanese will give the Philippine Islands their independence on the 14th of this month. Japan has already appointed an ambassador to their new satellite.

Yakasiji showed up today with the news that starting on October 9, ten prisoners every day will be permitted to have a personal broadcast sent to the States. The radio transmissions will be limited to one hundred words. I assigned Cross and Nelson to handle the operation and I was ordered to censor the messages.

October 8, 1943

The Japanese declared today a holiday. The only difference between holidays and any other day is that the working parties don't go out.

The newspapers are busy proclaiming the upcoming Philippine Independence Day. The new government will probably declare war on the United States immediately.

The reduction of personnel continues. I'm having difficulty retaining enough convalescent people to carry on the daily routine. It's beginning to look like only the very sick will remain in the camp.

October 10, 1943

Today is Sunday and Chaplain Wilcox held Protestant services in the upper compound. Wilcox is an Army chaplain of retirement age, a heart invalid and just recovering from dengue. I sometimes wonder if we are going to get him through this mess.

I began a survey of patients to weed out the permanently disabled. They may end up being the backbone of our organization. Nogi and Yakasiji came through on an inspection tour this afternoon. The wards really looked like a million bucks. Nogi commented favorably upon the hospital, but his determined interest in the convalescing patients was very evident.

October 11, 1943

Last night a patient was bitten by a sick cat. I'm trying to get rabies vaccine from Japanese headquarters. The patient is one of the men taking care of the Japanese "pig farm." The Japs have been keeping ten sows and a boar housed between the dysentery wards and the main galley. Naturally the responsibility for the care and feeding of the animals has been placed on our shoulders. Momota shows up frequently and has the boar put to the sows. Very stimulating. He takes photographs—close-ups.

I finally got around to writing my radio message today and censored several others. All the messages reveal one craving—to hear from home. Many of us are two years without a word. This is a living death, so completely divorced from the outside world and the life we have known. Most of us have "barbed wire" psychosis to some degree. The loss of memory for events prior to the war is universal among us.

Captain Ruge [Marines] dropped in to see me tonight about more food for his work detail. He has a crew of 52 men that are doing hard physical labor. They are all losing weight and can't last much longer.

Ruge can buy beans and bananas on the outside for his men if he can get the money. I'm trying to convince Nogi to increase the working party pay allowance.

The Japanese showed movies tonight—Walt Disney's *Pinocchio*. I never attend. Somehow, this policy of showing us movies when we need food so desperately always reminds me of the Pearson administration in the Virgin Islands. The natives were crying for work, wages, and better living conditions. Pearson gave them pianos, operas, and other cultural pursuits. The people finally cried out that they couldn't eat pianos.

To top the day off, Momota and Yakasiji informed me that we can only buy food from the store twice a week. There is no doubt that we are in the tightest denial period since we have been at Bilibid, and certainly the most isolated.

October 13, 1943

I worked most of the night on our permanently disabled list that we are to deliver to Nogi today. It's a 35 page report on 234 patients— by "page" I mean one about the size of a newspaper sheet. I also had a conference with Crews to learn if we can give the working party more rice without depriving the rest of the men. He said that it can't be done. Everyone is down to skin and bones.

I hustled up to the front office and, after a long talk with Nogi, I managed to get a small increase in the rice allotment for Ruge's crew. It wasn't much, but it will help.

My first difficulty to straighten out this morning was how to get the pesky Jap guards untangled from our hospital routine. Last night, one of the raccoons made the night shift cut off the hot water sterilizer and "leave it off." They have a marked incendrophobia. I tried to explain to the Japs that a hospital runs the same at night as it does during the day. We still need sterile compresses, instruments, etc.

I began a survey this afternoon of the clothing needs for the men. Most of us have been going naked except for a nine-inch "G" string in order to conserve our one or two shirts and pants. However, there are an appreciable number of prisoners who have enough clothes so that they appear neat, clean, and civilized. I believe I can acquire a certain number of shoes and other items of clothing, even if I have to redistribute the clothes available among the "well-heeled" of the camp.

General Miramoto showed up unexpectedly this afternoon and held an air raid drill. It was rather interesting although I don't like to be packed into any damn cell block during any air attack. I sweated out two of my longest hours of the war in a lockup like this on Corregidor. Give me a foxhole any old time.

October 14, 1943

Independence Day. Somehow I don't feel the least bit emancipated. We heard bands playing most of last night and early this morning. One group of musicians passed by the prison playing "America the Beautiful." Now try and figure that one out. The Japanese notified us that today will be a full holiday and tomorrow a half holiday. Ruge and his men can sure use the rest.

My examining board reported ten more officers fit for transfer to Cabanatuan. There will be much groaning and moaning, but it's an honest survey. There is no reason why the stuffed shirts shouldn't do their part. It's the unfortunate fortunes of war. All of us must take our turn. The strong and well cannot capitalize on the weak and needy. I seem destined for the job of son of a bitch throughout this entire war. I'm lucky that my happiness is not dependent upon a ward heeler's popularity.

Received word from Fritz Berley. He arrived at Cabanatuan O.K. Berley's working in the fields every day or else helping build roads— barefooted. He reported Sartin is doing fine. Bookman, Greenman, and Wanger are on carpenter detail, building an outhouse for the Japs.

I asked Hap Goodall to take charge of the men in the upper compound. He is one of the permanently disabled officers and will be here indefinitely according to our present plans. Hap was executive officer on the *Canopus*. He was wounded on my birthday, February 8, of last year. I operated on him that same afternoon. His last request before I put him under was not to amputate his leg. I didn't and he still has it—doing very well too.

October 15, 1943

Nogi showed up this morning and saw every damn one of the 234 men I had submitted as permanently disabled. Four hours later after the smoke cleared away, he had removed one case. However, before we were through, he allowed me to keep the man and also add Brown and Silliphant to the list.

The people in S.O.Q. raised a fuss when they learned of their eligibility for Cabanatuan. Manning, of course, gave me a long song and dance—politician stuff. He will go. There are no favorites in this league.

I dragged Frank Adamo out of his oblivion on the disabled list and put him to work as hospital statistician. He was glad to do it and the job will take his mind off his troubles. Adamo is a regular gentleman and has been a good shipmate from the beginning.

There have been scads of pigeons flying around the camp and a few of the boys knocked over a couple and made a stew. After two days of cooking, the birds were tender and very tasty. I'm afraid it's just too bad for the pigeon population from now on. I consider them fair game under the circumstances.

I managed to see a copy of the latest Manila newspaper and independence celebrations are still going strong. The new puppet government asked for recognition by the United States at once.

There is much conjecture as to what our status will be. I personally believe that the U.S. will refuse recognition as a matter of already committed policy. If that happens the Philippines will probably declare war on America. The possibilities are myriad. The paper also stated that in honor of Independence Day, the new government will be very generous and every family will be given one cake of toilet soap.

In order to maintain discipline in the camp it is necessary that punishment prerogatives be given to the Americans, to some degree anyway. I'm all set to put the idea to the "landlords" at the earliest possible moment. Unless I'm allowed a "big stick" it means that every time I have a matter of discipline to settle, I have to turn the problem over to the Japanese. I prefer that we do our own laundry. It's a ticklish point and will have to be handled diplomatically. We must maintain as much control over our own men as the Japs will permit.

October 18, 1943

The "landlords" were in early this morning and we held a conference. I presented my case and was given permission to handle the discipline problems. Several other matters of routine were also ironed out including this shortage of paper. My diary and notes are beginning to suffer.

October 21, 1943

I guess we are in the backwash of a small typhoon. There was no dawn this morning. We are handicapped all over camp on these dark days. The little light available only makes it more difficult to go about our routine.

I took on an invalid undernourished youngster to do my laundry and look after my bunk. I'm paying him five pesos a month. The extra money will permit him to buy a few limes and peanuts which he needs very much.

Wade and I spent most of the morning going through baggage in the storeroom. The personal belongings of the dead and the men that had been sent to Japan. We were looking for clothes for the needy. We found a reasonable amount of items, but only a few pairs of shoes. It was surprising how much medical department material we discovered among the personal effects. I plan to place a receipt in each box showing what was removed.

I continue to hear praises about the new galley crew. The chow has greatly improved. But as time goes on, the men will tire of it and bitch like hell again. After all, we are still dealing with human beings. Practically all day long I listen to gripes, complaints, and controversies arising over trifles. None of the problems amount to a hill of beans. The older men are becoming more senile. Although it has been my observation that the older fellows have done better than many of the younger men. The most difficult ages to handle seem to be the 40 to 50 group. I listen to their gripes, however, I have been telling them to take their problems to their immediate superior and not keep running to the "old man" all the time. I'm not trying to evade the issues, but it's the only way to maintain the station of the "old man." It's a basic principle of leadership and command.

October 24, 1943

Yakasiji showed up today and reported that we can't receive any more newspapers from the outside. They will be strictly forbidden. The only news allowed from now on will be "prison news" that the Japs will mimeograph up at the front office. There is much conjecture over the reason for this sudden edict. However, I think it's only because the Japanese headquarters have always objected to our having Manila newspapers.

I went over next month's prospects for food and reduced the individual buying power of the men. I could allow them a bit more, but they wouldn't spend the money for food. By adding more money to the general fund, I can buy enough limes so that each man will have a few for a weekly allotment. Vitamin C is our greatest deficiency at the present time. The men will probably bitch like hell but before the month is over I'm sure they will notice the benefits.

I had a long session with Nogi this afternoon. We wrangled over such items as bamboo brooms, rat poison, and mouse traps. I also repeated my request for writing paper. I'm beginning to doubt if the Japanese have any.

I did get on one sensitive subject. I asked Nogi if several of the men could buy watches out of the money on deposit in Japanese savings. Nogi asked what happened to their watches? I remarked that most of them had been lost due to the fortunes of war. He gathered my full meaning and changed the topic of discussion. However, I did get permission for those who have watches to have them cleaned in town without the expense being considered a store purchase. Nogi considers this a "great concession."

October 26, 1943

An officer from Japanese headquarters showed up today with another one of their great ideas. The Japs feel that anyone who has personal tools should buy them from the Japanese since the Japanese are the real owners. The reason for this is that tools are scarce and the Japs have none. I brought up the question of personally owned medical instruments. They are to be exempted. However, they must be registered with the Japanese so that they can issue us certificates of ownership.

October 28, 1943

About midnight last night the Japanese broke the galley crew out to receive a truckload of fish. They were in good condition for a change, but we will have to eat them all today because we have no way of keeping the fish from spoiling. The last shipment we received were so rotten that we couldn't eat them.

Our most serious clinical problems today are the beriberi eye cases. There is a great deal of blindness. We have begun a vigorous campaign against these eye conditions although in most instances the permanent damage has already been done. I issued orders prohibiting anyone from giving tobacco to a patient under treatment by the eye department.

Carey Smith is doing a bang-up job revising the diets. Putting Carey to work with a responsible job has yanked him out of his lethargy and the unhappy mental state which he has had since Bataan. Moreover, his health has improved.

The Japs came and got three of their pigs this afternoon—no explanations. I will be glad when we are rid of all of them. They are a fly breeding menace. And, allowing a minimum of four piglets per sow (all have been sired), just where the hell are we going to put 50 pigs?

A trifling incident occurred which undoubtedly will be treated as a grave offense unless we can dilute it in some manner. The Japanese have an old wooden sideboard which they have allowed to stand in an unlocked storeroom. During the week someone lifted two drawers out of it. The guards are afraid that Nogi will ask for the cabinet to be sent over to headquarters at any moment. I instigated a search to recover the drawers, but I'm quite sure they have gone the way of everything else that isn't nailed down around here. Schweizer tells me that he saw a Jap throw one of the drawers on a truck a few days ago.

We received a few medical supplies from Japan today—aspirin and cod-liver oil—Japanese miracle drugs. What we really need are amebacides. We have been able to acquire an appreciable amount of drugs by "shaking down" everybody coming in or going out of the hospital. Many of the prisoners are walking drugstores, dispensaries, and surgical supply houses.

October 30, 1943

Payday again and this Japanese farce ceases to be funny. I received 190 pesos, had to give the Japs back 100, put 50 in the indigent fund, and kept 40. Sounds good, but we are only allowed to spend three pesos a month. The balance has to be returned to the Japs at the end of the month. It's the silliest thing I ever heard of—perfectly ludicrous. Yakasiji realizes the system is ridiculous, but Nogi thinks it's a good idea.

October 31, 1943

Evidently there must have been a big argument up at the front office. We just received word that the extra pesos will be collected every three months instead of monthly. This means that everybody will be running around with pockets full of pesos that they can't spend. By the end of the third month I will have to give the Japs back more pesos than I receive. What a Mickey Mouse outfit!

The latest clothing report shows that we have 260 men without shoes. Wooden shoes can't be supplied because there isn't enough wood available.

Lieutenant Golden was returned as a patient tonight from Cabanatuan. He reported that conditions there are much improved. The men receive their full pay allowance and food is plentiful. Again it becomes obvious that this camp is singled out and given less food and privileges than the others. It's difficult to understand why this situation persists. It may be because we are directly under the nose of the Filipino mayor of Manila who hates Americans.

Our situation is desperate. We have only been able to survive because of the store, but since that has been cut down, our nutritional state has become worse. A Red Cross shipment would certainly help.

During September, Duckworth returned back here from O'Donnell. He has gone stir-wacky since then. "Ducky" has developed a persecution complex and feels that he is discriminated against by the Navy. He grows more cantankerous and childish every day. Even Carey Smith is losing patience with the Colonel.

Salt embalmed fish and moldy rice was the menu for the day. Most of the vegetables that arrived on the same truck were slimy and decomposed—just garbage. The food situation is worse now than I have seen it in a long time. And yet I'm told that there are plenty of fruits and vegetables in the islands. All we hear is the same old excuse, "All same, Jap soldier eat."

I went into a huddle with Ritter. Zundell is the latest man to develop optic nerve damage. Eye cases continue to be a major problem. The horrifying fact is that we have 840 men facing permanent eye damage. Nogi must increase our spending allowance so that we can buy more from the store. We can take hunger without a growl but to go blind is another matter.

November 7, 1943

Yakasiji showed up this morning. He wants a detail of 100 men, including 60 corpsmen, to go to Corregidor for a few days in order to make a moving picture. This will be a propaganda movie. Probably part of the "Down with the Stars and Stripes" epic they have been making.

An engineering problem also cropped up today. The drainage pipe from the pigpen is clogged. These pigs continue to be a thorn in our side. I don't know what we are going to do once the litters arrive.

A patient arriving back to camp from the port area reported that a ship anchored in the bay is rumored to have Red Cross supplies and mail on board. Then, about seven this evening, I received word to supply a working party to unload Christmas Red Cross boxes from the vessel. There was no information as to when they will be delivered to us. However, there are indications that the packages will be taken to a Japanese storehouse for further distribution. Of course, there will be the usual "shakedown." What we will actually receive is in the realm of speculation.

I learned about the Red Cross ship just as I was leaving for the upper compound. The "Bilibid Players" were putting on a little entertainment for the camp—songs and jokes. I had been asked to say a few words in support of the show. After a few remarks of appreciation for their efforts, I announced the arrival of the Christmas boxes. The men almost tore the camp apart with their cheers of enthusiasm.

Last year much hell was raised over the looting and selling of Red Cross supplies. This year every effort will be made to keep all the Americans free from any semblance of crooked dealings. We took a shellacking last year in a face-saving episode. We were just guilty enough to get our asses in a sling. I hope to prevent any trouble this year and we won't sign for anything we don't receive.

November 8, 1943

The Corregidor movie detail and the Red Cross unloading crew left camp this morning. I later learned that there were many Japanese women and children aboard the Red Cross ship and many of them gave the "V" for victory sign to the Americans. There are times I actually believe that the Japanese think this war is some sort of a game.

The prisoners put in a heavy day unloading the 47 pound boxes and the Japs were very meticulous about handling the packages. Every effort was made to keep an accurate check on everything received. Yakasiji informed me that there is a lot of mail on the pier including parcel post boxes. A system is being formulated to handle all the prisoners' mail.

The Red Cross cartons were placed in storerooms and the buildings were locked, but the Japs have all the keys. I stationed an American guard on the buildings all night. More of a case of guard watching guard.

The conduct of our men on the pier was excellent. The Japs were goggle-eyed. This shipload of supplies looked like the wartime allotment for a million men to them. The effect on Japanese morale was very noticeable. They can't get over the prisoners receiving so much.

November 11, 1943

Armistice Day. Twenty-five years ago Japan was on our side at quitting time. I spent the entire day counting every single box that arrived here. The Japs counted with us. We are 86 boxes over the count rendered by the unloading crew. So far the handling of the Christmas packages has been effected very well.

November 12, 1943

The Japanese declared another holiday. This gave me a chance to finish a load of office work which I have neglected due to the time required to check and inventory the Red Cross packages. All the boxes have to be recounted tomorrow.

I had a hell of a time getting rid of Momota last night. He insisted on opening several cases of recreational gear and clothing. He couldn't understand the stuff. He behaved like a kid opening Christmas presents under a tree.

The Corregidor movie detail returned to camp last night. I understand that the behavior of the men was exemplary. An entry will be made in their service records noting that they did not volunteer for this picture which will be used for propaganda purposes against their own country.

November 13, 1943

I blew my top at an officer in S.O.Q. for spreading gossip about the store and its personnel. I have always offered to explain any misunderstandings concerning the operation of the store and God help the individual who spreads demoralizing rumors and untrue remarks.

The Japanese want to increase Ruge's working party by one hundred able-bodied men. There ain't no such animal around here. Yakisiji now wants a list showing the population of each building. They only have several dozen of such lists.

I'm anxious to start distributing the much needed Red Cross supplies. But the Japs are dillydallying around in a fog. The guards are irritable over all the goodies in the storerooms. I can't say as I blame them. Their government gives them nothing. Anything they want they have to steal.

November 14, 1943

Rain! Rain! Rain! When will it ever quit! The Japanese now want lists of all available mattresses, blankets, mosquito nets, etc. It looks as if we are going to be right back to where we started months ago—a prisoner accommodating place.

I had a long conference with Nogi today, but got exactly nowhere—stupidity plus. He's now requesting additional data concerning the disability list previously submitted. Nogi now wants to know where the disability began and when.

November 15, 1943

A typhoon blew into camp last night with a heavy deluge of rain for about three hours. The wind abated somewhat about five this morning but the intense rain continues. Water rose nearly eight inches in the prison yard. All electric power is off and the entire camp, including the city of Manila, is in darkness. However, the galley is still functioning. Red Cross boxes sitting on the floor of the storerooms are water soaked.

Late this afternoon, Momota had the entire camp turn out shifting the Red Cross boxes under the guise of saving the supplies. He ruined more stuff than we can ever salvage because of his useless nuisance maneuvers. Besides that, he exposed the entire camp to pneumonia and physically exhausted the men.

Tonight it's still raining and everyone is cold and miserable. All bedding and clothing are wet. The Japs ordered us to bed at seven o'clock since there are no lights. They also redoubled the guard. Several of us sat around in the dark and sang songs. My contribution was "If I Had My Way."

November 16, 1943

About midnight last night I received word that the S.O.Q. was flooded, but nothing from the other wards. I discovered later that the Japs had locked up the night corpsmen.

As soon as it was light I made my inspection. Water was almost waist deep in the compound and halfway up the beds in some of the wards. The Communicable Disease Ward was especially bad.

I had no sooner returned to my office when I received a message from Goodall that Momota was "at it again" and moving heavy boxes to the top shelves. Those shelves are so flimsy that they will never carry the load. If we could only keep that guy off our necks and out of the way, we would be able to manage much better. Momota doesn't like Americans one bit, and Bilibid Americans in particular. He has stated on several occasions that all the Red Cross packages we receive will be wet or damaged. He's busy working at it.

The Manila water supply is contaminated and sewage is backing up into the hospital compound. We are boiling our water and have been notified to store drinking water as it may be cut off. That's great except that we have nothing in which to store water and neither do the Japanese.

There was a huge explosion in the upper compound this morning and an oil fire was started. The Japs are running around very excited. It seems that the buildings between us and the fire are filled with ammunition.

I was notified late today that no food supplies would be coming into camp for about a week due to the floods. We are handling sewage by means of steel drums that the Japs had placed near each ward and filled with sand for fire protection.

Water is continuing to rise in the food storeroom and much of the rice is already wet and irrevocably spoiled. I have a working party in there tonight trying to salvage whatever they can. It's still raining in torrents and the wind has increased. I don't know when I have been so wet, cold, and miserable.

There were no lights again tonight and everybody was ordered inside their barracks by seven. We huddled together like sheep in the pitch black, water-soaked building and shivered with the cold.

November 17, 1943

The water is receding, although it continues to rain hard. I slept in my wet clothes last night. They were no wetter than my mattress, blanket, or board bunk.

Momota has our boys busy as Chinese coolies moving rice out of the food storeroom. He tried to give us the wet rice as a food ration, but I gave him a cold ultimatum that we won't eat spoiled rice. We will go hungry first. Momota then decided to give us the wet rice to "make yeast." I told him we needed sugar to do that. He finally relented and permitted us to buy sugar in excess of our buying power. In the meantime he came through with our regular ration of good rice. I don't believe that I have ever been so mad with anyone in my life as I am with Momota. I think I'm allergic to the bastard. That midget-brained idiot is so flabbergasted with this penny ante shipment of Red Cross supplies that he's in a perpetual state of confusion. Every time he appears chaos follows. Castration definitely has its place.

By late this afternoon the water was down considerably, but the mist and drizzle continue. Discipline has remained good except in

S.O.Q. Those guys just can't seem to follow instructions and I have to ride herd on them constantly.

No lights in camp again tonight. However, a few glimmers are seen in the city. To bed early.

November 18, 1943

The skies are overcast but trying to dry up. The sewage situation is improving, however, we are still boiling our water. We have also been busy clearing away fallen trees and general debris.

Kubota, the chief interpreter, is back from Japan. He apparently was well indoctrinated while in Tokyo. He now refuses to deliver my messages to Nogi and is going completely by the book. At least I can reason with Yakasiji.

Early this morning, fifty members of the "gestapo" showed up to inspect the Red Cross boxes. It was the most gruesome, uncivilized demonstration that I have ever seen. They opened, pawed through, and destroyed. Cases of canned meats, cheese, and jellies were unpacked and searched with sticks and wires. Soap and chocolate bars were broken in half and probed. The bastards acted like a pack of wild animals as they mauled everything in sight. Cigarette packs were opened and the wrappers removed. Every shoe was practically torn apart.

Our patients and corpsmen, still worn out after a day of laboring like stevedores, were kept by Momota until way after dark moving boxes around. The Japs didn't even let the men take a break for dinner. Then to top it all off, Momota asked for another movie detail to move out for night pictures. I finally managed to grab a bite of rice by candlelight.

Everyone is tired and weary. I'm beginning to wonder if the Christmas boxes are worth the effort. Lights came on at ten o'clock.

November 19, 1943

The movie party was out all night and did absolutely nothing as it rained most of the time. The sky is dark and overcast this morning. We are still boiling water. Sewage is backing up into the camp from downtown Manila.

The "gestapo" arrived early and continued their sadistic search for whatever they are searching for. They raised a big fuss over the "Freedom" slogan on the back of the Union Leader tobacco boxes and confiscated eleven cases. However, all day yesterday they couldn't help but notice the same slogan on packs of Old Gold cigarettes that were in the food boxes. I have already moved the Old Golds into the hospital storage area.

The "gestapo" also went crazy mad over a label on the Palmolive shaving cream which read "Buy your cream in this Victory package." But they missed entirely five cases of Raleigh cigarettes that stated "Buy Liberty Bonds for Victory."

I began the distribution of food boxes this afternoon. But before I started, Momota noticed the Old Gold packs and directed that all cigarettes must be removed from the packages and the wrappers turned over to him. In addition he ordered every food box repacked in order to get equal distribution to the men. Eventually the job was completed and everyone was happy to receive the gifts.

I noticed a piece of crumpled newspaper in one of the cartons. It was a page from the Boston Post dated August 1943. I gathered from the paper that we have many European prisoners of war in the United States.

Momota approached me tonight in a very nervous manner. He wants me to sign for more boxes than we received. I flatly refused. Then he decided that perhaps he didn't need a receipt. I offered to recount the cartons if he believed there was an error—but no funny stuff. The fact is that this handful of supplies has the Japs all confused. They just are not geared to handle a job of this magnitude. Their records are all botched up and they have to keep accurate records or the "gestapo" will have their heads.

November 20, 1943

It was a long busy day. The wet cases of clothing and shoes had to be opened and dried. Momota at first allowed us to distribute the Old Golds after the wrappers had been removed. But this afternoon he ordered that all Old Golds be called in, repacked in the wrappers and turned over to the front office. It looked like an impossible task. However, word was passed and the camp responded splendidly. We worked far into the night repacking the cigarettes. When I turned the packages over to Kubota, he was embarrassed and suggested that I hold them for the time being. I doubt if the "gestapo" knows we have these Old Golds. I kept my force on the job tonight and replaced every cigarette returned to me with other brands.

November 21, 1943

In spite of my efforts to honorably and equitably distribute the food boxes, Duckworth instigated a secret investigation using several enlisted men to verify what the prisoners received in their Red Cross packages. He claimed that he had seen pilfering by my men during the "gestapo" inspections. Ten minutes after I heard what Duckworth was trying to pull, I made a tour of every building, assembled the men and reported what was happening. I told every person to give me the name of anyone who approached them on behalf of Duckworth. The camp backed me a hundred percent and I knifed that backstabbing cold. Duckworth was present in one of the buildings when I blasted his sneak attack. That skunk is no damn good. But like all of his crowd, run them out in the open and they are licked.

I had a talk with Nogi this afternoon and brought up the matter of increasing our food ration in order to prevent blindness among the men. Nogi's reply was his usual "luxury" argument. "Americans have been used to so much luxury that they must need more things than other people." I tried to explain that the physiological need of food for all humans was scientifically established throughout the civilized world. He immediately became hostile—the Japs always do when confronted with facts. They lose face by admitting they are wrong. I got exactly nowhere with Nogi today. However, I warned him that a written report on our eye cases was forthcoming and sooner or later he would have to answer for his stubborn behavior.

November 22, 1943

I woke up for *bango* but then went back to bed. I have a bad cold and feel lousy. Late this afternoon a couple of men from Ward One came in to see me. They delivered a scroll with the signatures of every man in the ward acknowledging that they were pleased and thankful for the manner in which the Christmas packages were handed out.

A short while later the patients in Ward Two sent Wade and me a bunch of their cigarettes. We felt embarrassed but realized that we couldn't return them. We decided to keep the cigarettes and reissue them to the boys when their supply ran low.

Dan Boone is now having eye trouble. I'm still afraid to have mine examined. I have headaches and my eyes hurt, but I can still see.

I heard this evening that 40 men in the upper compound are to be turned over to the Aircraft Bureau working party and we are to make bunk space available to them in the hospital barracks. I don't know where we are going to put this group as we are crowded now and have no extra beds or mattresses. Our own bedding is filthy, torn, and full of bedbugs.

November 23, 1943

Back on the job today and feeling much better. I'm still having difficulties with my S.O.Q. groaners and moaners. Lazy bastards calling themselves officers. They can't attend *bango* because of their "great ailments." They are a no good bunch on the whole. Several of the senior officers in S.O.Q. sent me a "confidential memorandum" asking to be separated from certain "obnoxious people who call themselves officers and are not." They further stated that by daily close contact with these individuals they "suffer constant insults and discourtesy from them." Dammit! I lived in a barracks with my junior officers and if I ever suffered any discourtesy or disrespect from any of them, I would sure as hell know that I was lacking somewhere. I'm doing nothing about this communication. I'm ignoring it. If that isn't confidential enough for them then it's just too bad. This letter is the most blatant admission of incompetency and lack of officer qualities that I have ever seen.

November 24, 1943

With the vast number of eye cases now among us, our limited food supply, and shortage of medicine and vitamins, the question of who is to receive treatment becomes paramount. The "military principle" will have to apply. The older cases offering little or no hope for recovery must be sacrificed in order to use our supplies in sufficient concentration to help those with a reasonable chance for recovery.

This was a tough decision to make, but there just isn't enough medicine and vitamins for everyone and we must do what is best for the greatest number.

The mounting number of eye cases among our own staff is eating into my crew to a degree where efficiency is suffering. More men are placed on the sick list every day. Certain eye cases have to be shifted to jobs they can perform. There are not enough dark glasses for everyone and eyes must be dilated as a treatment measure. I'm keeping a few men busy making eye shades out of cardboard. Tiny holes are cut in the heavy paper to see through.

November 25, 1943

Thanksgiving Day—just another wasted day out of my life in old Bilibid. The menu of the day was dry rice. I found a can of pumpkin I had been saving and this was as good a day as any to open it. I shared the delicacy with Wade and Cecil. The pumpkin was nothing to rave about but it was filling—and it wasn't rice.

We received four Red Cross cases of biologicals today. One box is slated for Davao. We are beginning to handle most of the medical supplies for further disposition to other camps. Unfortunately, all of this extra handling is under the direction of Momota. This means there is a lot of useless backtracking and coolie labor which is wearing everybody out. Momota is constantly ranting, "Get 10 men! Get 50 men! Get 100 men!"

Word from Cabanatuan tells that Colonel Beecher is unpopular with men up there. That must mean he's doing a good job. As near as I can learn, the only complaint against him is that he makes everybody work. So do I. I guess that makes both of us sons of bitches. That's O.K. by me.

The eye situation has become a menace to morale. Examination of the entire camp is in progress and the findings are alarming as hell. It has reached the point where everybody just sits around waiting to go blind—and wondering when. The eye exams are held at night. Each morning the boys routinely ask, "Who did they get last night?"

November 26, 1943

Held mast [disciplinary hearing] today concerning a stump case [amputee] by the name of DeMarco. He's a chronic bad boy. The common stump case philosophy: "I'm a cripple and you can't do that to me." He was charged with refusing a detail. I worked him over at mast until he was ready to obey orders and therefore let him off with a warning.

These stump cases are perfectly able to contribute their share of the work load. The job DeMarco refused was sitting at a table and sorting rice. I think he understands the situation better now. The Japanese brig isn't very comfortable, and he wouldn't be the first one-legged man to see the inside of it either.

November 27, 1943

A situation approaching panic has been reached regarding the eye problems. A review of the condition shows that this is not a sudden epidemic outburst, but is more the finding of a pathology that has existed for a long time. It has only come to light as a result of intense study and serious attention. Much of the fear among the men can be blamed on the fact that so many people are running around the camp wearing eye-shades and dark glasses.

Fortunately, the majority of the cases we are now seeing were caught early enough and should respond to treatment. I called a meeting with members of my staff and explained the situation in detail. I believe I succeeded in alleviating much of the concern.

I had a conference with Nogi regarding the delay in releasing our Red Cross medical supplies. This delay is serious as it is holding up much needed vitamin medication. However, explanation of the situation is hopeless. The "gestapo" are God and nothing can be done without their stamp of approval.

The "Bilibid Players" put on a show in the upper compound tonight. I was about to leave for the entertainment when Kubota called up on the phone. He raised all kinds of hell with me because he wasn't notified of the program and his permission wasn't given. The whole time he was ranting and raving the show continued and was able to finish. I finally got the Jap pacified and satisfied that no harm was intended. He was just saving face—an old Oriental custom.

November 28, 1943

Several days ago the Japanese passed around a questionnaire to find out who among the prisoners were aircraft oriented. Today, the men who answered the survey were interviewed as to their training and in what field of aviation they were proficient. Among the questions: "Can you identify the different kinds of American planes when you see them?"

Lieutenant Melvin [Army] was brought up before mast this morning. A Japanese guard caught him violating smoking regulations. Officers are the poorest disciplined people in the world. And most of those I have to deal with around here are dumb besides. It's a combination of ignorance and lack of innate qualities of leadership.

I spent a great deal of time today censoring mailing cards. The men insist on making taboo references and trying to be smart.

The Japs hauled in a load of minnow-size fish to fry tonight. These fish only waste cooking oil and provide us with nothing substantial. On paper, however, it shows that we were given "fish." The size is immaterial. They might just as well have brought in a load of rocks or seashells.

One of the guards discovered an illegal hot plate. I managed to grab it and hustled the plate up to the front office before the Jap made his report. It always helps to reach the authorities first. It avoids group punishment.

December 1, 1943

I made my weekly inspection of Bilibid today. Tsukahara, the Japanese district prison officer, came along with me. I showed him the empty galley shelves, empty refrigerator, empty storeroom, and empty stomachs. Tsukahara looked at me and shook his head, "Jap soldier hungry too."

Apparently, however, Tsukahara raised hell with Horani, the Japanese quartermaster. After inspection this morning, Horani hurried down to the hospital and spent most of his day following Wade and me around. He was continually crying and moaning, asking us what he had done wrong. "I'm only human," he said. "Maybe I have made mistakes. Tell me where I have gone wrong? What can I do to help in the future?"

Horani and I engaged in an Oriental bargaining session for about three hours. I finally managed to get a small increase in our rice allotment, sugar, and cooking oil. Naturally, of course, there was a catch to the concessions. Horani can't get his books to balance and wanted me to sign for receiving three cans of oil when we only received two. I refused and that riled the hell out of him. Horani has always been a big offender in chiseling off our food truck for use in the Japanese galley. He's a crooked little conniver.

Horani hung around the hospital for quite a while, probably because we were all smoking American cigarettes and he's the biggest sponger in the camp. I have caught him several times when he tried to pull phoney food deals on us. He knows that I will go to Nogi if I notice anything fishy going on.

December 2, 1943

The Japanese created another problem today by removing all the gas drums that we have been using for garbage—23 of them. The cans are leaky, rusted, and dented but the Japanese are hauling gasoline in them. That's what the Aircraft Bureau working party is doing this morning.

The "gestapo" finally got around to inspecting the Red Cross medical supplies prior to releasing them to us. They are very busy tearing off labels, unrolling the gauze and cotton, and in general ruining everything. There were quite a number of American newspapers used as packing in the boxes, but the Japs grabbed all of them.

Everyone in camp who could be fitted has been provided with a pair of shoes. However, we still have 200 large size pairs that nobody can wear. I managed to latch on to a pair of 9Cs and for the first time in a long while I am able to walk in comfort.

The Japanese want a Cabanatuan draft list submitted by tomorrow morning. The draft probably won't leave until God knows when. It's the old "hurry up and wait" all over again. Every time I submit a draft list to the Japanese they make changes. I will probably end up rewriting this list a dozen times before they are satisfied.

December 5, 1943

There was a theft in the supply department today. The amount is negligible, but it's evident that my men are involved. I was very disappointed and gave the guilty parties 24 hours to confess. No matter who it is, I will be sorry. All the men have done a good job but a breach of trust is a sad commentary on any supply department.

Momota showed up this afternoon and asked for all the Old Gold cigarettes to be turned over to him. I boxed and sealed them in cases and we both stamped our chop marks on the seals. They were then locked in the armory.

December 6, 1943

This morning, Henson came into my office and confessed the storeroom theft. I shook up the supply department tonight. All had knowledge of the affair and were involved to some degree. Shearer himself is no white lily. Little men are never good, especially those who knit. Shearer has never liked Wilson in the supply room. I let Shearer know that Wilson was my man and I put him there because I knew he was on my team, and he would stay in the supply department as long as I ran this place. The joint should click along pretty well now—for a few months anyway.

December 8, 1943

This is the second anniversary of our entry into the war. Today is a holiday in Manila and there are many planes in the air.

Our sickbed situation is going from bad to worse. We have eleven patients sleeping on the concrete deck without mattresses and more sick are due in from Clark Field and Pasay.

The Aircraft Bureau working party is using one of our wards. I tried to convince the Japanese to fix up the large building up front and move the crew over there. That would relieve the crowded conditions. But the Japs can't grasp the necessity of giving us more room. The reason, of course, is that they don't have any building materials nor any mattresses. I mentioned to Momota that we would be glad to build bunks and make our own mattresses. He refused as usual—afraid of losing face. That's just one of the problems that come up when you are prisoners of the "have-nots."

December 9, 1943

Yakasiji is asking for more radio messages. I thought that issue had died a natural death. There is a report that these messages have been used in propaganda broadcasts from Tokyo.

Nogi called me up to the front office this morning to complain that American cigarettes are appearing in Manila. He indicated Bilibid as the source but I beat him to the draw. I told him that we are searching all working parties and not permitting any American food or cigarettes to go outside the gate. I also informed him that on numerous occasions the guards have tried to intimidate the men, but without success. Nogi appreciated the information and stomped out of the office. Heads will roll in the guardhouse tonight.

A prisoner from the port area came into camp today for dental treatment. He cornered me in my office and reported that he had been "unable to buy any commissary supplies with the money that another officer and I had sent out."

I had never made any such request and was flabbergasted. Evidently somebody was using my name. I learned the identity of the other officer and straightened him out in short order. I wouldn't trust my grandmother anymore.

Momota stopped down this afternoon with the same cigarette selling story. He plowed through our indigent fund records, store account, counted all the money, etc. He finally gave us an O.K., wrote a meaningless figure in his notebook and shoved off. He doesn't know any more now than he did before. The Japanese receive a complete report of our financial status every month. They just don't seem to understand any information we give them. Everything is way over their heads.

Ruge brought a case to mast today, a private named K. C. Jones. This man is a mental defective, always in trouble wherever he goes. For the good of the camp he has to be punished, but it will never change the guy. He's that way and always will be.

December 10, 1943

It has been raining all morning and the sky is very dark. It's difficult to work during these gloomy days. No lights are allowed and the wards are dark.

Latest reports reveal that the food shortage in Manila has reached serious proportions and has every prospect of growing worse. Many people are leaving the city for the provinces.

Brokenshire stormed into my office this morning. He couldn't stay quiet any longer. "Broke" has never accepted the fact that the eye specialist has more say so than he does about the eye cases on his ward. Brokenshire doesn't agree with the eye doctor, his treatments, etc. Well, most of us have never agreed with "Broke" and his therapeutics, so that makes us even. However, Brokenshire had his say and now, martyr-like, he's satisfied. He has done his duty. He has objected. Now he's ready once again to submit to the iron law of those who inflict policies upon the common people. Situation—status quo.

I had to censure Ritter today and get his ward moving. Ed is a stubborn Dutchman. He's doing a good job but just can't seem to raise his eyes above the ground. He's very dogmatic with a narrow horizon for time and space. But he's a good man doing great work and he's no worse than all the other prima donnas around here.

Ritter was my only officer on Corregidor that I had to reprimand on one occasion. Even so, he did an excellent job. I can put up with human frailties as long as they are positive in nature. To hell with the "Yes Sir" guys. They give real trouble, not annoyances.

A "big shot" inspector from Japanese headquarters is expected sometime today. This visit is in answer to my request for more lumber. When Momota heard about the inspection, he immediately screamed for a ten-man working party and ordered the men to take sledgehammers and knock down all repairs, break windows, etc. The place apparently looked too good.

The "Bilibid Players" put on another show tonight in the "Bilibid Bowl." Not much talent and you can't eat the stuff, but it helps tighten the belt.

Momota had the duty tonight and as usual came around after lights out. As soon as he was spotted, the old familiar word was passed, "Air Raid." The other warning is, "Tallyho."

December 12, 1943

Father Duffy had a few disparaging remarks to make about last night's show and shows in general. This disturbed Clyde Welsh no end. The

Chaplain's comments were ridiculous. I will admit that the humor was a little lusty, but it's humor of a kind and we need it.

I wrote a letter to Clyde and his theatrical group, backing them up and encouraging them to do more. If Duffy was as wide open, aboveboard, and constructive as our "Bilibid Theater," he would serve a much more useful purpose around here.

The "Bilibid Players" offered their aid to the Chaplains in putting on a Christmas show. The padres replied with a beautiful injured-innocence tirade. The men decided to put on a show of their own anyway. I attended divine services this morning—sinner me.

The Aircraft Bureau is raising hell about not enough prisoners showing up for their work detail. Kubota barged into my office demanding an explanation. I tried to get the point across to him that they are using recently sick men instead of a healthy group. I further informed him that this is still a hospital, not a work camp. Kubota left in a huff.

December 13, 1943

The Japanese confiscated Turnipseed's and Pfieffer's swords. Yakasiji said, "The swords will be taken to headquarters for safekeeping and to prevent anyone from committing *hari-kari*." As a matter-of-fact, this is part of the same phobia as the tools. There is an inherent fear that we intend to gang up on our captors and escape. The idea is ridiculous but the Japs are dead serious.

Another example of the absurdity of the front office concerns our request for a new five gallon can to use as a rice and soup bucket. The one we are using has rusted through. I had a long talk with Nogi about the problem, but he said it was out of the question. He also refused to let me have any solder to repair the leaking container. Nogi suggested that we make wooden buckets out of the empty Red Cross cartons. I angrily asked him "What about the soup?" This rice bucket issue has really assumed epic proportions with the Japs. Nothing they do is ever simple. Decision making isn't in their vocabulary.

We started an agricultural project this afternoon. The Japanese have repeatedly mentioned that our prospects for vegetables are very poor. However, they will supply us with garden seed. I made a survey of the camp and designated certain areas for cultivation. Captain Jones [Army] was placed in charge of the "farm detail" and Sergeant

Edwards appointed his assistant. Labor will be supplied by convalescent patients.

December 14, 1943

I might have known. As soon as I had my farm program underway, every Jap from the top man at headquarters to the lowest ranking guard is now telling me where, what, and how to plant. They don't understand that certain crops do better in different places. I made up my mind that we will have a garden in spite of the "know it alls."

I made replacements in the Aircraft Bureau working party and rewrote the Cabanatuan draft list (again). All hands were kept standing at *bango* tonight because someone talked in ranks or some other insignificant thing. I think it was just the whim of the new Jap duty sergeant—big man on campus.

Ruge is very upset over four men in his work detail. It seems that they became involved with "liquor and women" while working at the Jap major's house. It would have been too bad for all of us if they had been caught. But somehow this doesn't strike me as a serious crime like stealing or lying. As I see the incident, it was only the wholesome desire in four denied men. A chance to have a few drinks and get laid. The consequences never entered their heads and the Major's wife didn't complain. I called the men on the carpet, however, and reminded them that all of us would have had to take the rap if they had been caught. They assured me that it would never happen again. Somehow I couldn't get myself worked up over the incident. I sincerely approve of earthly desires, but I guess I shouldn't forget that there is a time and place for everything. And perhaps a Japanese major's house isn't it.

December 16, 1943

It was cool and clear this morning and the Cabanatuan draft finally shipped out. I beat Nogi to the punch when he made his inspection by having all the eye cases concentrated in one ward. They made a very impressive showing for the doctor and held his attention for quite some time. As to what good this display of nearly blind men will do is anybody's guess. Nogi had to admit though, the hospital was in excellent shipshape condition.

Horani blustered into camp this afternoon to check on the pig farm. He said that headquarters might let us have a couple of them. I hope so, we need fats badly.

I did learn a sidelight on the war from Horani. He returns to Taiwan in three months to become a civilian for awhile and earn money to reimburse the government for money being paid to his wife. He then returns to the Army. Horani said that most of the Japanese who leave here for Taiwan become policemen. It seems that war is a natural way of life to the Japanese.

Horani also brought up the tool business again. The Japs are so darn afraid that we might use them as weapons that they insist we turn all tools into the front office each night. For some unknown reason the cobbler shop is exempt. I carry the keys to that building and if anybody eventually escapes by means of a shoemaker's hammer and stabs a guard with a shoemaker's awl, I'm in deep trouble. Meanwhile, in the galley we have meat cleavers and sharp knives out in plain view at all times.

December 18, 1943

I toured the "plantation" this morning and looked over the planting projects. I told the Japs that we can plant and outgrow anything they bring in if they will only let us run the farm our way. We can't get anywhere if they continue to meddle in the operation.

A draft of 60 prisoners from Palawan arrived this afternoon. They are ragged, dirty, shoeless, and most of them stir-wacky. We will attempt to shoe them, clothe them, clean them up, quiet them down, and start them back on the road to self-respect. One of the men in the group was a former Manila dentist who arrived on Corregidor as a refugee. He tried hard to convince me to take him on as a dental officer with the 4th Regiment. Naturally I refused. Anyway, after he was captured he told the Japanese that he was an American army officer in order to be placed on the prisoner payroll. He did the same thing upon arrival at Bilibid. I yanked him up short and had that changed in a hurry. There are too many phonies around here as it is.

I managed a bit of Christmas diplomacy tonight by sending a

holiday letter to General Miramoto. This will pay him back for sending flowers in memory of our dead each year.

December 22, 1943

My eyes have been hurting like the devil so I have tried to keep my writing to a minimum. The paper shortage is also acute.

There has been a lot of petty bickering among the officers. My barracks sounds like the inside of a kennel. Little things loom so large in prison life. The prolonged stress and strain is beginning to tell in the men. I'll work the hell out of them for a few days so they won't have time to bitch. So many of our young officers have lived their lives too much in the realm of self-imposed duties only. They are not used to community living. There is a good argument for military service early in life. I don't mean a milk-feeding military academy either.

"Neutral sympathizers" in Manila sent us a truckload of Christmas decorations and food. It was a most welcome contribution and I wrote a letter of appreciation. The local people have crashed through repeatedly, and darn well too. Many lives have been saved through their efforts.

Movies again tonight. Japanese newsreel, Japanese song reel, American movie—*Top of the Town* starring George Murphy.

December 25, 1943

Christmas Day in old Bilibid—very quiet. We made grab bags from all the odds and ends left over from the Red Cross supplies and the gifts sent in by the local sympathizers. Everybody received a present.

January 1, 1944

I didn't hear any bells at midnight, only a few firecrackers and the sound of a horn. Somebody in S.O.Q. woke up and beat on a duck [urinal] with a spoon. New Year's Eve sure isn't what it used to be.

I checked on the farm first thing this morning. Everything looks in great shape. The men are working hard at it and their efforts show.

This is the first agricultural project at Bilibid since the old leper colony days.

Late this morning I was notified that we now have eight baby pigs. Tsukahara rushed down from the front office to have a look at the new arrivals. He must have been celebrating last night. He was dead drunk and stumbled into the pigpen injuring one of the animals.

Several of the porkers are sick and the Japs are calling in a vet. There is nothing wrong with those pigs that a good nourishing meal wouldn't cure. The same holds true for us.

My eyes are bad. They ache like hell and feel hard as marbles.

January 11, 1944

The food situation becomes worse every day. The fish shipped in are the size of minnows and most of them are rotten. Horani is talking about sending expeditions into the countryside to try and locate food supplies.

The Japanese continue to demand more labor from us. They are not only using the sick for working parties, but are using our corpsmen as well. This leaves the hospital shorthanded. I took the matter up with Kubota. He says that there is "somewhat of an emergency." I heard that the Japs are moving gasoline and oil out of here in a hurry. If that's the emergency, can "Yanks and tanks" be far behind?

The front office wants every prisoner to write a letter to the Japanese—a sort of "thank-you note" for favors rendered. The letters will most likely be used for propaganda purposes. We are writing the letters under protest.

To top the day off, ants ate up our onions.

January 13, 1944

I spent part of the day editing letters the men are writing to the Japanese. It's a sorry commentary on the mental level of young Americans. Wait till the Japs get an eyeful of some of these masterpieces. Several of these boys are really getting malicious.

Recently the Japanese sent in a shipment of field corn. We almost wore out a grain mill trying to grind it. The Japs now insist that we

eat the corn after soaking the grain like beans. The men aren't tol-
erating the kernels very well, especially the dysentery cases.

January 18, 1944

The lightbulb situation is acute. At the present rate, the camp will be
in total darkness very soon. The shortage of firewood is about as bad.
The men are already cutting down trees without the permission of
the Japanese.

Kubota returned our Old Golds and each man received six packs.
He also handed over the boxes of Union Leader tobacco that were
confiscated by the "gestapo."

I have felt rotten all day. My eyes and head ache and I'm hungry.
Yakasiji stopped by. He's a civilian now and has been appointed ship
chandler for the entire Philippines. Quite a racket I imagine.

The Japs are complaining that there are no new piglets. They are
blaming the Americans. The vet reported that only one other pig is
pregnant and recommended butchering two that are of no value.

I had a run-in at the pigpen with a Jap guard known as "Slapping
Sam" and went directly to Kubota about the incident. The guards
apparently don't like me running to the front office every time I have
a problem with one of the raccoons. To hell with them. I don't do
business with "small fry."

January 24, 1944

More childish tantrums among the grown-ups over the fish ration.
One man got a larger fish than another. I'm supposed to be "King
Solomon" and solve all these ten cent problems.

It's another dark and dreary day. I can hardly see to read or
write. I'm clamoring for more garden seed but the Japanese now tell
me "they just ran out." We have either outfarmed them or farmed
them out. This is just another example of their inability to grasp any
project beyond the present or immediate future—mental nearsightedness. I explained to Kubota that I happen to know Cabanatuan has
plenty of seed. However, there seems to be interdepartmental difficulties in getting anything from another area. It makes you wonder if
they are all on the same team.

One of the sows came through with a litter of ten pigs, mostly boars. The father's doing well. He slept through it all—still sleeping.

January 29, 1944

Momota is screaming for coolie labor again. Today he's moving Red Cross boxes and medical supplies to Davao. He needs 60 strong men for the working party. Hell, we haven't got 60 strong men in the whole camp. I explained the situation to Kubota, but he's either stupid or is afraid to intercede. I finally stripped the wards of enough corpsmen to make up the detail.

The Japanese held air-raid drills most of the day. There was the usual noise and confusion. I have a hunch that the first time one of these Japs hears a bomb explode they will crap their pants. I understand that there is increased activity in Manila regarding air raid precautions and the press is warning the public to expect bombings at any time. There's a lot of camouflaging and foxhole digging going on. However, there are no foxholes in Bilibid. Everyone is herded into buildings and cells.

We had a mail delivery today. I received two letters. Everybody is reading their news from home. Some of the letters are amusing. The wives of two of our prisoners have met. One of them wrote: "We find we have something in common." Another fellow received a letter from his mother saying that his wife and baby are now living with her. The guy didn't even know he was married. One sailor missed the *Quail* when the ship left the Philippines, but he sent home his watch and ring. His wife wrote: "Received the watch and ring but you sure did miss the boat."

Several of the letters received from the States indicate that the American people believe that we are getting a Red Cross food box every week. That should ease their minds considerably, but it sure as hell isn't taking the wrinkles out of our bellies.

January 31, 1944

We have six new piglets today. That makes a total of 24 baby pigs and 10 adults including an old boar. One more sow is due anytime. The Japanese were worried that their pigs are underfed, so they shipped in a truckload of garbage from Santo Tomas. The prisoners picked through the trash and rescued potatoes, beans, and even coffee grounds which they were able to reboil.

Three men were caught drunk in one of the wards and raising hell. They evidently sneaked alcohol into camp from the outside. I fixed that good deal in a hurry. I surprised the working party tonight and had them empty their canteens before entering the compound. It's the laxity of the working detail officers and ward discipline that contributed to this problem. I preferred not to take the incident to the Japanese. I put the offenders in our psycho ward for observation.

Another case, Garcia, took a rope to bed with him—a hangman's knot already tied in one end. I also placed him in the mental section for safekeeping.

February 6, 1944

More mail today. God, but I wish I wasn't so sentimental and capable of such heartache. My imagination has always been a curse. I want these letters from home but I'm afraid of them. I thought I had adjusted to this living death until the real thing comes along, but I haven't.

In the mail bags up at the front office, somebody sent perfumed shaving lotion and chewing gum. I amble up there every now and then to smell civilization.

February 8, 1944

I'm 46 years old today and received a few more letters, a couple of them over a year old. One can remain content in spite of the delusion offered by the rest of mankind as long as one has the loyalty and love of those who matter.

The Japs finally supplied us with a mop. Their system—one hospital, one mop. Routine weekly inspection this morning. Everything looks remarkably good. This can only be done by prodigious effort and overcoming great odds. We have no brooms, soap, rags, bedding, or anything else that goes to make up a decent hospital. However, our men still manage to maintain some semblance of order and cleanliness. I'm proud of the whole lot of them.

Momota finally relented and gave permission to butcher two of the pigs. Japanese headquarters take one and we get the other. Now it's only a question of how much Momota and the rest of the front office grab out of our share. We will probably be lucky to see a thin film of hog grease on top of our radish water soup.

The Japanese told me that they wanted convalescent patients to do "light work" at headquarters. I agreed but then found out that they were using the men for heavy labor. I was mad as hell and served notice on the Japs that from now on only well men would be sent up there. I threw a monkey wrench into their plans for a change. There will probably be repercussions but it's about time somebody stood up to those bastards.

February 10, 1944

We had pig soup today and made cracklings. I directed Crews to increase the bean ration and brew the Red Cross coffee. We might as well fill everyone's stomach for a change.

Tsukahara showed up drunk tonight and began running the prisoners around the compound for exercise. I had to intervene and try to quiet him down. In the meantime I had an appointment at the front office on another matter. Tsukahara thought that I was going to report the incident. He started acting crazy and called up headquarters to report "All American sons of bitches ran away at exercise." The guards in the vicinity heard the ruckus and tried to reason with the drunk. Evidently they understood what was happening and were trying to play down the problem.

February 11, 1944

Tsukahara sneaked into my office this morning very repentant. He admitted that he behaved like an ass and must have gone crazy. Maybe we won't have any trouble with him for awhile. The less I see of the front office gang the better.

The Japs asked for the clothing measurements of 100 of the "biggest men" and then had them come to the front office to try on Japanese uniforms. It's hard for me to believe that they will issue us Army uniforms. It could be a propaganda move to show that clothing has been supplied. Kubota says he knows nothing about the request. If he does, he isn't talking.

February 16, 1944

My eyes are becoming progressively worse and I'm living behind dark glasses. I have had a bad headache all day and only ate about a third of a small fish and a bite of half-raw cornbread.

A few mail parcels arrived from the States this morning. One man received a football and a pump. We are trying to think of a practical use for those items. Another guy was sent a box of sanitary toilet seat covers. You can't be more practical than that. A rather disappointed prisoner opened his package to find a pair of pajamas that he sent to the States shortly before the war. At least he knows that his box arrived home O.K. Schweizer received a pair of hairnets—God only knows why. Another lad was sent several packs of spearmint gum and passed the sticks around. He gave me a whole pack. Hot damn! My biggest weakness! I have been chewing like hell all afternoon. Shades of the good old days in Western civilization.

Momota is busy having the "big men" try on Japanese Army overcoats and trousers. Heavy clothing is always an ominous sign. The boys are wondering if this means that a move to Japan or Manchuria is in the offing.

An unusual requisition for medical supplies was sent down from the front office about an hour ago. It was in Nogi's own handwriting, but the requests are different from any of their other want lists. Nogi asked for a large amount of morphine, several scalpels, vitamins, and such unusual items as camphor and stomachache pills. I think he's copying the Red Cross medical supply invoices.

I had a long talk with Nogi and for the first time he admitted that he couldn't meet our food allotments. He just doesn't have the supplies. That was a hell of a concession for him to make. It cost him a lot of "face." I asked him for soybean paste which is issued to the Japanese soldiers but he refused. That put an end to his constant excuse that we eat what the Jap soldier eats.

February 19, 1944

I toured the "plantation" with Captain Jones this morning. Everything has been harvested except some okra and odds and ends of the remaining greens. We planted a little garlic and onions. I ordered the rest of the garden to be planted with *camotes*.

We only have two weeks' supply of American canned milk in the Japanese storeroom. Momota tells me that when this is gone we will have to drink coconut milk. The Japs take the term "coconut milk" literally. To them it's the same thing as cow's milk. I explained to the Jap that in countries where coconuts are grown, the liquid is called "coconut water" and it's no way related to milk proper. Momota acted surprised—or was he?

February 21, 1944

The Japanese trucked 30 small ducks into camp today and insist we build a swimming pool for the birds. This place is beginning to resemble "Old MacDonald's Farm." All we need now is a couple of cows and a chicken coop.

The forced evacuation of Manila begins tomorrow. The puppet government has been trying to scare the people into leaving the city by citing the danger of American bombers. The real reason for the evacuation, however, is the food shortage. Famine is everywhere and there's nothing the government can do about it.

A Japanese officer at headquarters wants his boots half-soled with American leather. He brought the leather marked USA down to the cobbler shop. "Jap leather no good," he says.

February 25, 1944

I have been busy all day editing more "thank-you" notes to the Japs. The letters are lousy, horrible, and disappointing. The men will end up in all kinds of trouble if I deliver these compositions to the front office the way they are written.

Other matters to be taken care of include caring for the pigs and ducks, sanitation and material upkeep, the garden and, of course, the "small matter" of curing the sick—in that order.

Last night the President of the Philippines was given dictatorial powers and a national emergency was declared. The government has taken over agriculture, businesses, labor, and wages. There is open rebellion in the provinces against the Japanese. The present situation in the Pacific is fast becoming critical. We are in a tough spot—right in the center of the bull's-eye.

The Japs are sending all the patients they can get their hands on to Cabanatuan, and are still calling for large working parties. They continually request corpsmen for their work crews, and this puts additional strain on patient care.

February 27, 1944

I recommended that two baby pigs be killed due to roundworm infestation. All the sows are probably infected, but Momota insists we keep all the pigs. He also wants us to plant *camotes* in the dysentery ward area—I flatly refused.

After lights out tonight a truck rolled up loaded with Japanese soldiers and two cows. One of the cows arrived dead and Horani permitted us to butcher the animal. We were allowed 60 pounds of the beef and the front office took the rest.

March 4, 1944

One of the reasons for our present food predicament is due to the large number of men in camp awaiting shipment to Cabanatuan and Japan. I completed my monthly report to Nogi setting forth the deplorable conditions. I'm also preparing a letter to the new Japanese commanding general of the Philippines, General Koa, with recommendations for improving the camp.

I had a long talk with Nogi this afternoon and was very firm with my demands. He finally granted a few concessions. We can now spend all of our pay allotment. In addition we received, through Japanese channels, a donation from the Pope of over 300 pesos as our portion of a fund for war prisoners. However, the fact remains that there are very little extras available to buy.

Ruge showed up tonight. More trouble with K. C. Jones. I'll get them both together tomorrow in the "Court of Human Relations."

March 5, 1944

I put Ruge's problem child, K. C. Jones, on the next draft leaving for Cabanatuan and took him off the Aircraft Bureau working party until then. I also asked Kubota to exchange 20 healthy men from Cabanatuan for 20 of our worn out boys.

A new Japanese medical officer visited the hospital this afternoon and I showed him around. He was rather intelligent and was very affable and polite. He had a young Caucasian-looking interpreter with him. The fellow was a well built handsome man wearing the insignia of the administration corps. He left us with very respectful and kindly remarks. And his attitude was quite considerate.

A work detail returning from the port area reported that they were made to clean out the hold of a 4,000 ton merchant vessel that was armed and painted battleship gray. The ship was unmarked and the description fits the *Lima Maru*. Most likely another load of prisoners will be on their way to Japan.

Kubota stormed into my office tonight complaining about certain statements made by officers in their letters to the Japanese regarding the handling of Red Cross packages. In many instances Kubota was justified. The statements were half-truths and in some cases completely wrong in the picture they created. He objected somewhat to criticism about the food in camp, but had to admit that the chow wasn't good.

March 6, 1944

Wade and I spent most of the morning looking over the compound. There are a lot of odds and ends to take care of. We checked into the possibilities of more pig runways as four more sows are pregnant. The gardening project looks good and the *camotes* are healthy. I'm having one of the barracks buildings cleaned up in preparation for the arrival of 300 men for further transfer—probably Japan.

Last month I used money from the indigent fund to buy beans and peanuts since they were available and hoped the camp would donate to cover the expense. Well, the men refused. They had already spent their money on nonessentials. Of course, that put a crimp in my efforts to help the needy. I had no choice but to take back five sacks of beans from the galley. When the chow offering gets slimmer in a couple of days, the guys will yell bloody murder. They refuse to see how they defeat their own ends by never looking beyond their own selfish needs. They don't understand that the donations are used to feed them. If the men would only show a willingness to momentarily curb their own immediate desires, then we could materially improve conditions. But they won't do it and are stupidly cutting their own throats. When the rude awakening does come, they will put the blame everywhere but where it belongs—themselves. Thank God I lost any flattering ideas I might have had of "Adam's Breed" a long time ago. Otherwise this war would have been one big disillusionment.

The 300 man draft arrived this afternoon from Cabanatuan. The men were the pick of the camp physically. Major Christenson and Captain Underwood are in charge. I made arrangements for the draft to make purchases through the store and also held sick call for the men.

March 7, 1944

The Japs took one of the pigs to headquarters this morning. They are having a pig roast. My main concern, however, is the theft situation in camp. The guys have been stealing mail, clothes, food, and money. Somebody even stole Tsukahara's sword belt. They will have his sword next.

Nogi showed up but took all his time with the new draft. There was no chance to go to bat on the chow problem. I slapped a ten percent tax on the store buying. It's the least painful way of making the men do something constructive for themselves and the others.

I invited Captain Robinson [Army] with the draft over to our quarters for supper. This was the day to cook our weekly budget of beans. I also managed to acquire a handful of green onions. This was a big feast for us. I really put on the dog for company.

March 9, 1944

We were busy all day with medical cases arriving from outlying camps, either for admission to the hospital or for examination. A number of civilians from the port area were admitted to sick bay.

I heard several diverse reports concerning the execution of a few men, incident to the torpedoing of Japanese ships leaving the harbor. However, I later learned that the men are being held at Fort Santiago and are charged with espionage along with 15 Manila residents and one rich Japanese.

Information from "over the wall" indicates that the situation on Corregidor is going from bad to worse. The Americans are fighting among themselves and there are rumors of executions incident to escape attempts.

Word was passed that a big inspection is underway and will hit here soon. Probably General Koa is making a tour of the Philippine prison camps. I'm loading my guns to give him an earful when he shows up at Bilibid.

New blackout orders were issued today. All lights are to be shaded. There are increasing rumors from abroad telling the Filipinos to prepare for the bombing of Manila. Personally, I doubt if the city will be bombed but nearby airfields and military installations will no doubt be "visited."

Wade and I saw Kubota this afternoon and explained that something had to be done about the food problem. Kubota agreed to go to headquarters in the morning and mention it to Nogi again. I expect Nogi to dash over here tomorrow and the fight will begin.

If and when Nogi shows up, I also have another matter to take up with him. It concerns the herding of all the medical personnel into one building during an air raid. I want my men scattered throughout the camp rather than all bunched together. A direct hit on the building would wipe out the entire hospital crew. These Japs have never been through a bombing attack and have no conception of what takes place. I wonder if American bombs sound any different than the Japanese variety?

This evening, Kubota and Horani stopped in my office and we went into a detailed debate over our food allotment. I presented the situation with facts and figures. There was much argument and counterargument. I told Kubota that I intended to file a complaint with Swiss agencies in Manila for further transfer to Washington. I presented the facts that we are not eating as well as the Japanese soldier and that we are the poorest fed camp in the Philippines.

Horani brought up the old Japanese claim that the Americans are sinking Japanese hospital ships. I told him that it was propaganda and the only thing he knew was what he read in the Jap controlled newspapers.

The conversation was soon joined by Wade and Crews and continued long into the night. I managed to control my temper pretty well and kept my voice within the bounds of diplomatic pitch, even in the face of gross stupidity and their Oriental refusal to see the truth.

The conference ended without open hostilities but I doubt if the matter is cleared up. Nogi will be in tomorrow, stamping around and acting hostile. However, the time has come to act decisively about our situation. I might as well get it over and done with.

March 10, 1944

I spent all afternoon in a long, boring, stupid conversation with Nogi and Kubota. The fight began when I casually asked if Christenson's draft could be allowed more buying privileges. Nogi blew up and began throwing around accusations that the draft already had more money than they received. Well, he had me there. Nogi demanded that Christenson be brought to my office and explain where the money came from. Chris gave the Japs reasonable explanations but Kubota called him a liar. The Japanese had suspected, and rightly so, that the draft had received a large sum of money before they left Cabanatuan, but the Japs can't prove it.

We sat tight and answered questions cautiously, but the truth was told in every instance. There's an art to asking questions and answering them. However, for a while things were sure as hell in the balance and could have fallen either way. We never really had a chance to discuss the food problem and the air was too tense to bring it up at this time. Nogi was already worn to a frazzle. I'll catch him again when he's not so excited. After the Japs left, I invited Chris to have chow with us. It certainly was a long afternoon.

March 11, 1944

I received five letters today. One contained a picture of "Barnacle." He's a big boy now. I regret that I'm denied these years with him. My dreams of teaching my son how to swim, sail, fish, and hunt are now shattered. That time of his life will be over if and when I ever see him again.

We had another blackout drill tonight. It indicates the changing events and progress of the war. The sirens have a familiar scream but tonight they are thrilling rather than frightening. All of us think and feel the same thought: "Come on—blow the hell out of this place. We welcome the bombs. We want action—now!"

March 12, 1944

General Koa showed up for inspection today. He's a Reserve General with a load of campaign ribbons and the "Second Order of the Rising Sun." The inspection was uneventful, however I did notice that none of the Japanese wear their American World War I Victory Medal anymore.

I talked with Kubota this afternoon and learned that the General found defects in his inspection, but he was shrewd enough to notice and understand the situation. I offered to correct any faults on our part if the General would let us know what was wrong. Kubota admitted that there was nothing for us to correct. In fact, the Japs at headquarters were quite surprised that General Koa knew so much about the operation of the camp.

Kubota also mentioned that the General asked about Wade and me and the other Americans. He wanted to know how much grumbling we did and about what. Kubota said he told the General that we only complain about food. That's great if it's true. This is the very impression we want to present to the Japanese. That of Americans who admit they are prisoners, do not whine, are willing to abide by the rules of warfare, and expect fairness and civilized treatment as prisoners of war—no more, no less.

We have endeavored to maintain the welfare of our men, but have never believed we could accomplish this mission by presenting a grumbling, whining front. Our attitude is under test now. Heretofore the reputation of the Americans was lousy. Now, however, with discipline and open dealings with the enemy, this may prove to the betterment of our situation. If not—well, it hasn't hurt us. The laissez-faire chaotic morass into which the Americans had sunk before we cleaned up the place was suicidal.

I held a long disciplinary mast this afternoon: a series of stupid miscreants who still haven't been yanked out of their "reversion to pack" instincts that followed the surrender. The difficulty in handling many of these problems is that we have American interests to protect and yet must satisfy the Japanese and keep them in accord with our actions.

Nogi caught me as I was leaving my office this evening and said that we would have to find a substitute for toilet paper. A lengthy discussion followed as to the relative values of high gloss magazine paper, common rag paper, catalogues, corncobs, and leaves. I suggested he supply a quantity of white geese, remembering that the use of feathers is an old Japanese custom.

Next came a long discourse on sewage systems in general. I had to explain to Nogi the system as used in America. He was very interested and continually replied with a series of surprised grunts. I explained to him that most of the city of Manila was too low to permit septic tanks, however Bilibid does have a septic system. I believe Nogi was concerned about what we would dump into the city sewers but since the camp has septic tanks, he doesn't give a damn what we use for toilet paper.

March 13, 1944

I had a talk with Jones this morning about increasing the garden space. We now have everything planted in *camotes*. The little Jap veterinarian is now complaining that the pigs won't eat the vegetables that headquarters are sending into camp. That's nothing, we can't eat them either.

I'm depressed as hell today. As far as my life is concerned, for the first time I'm beginning to have doubts whether I'll ever get back to America. If I do return, there will be no pieces to pick up. Everything will be new and I'll have to go it alone. But there will be many of us in the same boat. I will fare as well as any of them. The futility of love, service, loyalty, sentiment—even life, coldly reveals itself like an icy blast from the dark poles. However, war has prepared me for it. I was destined to such a return (if I return) from the beginning. I can even recall the very moment when I realized my earthly life was over. To all intents and purposes I died a couple of years ago. I'm thankful for the brief bright flame:

> My candle burns at both ends,
> It will not last the night.
> But Oh my friends, and Ah my foes,
> It gives a pleasant light!

March 14, 1944

This morning I received a report that Horani had kept a working party busy last night filling rice sacks with dirt. There's something fishy going on, that's for sure. I'm debating at the moment whether to upset his apple cart or not. I will wait and see what develops.

Wade received a letter saying that he's promoted to full commander. Others have also received promotions. These kids have finally caught up with me. Apparently I have been forgotten. Screw it! I can't do anything more with four stripes than I could as an ordinary seaman.

This afternoon Horani accused the Americans of stealing shelter halves out of a storeroom to which he has the only key. By the time I was through investigating the matter I learned that Horani recently had a shelter half collar sewed on his shirt at our tailor shop. Not only that, but I discovered the little bastard has been changing figures on the food reports he sends to headquarters. That guy has been screwing us from one end to the other. It's no wonder we have a food problem. Everybody's on the take.

Wade and I hustled up to the front office and saw Kubota. I told him of our trouble with Horani and also brought up the fact that Horani had a working party fill rice sacks with dirt. Kubota was visibly angry and promised to look into the problem. The fur will probably fly at headquarters tonight.

March 15, 1944

Mail from the States is beginning to have a detrimental effect. If the letter writers would tell the prisoners that everything is O.K. at home, then mail would be a morale booster. However, people can't write freely under censorship. Awkward incomplete statements cause misunderstanding, worry, and concern. So instead of being a help to morale, the mail becomes a kick in the pants and does more harm than good. Even under normal circumstances letters can be misinterpreted, but a phone call or wire can relieve the anxiety. Not so under these conditions.

Christenson's 300 man draft is slated for Japan but there's no word as to when they will leave. Rumor has it that the men on the previous Japan draft are still aboard ship in Manila Bay. Practically every vessel leaving port is sunk by American submarines.

March 16, 1944

Wade and I see eye to eye about the coming postwar situation. We both sense the fact that life has gone on ahead of us and future plans have not taken us seriously into consideration. In these past few years the trend of life back home has been set and we are a forgotten issue. I can remember the pathetic instances of the last war where men returned and tried to pick up where they left off. They couldn't. The past is past and no matter how it hurts, we must realize the fact, accept it, adjust to it, and start out new as a stranger.

Momota tried to convince me to take shoes away from the patients and give them to the working party. I refused. I told him that this would only result in a shoeless camp and the demand for shoes for the working party would be endless. He finally agreed with me and said he would try to find "used" Jap shoes.

Momota, however, is one of those guys that doesn't know enough to quit when he's ahead. He next asked me why the working party wasn't getting enough food. He sure enough opened a "Pandora's box" with that question. I buried him with facts and figures and by the time I finished he left here with his tail between his legs and lost a lot of face in the process.

There's a hell of a lot of stirring around just now about this food business. The only person left to tackle is General Koa and I wouldn't be surprised if I got a crack at him soon. I'm fed up and worn out after several days and nights of constant fighting and sweating over conference tables. Today was the first time that I let these bastards get my goat. I lost my temper and let go at Momota with both barrels.

This is the worst mosquito season in years. I had planned to get under my net in self-defense. However, before I could even try to relax, word was received that the Japanese now declare Red Cross material as "Jap issue." I'll knock that crap into a cocked hat tomorrow.

March 17, 1944

St. Patrick's Day. I'm wearing a four leaf clover, but I don't know for what. My good luck deserted me when I lost my rabbit's foot at Mariveles.

I directed all Americans to declare any Red Cross items as personal property and to report to me any Jap instructions to the contrary.

We received four sacks of sugar and I have been trying to figure some equitable way to distribute it to the entire camp. The responsibility of doing what's best for the men and yet keeping everybody happy is not always easy. Sugar will be issued to each person today. It will be a pitiful small amount but the boys will have the sugar in their own hands and can do what they want with it.

The most beneficial method would have been to issue the sugar through the galley, but Japanese bookkeeping has to be satisfied and the prisoners must be assured that nobody is trying to flimflam them. Then, of course, there are a certain number of individuals that must be convinced that they aren't contributing one darn cent to the next guy's welfare. Heaven forbid! Perish the thought!

March 20, 1944

The Japs must know I'm on the warpath. They are steering clear of the hospital. As long as I'm on the offensive I intend to press my attack. I barged into Nogi's office today and told him in no uncertain terms that I can't prevent the men from going blind unless our food allotment is increased. Nogi tried to bring up the old "luxury" act again but it didn't work this time. I brought up the business of Horani's crooked food reports and the 26 bags of rice that Horani had the men fill with dirt. He intended to pawn the sacks off on the galley crew as our rice allotment. Kubota was supposed to have given all this information to Nogi but evidently he "forgot."

There seems to be an increasing Jap-American tension of late and also squabbling among the prisoners. It's all the development of hunger and the fight for food. The Japanese are forced to steal from us in order to have enough to eat themselves. My job is to keep my "children" from fighting with each other and at the same time fight the Japs in their behalf.

March 22, 1944

Just when I have the enemy backed up against their own goalpost, somebody fumbles the ball. The Japs caught a note carrier last night.

The man, Harry Rapp, was thrown in the brig. I don't know for how long or what the status of the case will be.

There was a long conference up front as the "gestapo" interrogated Rapp. Americans were not allowed to be present. The Japs apparently made the poor guy talk because later when I went up to the front office I overheard Nogi explain to a guard that the notes were passed to a Filipino in the toilet. I knew that part was true as this method has been used for a long time.

The silliest damn part of the whole affair is that the messages Rapp had on him were love notes to a Filipino girl. This type of irresponsibility can only get everyone in trouble and break up an excellent system that can serve for important things.

March 23, 1944

This afternoon I went up to the front office to see Nogi and complain about the latest incident of guards slapping patients around. Nogi cornered "four-eyes" and gave him holy hell. He really jumped down Kito's throat. Nogi then told me to report any more slappings directly to him. I guess he has his personnel problems the same as I do.

I hung around the office awhile to see if I could find out anything more about the Rapp case. The Japs are convinced that there's more to this than simple love notes. They are very suspicious people and always assume sinister things are going on between the Americans and Filipinos. Important items they miss or disregard entirely. They can't see the forest for the trees.

Nogi collared me as I was about to return to the hospital. He wanted me to try out a new calcium preparation on the American patients. I asked him if it was a proven medication or another one of his "Jekyll and Hyde" experiments. He admitted that this was a "try out for what happens." The situation became a little tense as I explained that Americans don't experiment with drugs on humans and abhor such practices. Nogi was annoyed but I cooled him down a bit by offering him the use of our new textbooks.

March 27, 1944

I stood by while the Japs rummaged through Rapp's personal effects looking for evidence. Rapp is still holding out and won't reveal the girl's name. The guards are letting him have a little water in the brig but no food.

I received 113 mail parcels today addressed to men we have no record of or those who are known dead. I'm going to inventory the packages and distribute the contents to the prisoners who have received nothing from home. It's a darn shame this mail can't be delivered. I'm saving all the names on the packages and hope to notify the senders what we have done.

I have been so darn hungry for three days that I'm hurting. I haven't eaten enough today to keep a bird alive. I nibbled a few radish roots and had a little rice and bitter soup.

I sent a note up to Kubota that the ducks and pigs are dying from starvation. The animals are more important to them than human lives.

March 28, 1944

Rapp was questioned again today but continued to hold out. However, Nogi finally weakened. He was getting nowhere in his investigation. Kubota saved face by making a statement that the "gestapo" found the information they were looking for "elsewhere." Rapp was sentenced to 30 days in the brig. As far as I'm concerned, he got off lucky.

It was a long thankless job passing out the undeliverable mail packages. While I was sorting through the boxes I noticed much evidence of tender care, remembrance, and concern for the welfare of sons, husbands, and lovers. In other instances there was a cold impersonal feeling about the contents. These parcels have a definite tone. You can read them like a book. I'm still not completely hardshelled. I felt a lump in my throat several times today. All the prisoners of this war aren't in prison camps.

The eye department insisted that I have my eyes examined this afternoon—caught at last. You can see by my handwriting that my eyes are dilated to beat hell and I'm having a tough time visually. My nerve heads are involved and blind spots greatly enlarged. I'll be damned if I'll be an eye invalid in a world where everybody else is active and healthy—to hell with it. A half-blind bastard is no good to anyone. My mind is made up.

Tonight I'm wondering if it wouldn't be best for all of us if we just disappeared when this war is over—those of us who are still alive.

I can see so much evidence of deterioration in the prisoners. I know I show it too, but haven't the insight to appreciate the fact.

March 29, 1944

Mosquitoes and flies have become impossible. The weather is hot, dry, and dusty. The wind blows constantly, covering everything with sand and dirt. Our half-naked bodies are caked with dried mud. We are out of brooms and the Japs have directed us to use tree branches and palm leaves instead.

I received a report that most of the medical supplies we ship to other camps are stolen before they arrive. I suspected we were taking a screwing on that deal and now I know it.

Nogi inspected the hospital this morning on one of his quick tours. He asked me if we were receiving enough ice. I told him more than enough. It serves to keep the icebox cold, but only the box. We never have anything to put into the cabinet to preserve. That ended the conversation. Nogi went away mad again—tough.

The men are referring to the provision truck as "incoming garbage" and the garbage truck as "outgoing garbage." The only difference is that one truck comes in loaded and the other goes out loaded.

Ducks are continuing to die of starvation and the pigs are deteriorating rapidly from lack of food. But the Japanese still want the sows bred. Yesterday, one sow was so weak that she couldn't hold up the boar. I recommended that all the pigs be killed while there was still meat on their bones.

Schweizer has been after me for a long time to sneak him a hot plate from the storeroom because the Japs grabbed his. I told him that the plates were private property and he would have to ask the owners. Well, today he sent me a note saying that Tsukahara ordered him to get a hot plate from the storeroom. I confronted Schweizer with the fact that the Japs couldn't have known I had these hot plates if he hadn't told them. I not only refused to give him a plate, but I was so damn mad that I carried the whole box of them to headquarters and told Tsukahara to pick out his own hot plate.

April 1, 1944

April Fool's Day. I get fooled every day, so I can't get worked up over this date. A red and white alert flag was hoisted over the camp this afternoon and the guard was doubled immediately. The walls are being patrolled and a lookout established on top of the tower. I received word that a blackout drill would take place tonight. American planes have been reported over the Philippines.

April 2, 1944

The air alert continues today. Last night the Japs at the port area slept in foxholes. Any soldiers going outside the Bilibid front gate must travel in groups of three and carry rifles. I learned that about a hundred American planes "visited" Davao last night. It seems to me like a hell of a lot of hysteria over a group of planes 600 miles away.

We were ordered into our barracks at seven o'clock this evening. It's so hot and dusty that I asked Kubota if he would allow us to stay outside a little longer to cool off. He finally consented to let us sit outside but not walk around.

April 5, 1944

We aren't allowed in the guardhouse anymore. Any business with the guards must be done through a Camp Warden. Yesterday the Japs raised hell with Schweizer because he happened to walk behind a Jap sergeant's chair. The Japanese are becoming very suspicious of us and trigger-happy nervous.

It's open season on cats and rats. The prisoners kill and eat them. We are eating everything and anything. The latest news from "over the wall" tells of a big naval battle in the South Pacific—both sides losing heavily. The shelling and bombing of islands to the north of us is also reported.

I submitted my monthly sanitary report today. It's the worst report I have written since I have been in charge. I find it difficult to concentrate and carry on a thought for any sustained length of time. I had the same trouble on Corregidor when beriberi hit me. I realized the report was a mess when I dropped it off at headquarters. There is a lot of information in the letter but it's poorly done and not put together well at all. In dealing with the Orientals, this is important. I must snap out of my lethargy and get ahold of myself.

April 9, 1944

Easter Sunday. Bataan fell two years ago today. It seems like a million years ago when the earth rocked like a bouncing ball and tons of steel ripped mountains apart. And the whole world was a mass of torn flesh and blood. Almost everyone was dead or dying and the living were waiting for their day.

I have been ordered to put another draft together for Cabanatuan. I decided to send our sick that we would ordinarily keep. I'm convinced that the men will die if they stay here and the food is better at Cabanatuan. They might stand a better chance for survival there.

All the Mexicans are lining up to join this latest Cabanatuan draft—even one-legged Sanchez. This sudden decision all revolves around the fact that Garcia is on the draft. Garcia is a leader and has taken care of most of the Mexican group. He's a hustler and a racketeer, but has shared his wealth and gains with the needy. A sort of Mexican Robin Hood in this Sherwood Forest. Even before the war, Garcia was an enterprising fellow, running cabarets, etc. The others look to him for leadership and support. The Mexicans are not without their wrong side and do have their intergang differences. But I would rather deal with them than some of the other factions in camp.

April 13, 1944

I have had a severe headache for about two weeks and last night it became so bad that I had to take codeine. Today the boys are giving me massive vitamin therapy for my eyes. I hope it helps, but I think more nourishing food is the only salvation for my sight.

Nogi and Momota stopped in late today. They want me to sign a receipt for all the Red Cross supplies. The figures are approximately correct and the Japanese feel that it would be in the best interest of all parties if I signed the document. I signed the receipt. At this stage of the game there is no point in raising a fuss over something we can't do anything about anyway.

I feel weak tonight but I'm able to get about and handle the usual problems as they arise. I'm still hungry.

April 15, 1944

The Japs showed a movie last night—*Vivacious Lady* starring James Stewart and Ginger Rogers. Everyone was enjoying the picture when I was suddenly called to the dispensary and informed that a prisoner had been caught trying to escape under the charged wire near the carpenter shop.

Wade and Schweizer were already up there. The Jap guards had become hysterical and were running around like a pack of wild dogs, slamming everybody with their gun stocks. Wade missed being bayoneted by inches.

I was about to leave for the scene of the commotion when I met Wade coming in the dispensary door. He started to tell me what had happened but suddenly the crazed Jap guards charged into the mass of men sitting on the ground watching the movie. Whistles pierced the night along with fanatical Japanese screams, as the guards stampeded like a herd of wild buffalo into a thousand defenseless men—many of them invalids and on stretchers.

Wade and I stepped back into the dark of the dispensary and ducked under the window to be out of the line of fire in case shooting started. Many men were trampled in the wild chaos of the night, and their cries tore through our guts. Wade attempted to tell me the complete story of what had happened but it was almost impossible to talk above all the outside noise.

R. D. Parker, a Marine sergeant, had tried to escape by sneaking through the charged wires. However, the wires began to spark as the Marine crawled under them. A guard found Parker lying dazed on the other side. Wade immediately cut off the juice. When Parker realized that the electricity was off, he picked himself up and climbed back through the fence.

By this time about two dozen guards had gathered at the spot. They instantly jumped Parker and began working him over. Wade, Schweizer, and Dwyer were mauled in the melee. Moments later the entire Jap garrison became unglued and began their rampage.

Wade and I had just started to venture outside again when we heard Schweizer ordering everybody back to their barracks for *bango*. After an hour of count and recount we were one man short. I talked with Kubota and suggested that my officers conduct a "sight" roll call. However, this proved unnecessary. Schweizer talked to Parker and learned that a Marine corporal by the name of J. W. Carrington had slipped through the wire twenty minutes earlier.

By midnight everyone had calmed down and the Japs let us bring Parker up from the brig and dress his wounds. He was badly banged up but was still alive—for now anyway.

The Japanese method of group punishment means that every man who escapes, or attempts to escape, places the lives of his fellow prisoners in jeopardy. Many men have paid dearly for one man's break for freedom. This entire camp will now suffer reprisals and our lot will only get worse. Moreover, it shows the Japs what we have known all along—that the wire they depend on is far from foolproof. As long as they had faith in the wire, we were guarded less and had more freedom of movement. Now that the cat's out of the bag, our every action will be watched.

April 16, 1944

Early this morning I sent word to Kubota to cancel all gatherings until further notice. I thought it better to have word originate with us first. In this way we will be in charge of the situation.

The camp has quieted down somewhat but the tension is still there. It's like waiting for "the other shoe to drop." General Koa showed up this afternoon and Parker was brought in for questioning. He was returned to the brig this evening. The Japs untied him, permitted him a bath, and gave him a meal. They also gave us permission to change his bandages. There are no reprisals in evidence—yet.

Late tonight all officers were assembled as Nogi read off the punishment: "All entertainment privileges revoked. All officers are reminded to take more precautions against escape. The guilty men will be punished in accordance with Imperial military law."

There has been an astonishing lack of strain as a result of this escape attempt. I'm inclined to believe it's the influence of General Koa. I imagine that the Japanese are postponing action in Parker's case in hopes of catching Carrington and placing them both on trial together.

I had a long talk with Nogi after his speech and he agreed to let us organize a squad system along lines which we believe will be effective. The squad punishment system is deplorable but it's up to us to have a program that will work—otherwise group punishment is assured.

During our talk, Nogi said that he realized we were not getting enough to eat but he was doing everything in his power to remedy the situation. He remarked that he knew our lot was a hard one and he was willing to let "bygones be bygones."

April 17, 1944

Smack in the middle of this hot torrid season we now have rain and overcast days. The cloudy weather has been a welcome relief for those of us with dilated eyes. Trying to move about in a world of blurred vision is hell. Even as I write, I can hardly see what I'm doing.

Last night we received four sacks of sugar we had paid for. The trouble began when a Jap guard insisted on loading cans of insecticide on top of the sacks, although it was obvious that the cans were leaking. I had a hell of an argument with the front office gang but they refused to replace the sacks. We are trying to salvage the sugar by boiling the mess and turning it into syrup. Sugar is such an important item that we can't afford to lose a drop.

April 19, 1944

The Japanese doubled the guard permanently today. Everywhere I go I bump into one of the raccoons. Kubota warned the working party to be careful of their conduct on the outside and to stay clear of the guards.

Kubota is busy erecting buildings for soldiers that are to arrive soon. He moved most of the guards into a barracks in our compound. The guards plainly have the jitters and feel safer behind these walls than over at headquarters.

Filipino sentiment is running high and the people are becoming bolder and more demonstrative as the war approaches their own shores. Reports from "over the wall" reveal that Formosa has been under heavy attack for the past ten days. Most of our guards are Formosan and that places the Americans in a precarious position. Kubota has remained outwardly calm but the others are noticeably nervous. The frantic wild episode that occurred the night of Carrington's escape shows very well what we will have to deal with when a real crisis arrives.

April 20, 1944

It never ceases to amaze me how small incidents can assume great significance. All these months while I have been fighting, conniving, and beating my brains out trying to drag money from the wealthy around here, in order to feed the indigent and sick Americans, an unexpected surprise dropped in my lap.

From out of the blue this morning, Staff Sergeant J. F. Zagorri (leaving today for Cabanatuan) turned his pay for the month over to the indigent fund—60 centavos. Only a pittance, but the spirit—it was like the sweet breeze of orange blossoms to a man in the sewer. I called Zagorri to my office and thanked him personally. He will never know the lift he gave me this morning.

April 23, 1944

Nogi stopped in my office today and asked all kinds of medical questions. These Japs are trying their darndest to acquire a medical education. Well, they have a captive teacher so why not. One question asked: "How many meters of suture thread is needed for an appendectomy?" I tried to explain that each case was different, depending upon who was operating, what incision was used, and the case itself.

Wade and I made our weekly inspection of the hospital compound this afternoon. The camp is being maintained as well as we are permitted to keep it. The general condition, however, grows steadily worse. Garbage and refuse are not cared for as well as before. Only wooden containers are available and they are not satisfactory. Flies and mosquitoes are a pestilence we can't control. This place is just naturally falling apart. However, conditions are generally bad throughout the Manila area.

April 27, 1944

The Japanese have announced that they wish to pay respect to our war dead on Sunday. This marks the beginning of their shrine period.

They have held this ceremony for the past two years. The general sends in a wreath and we are permitted to buy one. The roll call of the dead grows longer each year. We stand uncovered under the broiling sun and listen to it read. This year I'm limiting the roll call to only those men who have died during the past year. Most of the very sick can't stand under the hot sun for too long a time.

We had another air alert this afternoon. Blackout is the order of the day from now on. Our forces are apparently near enough to constitute an immediate threat.

Wade continues to look bad and has a hellish cough. I placed him on a special diet and gave him a box of Red Cross food. He feels that he is robbing a patient by eating it but I convinced him of the importance of our mission and the need for him to keep well.

April 29, 1944

The Japs rousted everybody out at three in the morning for *bango*. Somebody heard an alarm bell, or thought they did. The whole headquarters outfit showed up and added to the confusion. Nobody was missing—back to bed. Occurrences like this make a person wonder about the Japanese. How these guys who don't know which end is up can create so much trouble in the world. Come to think of it, maybe that's why.

A recent Davao prisoner list shows 19 escapes. I think that's what has the Japs skittish. The medical department occupies a peculiar position in this prisoner of war game. Escape is O.K. for everyone else. I can't blame the prisoners for trying to get away if the prospects are within reason and the rest of the men are not endangered. But our job is not to escape. Our job is to stay and take care of our own. The Japs can't understand that at all. However, here in Bilibid, escape is too far beyond the realm of reason to warrant jeopardizing the lives and welfare of the entire camp. In Davao the situation is different. The prisoners are not located in a large city that is loaded with Japanese soldiers and Jap sympathizers.

Today is the Emperor's birthday and Nogi showed up at my office in full dress uniform and acting very formal. At first I thought he was going to confer the "Sacred Order of the Second Kite" upon me. However, he told me that on the Emperor's birthday certain grants were made and, in accordance with this spirit, he would lift the ban on amusement gatherings. Of course, under blackout restrictions no amusements are possible. But, nevertheless, the gesture was made and Nogi said he hopes we will show our appreciation by not attempting any more escapes.

April 30, 1944

Memorial services were held this date at our Bilibid cemetery. There was 60 seconds of silence and then roll was called of the men who died during the past year. A psalm was read by Chaplain Wilcox and prayers were recited by Chaplain Duffy. Wreaths were placed on the graves and Private Raymond Beck sounded taps. The Japanese sent two beautiful baskets of artificial flowers and the merchant donated a wreath of fresh flowers.

After the ceremony, I conducted a special prayer service at our chapel for the Japanese war dead. I also wrote a letter to General Koa, thanking him for respects shown and mentioned our services for his country's war dead.

In the spirit of their holiday celebration, the Japanese sent in 50 pounds of carabao meat (counting bone). Divided among 900 men, it wasn't more than a taste. But we were darn glad to have any kind of meat. We made soup from it.

May 1, 1944

Five Americans were brought in today who have been driving trucks for the Japanese at Naga in southern Luzon. This is the first contact they have had with their fellow Americans in nearly two years. They lived with Japanese troops the whole time. The men reported that Japanese rolling stock is in bad shape. There's a shortage of parts and gasoline. The enemy defense lines are thin and there is very little artillery. There is also a shortage of food and ammunition. They said that most of the Japanese soldiers seem to be concentrated in the Manila area.

May 3, 1944

The "neutral sympathizers" were allowed into camp today with a marvelous donation—beans, peanuts, sugar, limes, bananas, tomatoes, clothes, shoes, writing paper, and 200 pounds of beef. Thank God!

Mrs. Margaret Utinski negotiated the delivery with Japanese headquarters. I wrote a receipt for the gifts and also a thank-you note to all the people involved in putting the project together. I also wrote a note to the Pope, thanking him for his recent donation. In fact, I even had to thank the Japs for a donation of 65 pesos to the indigent fund. They obtained the money by returning the floral offerings for a refund.

I think Shakespeare said it best: "As a tiny candle throws its light, so shines a good deed in a naughty world." There has been nobleness and good deeds, and they do stand out like mountains in a naughty world.

May 4, 1944

For the first time in a long while I'm not hungry. These gifts were certainly a boost for morale—we needed it. The galley crew performed excellently serving the donated food. I wrote them a letter of appreciation and gave each man two cigars. The boys in S.O.Q. even wrote the galley force a commendatory letter. I was glad to get that group on record. It does my heart good to know that the majority of the camp realizes that what goes into the kitchen comes out to them—all of it.

The Japanese uncovered a drug racket involving the working party. As a result two men are in the brig tonight. The Filipinos engaged in the drug trafficking were severely beaten. Fortunately I was able to show that there was no leakage from our stock. Evidence points to other sources, except for a few tablets that may have been saved up by patients over a long period of time.

May 6, 1944

Nogi sent five Japanese soldiers down to the hospital for eye examinations. They show definite signs of optic nerve damage. This should prove interesting when I send the men back to the front office with my diagnosis.

Headquarters reduced our food issue since we received the donation from the "neutral sympathizers." At least we had two good meals before they lowered the boom.

I'm still writing through the blur and haze of dilated eyes, and have trouble reading any of it. This living in a half-blind world is agonizing and frustrating.

I'm convinced that life at home has now gone on too long without us. We will never fit in again. Adjustments have undoubtedly been made and our loved ones have detoured their lives around the missing. We would be an ill-fitting part in the smooth running machinery of their daily routine. At times it seems silly for us to suddenly barge in and disrupt lives that have become used to being without us. Wade talks of going to Shanghai. I'm thinking of Singapore. Cecil says that Australia is in his future.

May 13, 1944

Morale among the medical officers is at a new low. The will "to do" is sagging. Another six months and most of my boys will be cutting out paper dolls. Small petty things are becoming too important. I realize that I have to do something about the problem. However, in most cases there isn't any basic material to work with. The men suffer from starvation and weak eyes and are bored from their long confinement within these walls. It takes guts, early discipline, and more to keep the old body functioning after two years of this grind. The prewar life and training of most of the officers didn't fit them for this kind of ordeal.

Nogi appeared late this afternoon and announced that he would inspect the personal effects of the entire working party. It was a long, hot, tedious, and disgusting search, carried out in the usual unorganized manner. The project was unplanned and with no conception of how to go about a thorough systemic search—hence nothing accomplished. The only major question that arose was where one man acquired a jug in which he was making vinegar.

It's a hot sultry night and walking back from the upper compound, I paused for a moment under the mango tree and looked up at the stars. My eyes fixed upon an old familiar constellation that always seemed to free the night over Williamsburg and Yorktown.

May 15, 1944

The long hot days drag slowly by. Our adobe barracks bake in the blazing sun to make nightly ovens in which we are packed—to cook. One of these mornings I'm going to awake so hungry that I'll roll over on my sleeping platform and find Cecil baked to a nice rich crusted brown and basted in his own dripping sweat. I'll take a big juicy bite from his short ribs and find them tasty—even without salt and pepper.

The food truck arrives with a little less each day. A few squash this morning and one basket of pineapples for over a thousand men. Our *camotes* are running out and no grain is expected in the immediate future. Momota says, "You have more food if Roosevelt dies." The ridiculous talk of a babbling idiot.

Momota wants to increase the size of the farm but the only soil available is hard and rocky. We would need picks and shovels plus men strong enough to do the labor. All he ever says when he looks over the garden is, "More plant! More plant!" The Japs are so childlike that they have no mental conception of what's entailed in any project.

May 19, 1944

At four o'clock this afternoon I was notified that a Japanese guard [Formosan] had shot a patient in Ward Sixteen and then shot himself. Wade and I rushed to the scene but met a stretcher party bringing both men to surgery. The American, Sergeant J. W. Griffin, had been shot through the neck, while the guard had part of his face blown away.

Captain Paul Ashton [Army Medical Corps] reported that he had been present at the incident and heard the guard and Griffin arguing outside the ward. Ashton heard the guard cry out, *"Me patai! Me patai!"* Griffin, apparently not understanding or caring to continue the conversation replied, "O.K., you *patai!*" Ashton then heard the bolt action of the guard's rifle and a shot. Paul rushed outside and saw Griffin lying on the ground. Ashton struggled with the guard and tried to take the gun away from the Jap. However, the rifle went off again striking the guard under the chin.

I immediately notified Kubota and the front office. Kamura rushed down from headquarters and began an investigation by taking statements from Ashton and other Japanese guards. All the patients in the ward were also questioned. One man saw the guard shoot Griffin and another patient noticed the guard shoot himself. By six o'clock, Kamura informed me that the affair was a result of a misunderstanding on the part of the guard and that I shouldn't be concerned about the incident.

Not satisfied with Kamura's explanation, however, I conducted an investigation of my own and came up with the following facts: This Japanese guard has had gonorrhea for about four months and has been continually trying 'o buy sulfa drugs from the Americans. A short time before the shooting, the guard called to an American outside the ward to come in and he passed the prisoner some money. However, the Jap was se⁻n by the Sergeant of the Guard. Fearing he was caught, he threw the money on the ground and tried to shift the blame to the American. The Sergeant of the Guard did nothing about the incident, nor did he mention it under questioning by Kamura. The American involved is named Howell and he is due to leave on a draft tomorrow to Cabanatuan. The wounded guard has a reputation for having been always friendly to the Americans. "*Me patai*" is pidgin Tagalog and can be interpreted as meaning "I die." It looks to me as if the guard was telling Griffin that he, the guard, was about to die. Griffin, not understanding, replied, "O.K., you die."

I interviewed the patients from Ward Thirteen who had a complete view of the whole area. But they only noticed what took place after the second shot was fired. The men said that the wounded guard was convulsive and was lying on the ground between two other Japanese. The rifle laid near the fallen man. Griffin has been placed on the critical list. There is little hope for his recovery.

May 20, 1944

James Griffin died about ten o'clock tonight. He had been attached to the 192nd Tank Battalion and was an outstanding soldier. He was wounded twice—once when his radio operator and driver were killed. Griffin's father and mother live in Chicago. He has two brothers still living. I understand that his father is a judge and Griffin was studying law while at the same time working in the police department.

Nogi came in late and asked if my investigation of the shooting had revealed anything new. It's plainly evident to both of us that bartering and wheeling-dealing has been going on between patients and the guards. I have reason to suspect that certain of the "big wheels" around here are also involved. I'm still not ready to accept any ready answer to the question of why this particular guard shot this particular prisoner.

May 26, 1944

There's a report that the "gestapo" intercepted a shipment of money being supplied to the men at Cabanatuan. Several prisoners are in custody. One of them, a Colonel, was yanked out from under a shower and not even allowed to put on his clothes. He was told that "he wouldn't need clothes where he was going."

May 27, 1944

Mongo beans are no longer available at any price and peanuts are beyond our buying power. Japanese money has flooded the marketplace and the Filipinos are now refusing to accept it. They are calling Jap money "*benjo* paper" [toilet paper].

I'm having minor problems with Jerry Crews. He's had so much trouble with the working party that he's developed an aversion toward the men. If anyone takes issue with him, it's like waving a red flag in front of a bull. All day yesterday I had to keep a tight curb on Jerry and try to keep him on an even keel until he gets his bearings again. He went to bed still smoldering and not at all happy with his little world.

The usual minor bickerings and problems of prison life continue to occupy my time. One man received more tobacco than another, or one person has pencil and paper while another doesn't. All these issues are momentous to the people involved. Alas, they have nothing but themselves on their minds—there is certainly no one more important.

Duckworth didn't receive any bananas on a recent distribution. The Japs had designated the bananas for the sick and "Ducky" claims he's sick. Duckworth became peeved and wrote a memo to Nogi asking permission to withdraw his contributions to the indigent fund. Nogi agreed to let him take his money out. The Japanese realize that the fund is in the best interest of the camp as a whole, but they can't force a person to contribute to it. I told Nogi that someday there would be an accounting of all the officers who took an attitude of personal selfish interest at the expense of their men.

May 29, 1944

Nogi spent the last two days snooping around the hospital, making chicken scratches alongside each name on the patient list. It turned out to be a 250 man draft for Cabanatuan. He gave me the list to organize, but I have plenty of leeway to substitute. In the end we will send who we want.

Toilet paper, a lowly commodity, assumes major proportions by its absence. In fact, there's no paper available for this civilized necessity of the western world. I took the matter up with Kubota—usual answer: "Jap soldier no paper too."

Momota now states that the *camotes* are for the pigs. The animals are only fed about once every five days and are slowly starving to death. The prisoners aren't in much better shape. We have been cut to three spoonfuls of rice for each meal and the men are growling. Their natural reaction is to look upon me as the one who starves them. I have been able to maintain an understanding attitude toward the "children" so far, but my respect for most of the officers is lowered daily.

Several months ago I reminded my staff that there was tough going ahead—and I meant tough. I considered it the duty of every one of them to maintain a posture of calm assurance and set an example for the rest of the men. There are a few officers who don't complain. However, most of them are pampered children, born with silver spoons in their mouths, untrained in self-denial and undisciplined in childhood.

The desperate frustration of the men is evident everywhere. They will fight over a banana, over the garbage barrel pickings, or over a spoonful of sugar.

June 5, 1944

I took the bull by the horns today in an attempt to alleviate our condition. I conferred with Nogi and requested permission to contact the neutral agencies in Manila for help. I also requested that the money everybody has in savings be deposited in the general fund to buy more food for the camp. Nogi demanded to know how many depositors would be willing to contribute their money. Accordingly I wrote a memo to all depositors asking them to answer Nogi's question. Out of 242 depositors, all but 18 agreed to cooperate. Of course, the dissenters were most of the boys in S.O.Q. They refused to contribute without certain provisions. They insisted that the indigent prisoners should not have any spending power in the store, while they, the dissidents, would have the right to spend whatever they wished.

My policy is, and always will be, that I will never sacrifice the welfare of the enlisted man for the officer brass. In fact, it's the duty of the officers to take care of the men. I consider their proposal unbecoming an officer, un-American in principle, and another disgraceful commentary on officer conduct in general. My answer to their request was to completely ignore them. Those bastards should know me by now. I don't make deals—not where the welfare of the camp is concerned. I'll make that bunch of stuffed-shirt parasites help support the needy if I have to dig up Jesse James.

June 15, 1944

I had to remove Weisblatt from the library detail at the request of Chaplain Wilcox. However, I feel that the problem was only a case of misunderstanding on Weisblatt's part. I have written him a letter expressing my appreciation for the work he has done. After all, he's also hungry and irritable. Everybody rises to the level of their own incompetence—some sooner than others. Chaplain Duffy takes over the library duties today as assistant to Wilcox.

June 17, 1944

The rainy season is upon us and presents its usual headaches. I have tried to convince the Japs to prepare for the wet weather, but to no avail. The dysentery wards and pigpens are already in danger of flooding. Wood lies dripping wet in the open with no place provided to store it out of the rain.

Bango regulations were changed tonight. Roll call is not allowed in front of the guardhouse anymore. The Japs are afraid we might rush the place. *Bango* is now held in the rear of the compound and in small groups.

Another silly regulation from headquarters states that only bedridden patients are to be allowed in their bunks from reveille till evening *bango*. Here in this hospital everybody needs bedrest if for no other reason than to combat starvation.

June 20, 1944

A 150 man draft from Cabanatuan arrived this morning for further transfer—destination unknown. One officer is with them, Captain Lilles. After looking the group over, I noticed that it was composed of all the misfits and troublemakers that I had known over the past couple of years. After talking with Lilles I got the impression that things have changed for the worse up there. It's not the "paradise" anymore that some people pictured the place. They are also beginning to feel the food shortage.

Our *camote* crop isn't doing well in this rainy weather. It's all vines and no *camotes*. We are eating the vines and sharing them with the pigs. The ducks continue to die and the porkers grow skinnier every day.

The working party returning to camp tonight reports that the Manila papers are telling of a hot naval battle in progress and Americans have landed on Saipan. The Japanese are admitting large losses, but say our losses are "gigantic." The Japanese claim that the supremacy of the Pacific is at stake.

June 24, 1944

Nogi called me to the front office this morning. He said that he can't contact the neutral agencies in Manila on our behalf. The Japanese Army doesn't recognize any neutral agency. I looked at him with disbelief. "You mean to tell me that you don't recognize the Swiss Agency in Manila?" I asked. Nogi shook his head affirmatively.

I then asked him about the return of the deposit money. He refused that request also. However, he did have another stupid demand. He now wants a sample of every item we received from the Red Cross. I left his office very depressed. I'm beginning to feel like I'm back on my own two yard line, fourth down and goal to go.

June 25, 1944

We had two litters of piglets last night. That makes a total of 57 porkers. The sows have no milk and have to be watched constantly to keep them from eating their litters. The Japs brought in 10 sacks of rice bran for the pigs and asked me "how many days one sack would last." I nearly laughed out loud. Shoestring administration is all they know. They can't think in any terms other than small.

Lilles's detail is still with us. Kubota indicates that they may be here for some time. In the meantime, the Japs are moving soldiers into our barracks and wards. We are forced to keep doubling up. It won't be long before we will have more Japanese than Americans.

Late today, Nogi showed up very excited. He told me that 130 sick men would be arriving and we must house them in "what wards we have left." The Japs have already cleaned us out of beds, mattresses, and blankets. The only room we have left is the concrete floor. However, never let it be said that the Japs aren't innovative. They confiscated blankets from Lilles's draft to give to the incoming patients when they arrive.

June 26, 1944

Late this afternoon, 1,234 prisoners arrived from Davao after spending 21 days in the hold of a small ship. For the last three days the ship had been anchored in the port area with its human cargo aboard. They were a horribly miserable lot when they stumbled into camp. One man immediately died from heat exhaustion and 200 others were admitted to sick bay.

In general, the poor condition of this Davao group is mainly due to their rigorous trip up here. They had a bad record of escapes and

attacks on guards. The Japs are handling them as desperate characters. The men are hostile and there is a complete lack of organization
and discipline. It's a real dog eat dog outfit.

I noticed several familiar faces among the Davao people, but most
of them had changed almost beyond recognition. A few of the "high
and mighty" Colonels who treated me so shabbily on Corregidor were
among the group. They greeted me like a long lost friend. I was
reminded of the old adage, "Be kind to those you meet on the way
up. They are the same people you meet on the way down." I refuse
to let such experiences influence me in respect to their present
needs—but I will not forget.

Another group of 450 men arrived from Cabanatuan tonight.
They will join Lilles's bunch and the Davao draft. The whole lot of
them are scheduled for Japan. No definite word yet as to when they
will leave.

July 4, 1944

Independence Day. That's a joke. A big inspection is slated for this
afternoon, creating the usual confusion among the Japanese. Wade
and I are to be at the rear of the inspection party and Nogi is to be
the "lead off man." Haase was ordered not to be in the group. He
speaks and understands Japanese too well. All our ragged clothes and
filthy mattresses were directed to be "out of sight." The only major
variation to this inspection is that usually the Japs serve an imposing
chow for the benefit of the visiting dignitaries. Not this time however.
We were issued a hundred pounds of fish for over a thousand men.

The General's tour proved uneventful. This dude at one time was
a military attaché in Washington. He spoke perfect English and asked
a lot of questions, but was unconcerned with the answers.

Chaplain Wilcox is not doing well at all and I placed him on
complete bedrest. I heard a report tonight that the Japanese top brass
are considering sending their sick men to this hospital. If that's the
case, we are going to need a ten story building.

July 6, 1944

The entire Japan draft moved out yesterday. Over a thousand men
bound for Tokyo and Osaka. I learned that their ship is a very small

craft and all the men are jammed into one hold. There was no latrine facility on the vessel, so I had our carpenters up all night building a latrine for them. One of the boys in the front office told me that Tsukahara is leaving for Japan with the group. I never would have figured that.

We held a general cleanup around the camp after the draft left. However, it will only be a short time before another group arrives. The wholesale migration to Japan is underway and practically everybody will pass through these gates. It won't be long before the only people left here will be the absolute invalids.

Our hospital census is 920 and over a third of the ward space is taken over by the working party and Japanese soldiers. We have patients sleeping everywhere—on concrete decks, between the bunks, under the bunks, and on stretchers. Mattresses, blankets, and mosquito nets are out of the question for most of the men.

I realized today that I have been within these walls for over two years. The job of maintaining self-respect, personal appearance, and a philosophy of life that's constructive and compatible with prison living, becomes more and more arduous and taxing. One comes to the point where it's hard to know whether to drive, lead, request, praise, or damn.

July 9, 1944

I'm downright sick today—afraid my eyes are going bad again. I had to get up from my "invalid couch" this morning to settle a problem between Crews and Hanson. Personality differences have to be ironed out daily.

The Japanese are actively combing the provinces for food. They managed to acquire a small quantity of coconuts and *camotes*, but little else. We have replaced practically the entire farm with Tillandsia [Philippine chrysanthemums]. They are the most productive plant we can grow and we are using them to make soup. The taste is semibitter but it at least helps us swallow the bland tasteless rice. I doubt whether there is any food value to the plant, but even a bitter taste is better than no taste at all.

July 10, 1944

It rained most of the night and is still raining this morning. I feel a little better but am weak and lightheaded.

Our diagnostic report today indicates 1,029 medical conditions among 1,052 people. This is an understatement. Many of the men have ailments other than the categories reported. Everyone in Bilibid shows some disease or malnutrition disturbance. Neither my name nor Wade's shows in the statistics, yet both of us have definite pathology.

One of the front office flunkies, Agowa by name (we call him Captain Bly), was recently promoted to corporal. He suddenly developed a Napoleonic complex and has been driving everyone up a wall. I complained to Nogi about the man's attitude but Nogi's afraid of his own shadow. One prison camp—fifty bosses.

I'm making further efforts to snap my staff into line. As usual, the most difficult group to handle are the officers. Most of them are suffering from metabolic changes. Their internal secretion glands are going haywire—or something.

The Japan draft still sits in the harbor. They made one start but returned. For the past eleven days their ship has remained anchored in the port area. We receive new patients from them every day.

I learned that the men are packed in the ship's hold so tightly that the only way they can lie down is to flex their knees. The Japs serve them a cup of water and a handful of rice once a day. The prisoners are allowed out of the hold for a 20 minute period every three hours. Whenever it rains, the Japs close the hatch with a tarpaulin, cutting off all fresh air. Men are continually fainting from heat exhaustion and disease is running rampant.

July 11, 1944

Horani went off the deep end today. He stormed down to my office demanding that I change the figures on my recent sanitary report in which I indicated a shortage of *camotes* that were supplied to the working party. I refused, but Horani decided to pull a fast one and ordered Haase to change the amount. When I heard what that damn Jap quartermaster was trying to get away with, I ordered Haase to cross out my signature at the bottom of the report. That was the last thing

Horani wanted me to do. He started to throw a tantrum and demanded that I feed the working party with the *camotes* from our garden instead of using the regular Japanese food allotment. This would take care of the deficiency on my report but would also have the effect of cutting our food allowance. I steadfastly refused to budge an inch as Horani continued to stomp and bluster around the office.

Finally when he saw his threats and table pounding were all in vain, Horani issued us a thousand pounds of *camotes*. It was exactly the same figure I showed as deficient. To add insult to injury, I still refused to change my report.

Later in the day, I heard that Horani really got his ass in a sling when Nogi read the document. He was chewed out good. The bastard deserved it.

July 12, 1944

We are out of firewood. The men are using tree limbs, old doors, anything that isn't nailed down. However, the general condition of the camp is good despite overcrowding.

Over 400 human derelicts from Pasay and Las Pinas arrived on open trucks through a cold and miserable rain. They are an ugly mob of disorganized, degenerated, misdirected robots—reflex animals mostly. The frantic desperate survival urge is uppermost in their minds. They are predatory creatures, taking advantage of any situation to defy the bounds and limitations of normal society. Still others are indifferent to life, destiny, suffering, or anything else.

I admitted 21 of the group to the hospital immediately and scrounged up blankets for them. The senior officer among these men is an Army Warrant by the name of Kipps. I gave him the job as leader of this motley crew. The guy took immediate charge. He was forced to knock a few boys on their ass, but by nightfall he had the group under control. That was no small job either. In fact, I'm rather proud of him—a regular "Daniel in the lion's den."

July 13, 1944

I held a conference with Nogi and Kubota at the front office early this morning. I explained to them that this latest draft from Pasay and Las Pinas were a mess. All of the men are sick with beriberi, pellagra, pneumonia, amebic dysentery—you name it.

I told Nogi that we were aware of the arrival of a sick draft, but this was ridiculous. There is no way we can accommodate over 400 more patients. Nogi became very nervous and upset. He immediately hustled down to the hospital and quickly reviewed the mass of men who had been dumped upon us.

After the inspection, Nogi threw up his hands in disgust. He grabbed his hat and sword and beat a quick path up to headquarters. Meanwhile, Kubota authorized me to keep admitting the sick. But where to put them. We jammed the aisles, doubling up everywhere. We now have 1,400 patients crammed into the few available wards. Even as I write, five more truckloads of a hundred men each have just arrived. Our galley is already overtaxed, but we will find a way to feed everybody.

July 15, 1944

This morning Wade and I stopped in at the front office. "Captain Bly" was seated at a desk reading a Japanese newspaper. Nogi arrived moments later with a disturbed look on his face. He didn't even notice us, but proceeded to give Agowa a chewing out for reading on duty. The war situation can't be too bad for our side if the Japs aren't allowed to read their own newspapers.

Nogi and I went over the Pasay draft list and picked out 156 men to go to Cabanatuan, sick or not. He also formed another Japan draft. By the time Nogi was finished, over 800 men were scheduled for transfer.

All the Aircraft Bureau working party was also added to the Japan draft, with the exception of the officers. Haase was put on the list too. I didn't like that decision because it means that we will lose our only Japanese speaking American.

July 16, 1944

Trucks were pulling into camp all through the night bringing more prisoners for transfer to Japan. The drafts are leaving here as fast as the Japanese can put them together.

Whle we were at *bango* this morning, several explosions were heard in the port area and a large column of black smoke could be seen. I learned later that a Japanese ship was torpedoed in the harbor.

I talked with Kubota in an effort to keep Haase off the Japan draft, but no luck. They don't want him and his knowledge of Japanese around here anymore. Wade and I had Haase over to our quarters for coffee. I thanked him for a job well done. I also told him that I would write a letter in his behalf, stating that I consider him as a man of tremendous value during this period of captivity.

July 17, 1944

All the scheduled drafts left early this morning and the front office is closed until noon so that the Japs can get some rest. They worked most of the night. This respite will give me a chance to get the camp organized and back to our regular routine. I appointed Kentner as our medical representative in the front office.

A working party of 95 men were marched into camp from the port area this afternoon. Commander Harrison is in charge of the group. I believe that they will continue working in the harbor, but will be billeted in Bilibid.

Nogi didn't show up today so I asked Kubota if he had any information on Harrison's crew. Kubota said he didn't know anything about the group. He didn't even know they were in camp. Everything is so secret that the Japs don't even tell each other.

I had a talk with my "troops" before *bango* tonight. It was a little pep talk to the boys to pass along the praise we received from the Davao Army bunch. Their favorable comments on our discipline and courtesy is a great tribute to the Navy. My men upheld the best traditions of the Service and the Corps. We were certainly judged by our "severest critics."

July 21, 1944

Neither Harrison nor I have heard anything yet as to the future of his dock working party. They are an excellent organized group and I have been busy trying to find beds for them.

A serious sewage problem developed today. We can't get the lines unblocked due to the continuous rains. Garbage also gathers a week at a time without being collected. The Japs claim they have no fuel for their trucks.

The Warrant Officers are quarreling again. Crews is taking the brunt of the attack because he's a hundred percent behind my policies. That's more than I can say about the rest of that gang. I had to call Schweizer and a couple of the others on the carpet. I let them know "whereon they trod" and what to expect when the axe falls. It looks like the "deep-six" for a few of them.

July 26, 1944

Late yesterday, Chaplain Brewster arrived from Cabanatuan to take over Wilcox's duties. Brewster seems like a good man and will be a welcome addition to this place.

We still have all our patients crowded into the few remaining buildings left to us for hospital space. The Japs are holding one building for a Japan draft and the working parties take up three other wards. It's common practice for the Japanese to dump patients on the deck and take the beds for arriving soldiers.

Headquarters now wants proper identification for each prisoner. Kubota says that when we were first captured, the Japanese didn't know what to do with us or how to treat captives, but now, etc. That's just an old Oriental way of saying that when they captured the Americans they never thought about facing retribution. The handwriting is on the wall now and most of the Japs are worried—they should be.

July 30, 1944

Chaplain Brewster gave his first sermon today [Sunday]. There was a big turnout to hear him. I feel very much encouraged in having Brewster with us. He has restored my faith in men of the cloth. I was flattered to hear him quote my words to the effect that rank has its privileges insofar as rank assumes its obligations. I think Brewster is going to fit in very well with my policy of one for all and all for one.

This afternoon eight British sailors were admitted to the hospital. They were taken off a prison ship bound for Japan from Singapore. The ship had been en route for 40 days and has spent the last 16 days anchored in Manila Bay. The men are in rotten shape—everyone of them. They had been working on railroad construction in Siam and Indochina. There are still 750 of their shipmates aboard the vessel. No telling when that ship will try and run the American submarine blockade to reach Japan. There is reason to believe that three of our Japan drafts are also still at anchor in the port area. Japanese destroyers have been seen returning to port with survivors of sunken ships.

I had quite a long discussion with the Britishers about the battle for Singapore. They said it wasn't much of a fight. The English had very few regular army soldiers there. Most of the defending force was composed of militia. They put up a good showing, but it was no use. The Japanese Navy was in their own backyard and there was nobody to stop them.

The British sailors also told me that 26,000 men died of cholera building the railroads—English, Americans, and Dutch. There were also about 80 survivors of the *Houston* with them in Indochina.

From the stories these sailors related, I was impressed with the decisive part our Asiatic Fleet played in breaking up a Japanese convoy bound for Australia. They did not go down in vain.

August 2, 1944

It looks as if the Japanese are taking a possible American bombing of Manila seriously. They are painting red crosses on the roofs of all the buildings. Headquarters passed the word today that we must save all charcoal to be used as filters in case the Yanks bomb the waterworks. Momota sent an order down to the hospital for us to "dig a well." Holy crap! With what? The ignorance and childlike naiveté with which these morons speak and direct. They become more unbelievable every day. I don't know how they will handle losing this war. Maybe commit national *hari-kari*.

August 5, 1944

Another draft of 600 men left early this morning for Japan. Our census is now down to 769 but more men are due to arrive. No rest for the wicked.

Over 20,000 letters for prisoners arrived today. Sorting them out is an impossible task. Most of the men are either dead or on their way to Japan.

The Japs are searching Filipinos in the streets for concealed weapons. It's "nervous time" in Manila. The food situation has collapsed. I have lost four more pounds and am weak and on the sickly side. However, I still manage to keep up my appearance and carry on.

A few parcel post packages arrived for deceased prisoners. In view of the fact that the British fellows have nothing of this kind, I gave the packages to them to divide.

August 12, 1944

I made my weekly inspection this morning. The place wasn't as ship-shape as it has been. Long rains, overcrowding, and continuous Japan drafts moving in and out have all tended to disrupt our routine. However, we must now bear down harder and get this place back in shape.

September 17, 1944

Writing paper and my eyes are both about gone. Latest reliable reports indicate that 18 Japanese ships have been sunk recently trying to leave Manila Bay. God, I hope none of our boys were on them.

A typhoon has been raging here for five days. We are all cold, wet, and hungry. The store is useless—nothing to sell. A 2,000 man draft from Cabanatuan is due to arrive anytime this afternoon—destination Japan.

Commander Hayes's diary ends with this last entry. However, his odyssey was far from over. The final test of courage and perseverance was yet to come.

IV.

Aboard the Hell Ship
December 13, 1944 to Early 1945

During the latter part of September 1944, American bombers began daily attacks on the city of Manila and its port area. Prisoner drafts to Japan via Bilibid continued at a breakneck pace. The Japanese were in dire need of manpower to work their mines and factories. An order was issued from Tokyo to transport all able-bodied prisoners of war in the Philippines to Japan for use as slave labor. The Japanese criteria for able-bodied was simply, "Can he walk?"

Transfer of the prisoners had to be accomplished at the earliest possible moment. General MacArthur's Army was already advancing on Manila.

On November 28, 1944, American air attacks ceased and this respite gave the Japanese a chance to sneak a few ships into Manila Bay.

Early on the morning of December 13, 1944, a group of approximately 1,619 prisoners, including thirty-seven British, were marched out of Bilibid and formed in a continuous line around the prison walls. The Japanese officer in charge of this Japan draft was Lt. Junsaburo Toshino. His interpreter was the hunchback dwarf Shusuke Wada. Both Toshino and Wada had amassed a gruesome record at Davao and their reputation was well known at Bilibid.

The Japanese guards were mostly Formosan and were under the command of Kazutane Aihara. Aihara had been stationed at Cabanatuan and received the nickname of "Air Raid" because of his practice of sneaking up behind prisoners and beating them unmercifully with a bamboo staff.

Included in the Japan draft was Commander Hayes and 225 men of his Bilibid hospital unit. As the pitiful procession wound its way through the bombed-out streets of Manila, thousands of Filipinos lined the way. Most of the local people were silent or crying. There was an occasional flash of the "V for Victory" sign. Any stragglers in the slow-moving column were beaten with rifle butts by the cruel guards. Sympathetic civilians who ventured too close to the prisoners were beaten back by the overzealous captors.

When the ragged half-naked column reached the waterfront, the prisoners could see the devastation that the American planes had inflicted on the port area. The shimmering surface of Manila Bay was broken by the masts of over sixty sunken Japanese ships. The captives were marched to pier seven, Manila's famous "Million Dollar" pier, now only a mass of unrecognizable rubble. On one side of the burned out structure stood the fire-gutted hulks of two cargo ships. On the other side was an untouched Japanese passenger-cargo vessel. Milling about the pier were 2,000 women and children preparing to return to Japan aboard the *Oryoku Maru.*

The vessel carried no markings of any sort, but was armed with numerous antiaircraft guns. The Japanese civilians were loaded into living quarters on the ship's superstructure and the prisoners were lined up preparatory to boarding the vessel.

General Koa and Doctor Nogi were on hand at the pier to wish the captives a safe journey. In spite of numerous misunderstandings, Hayes and Nogi had a mutual respect for one another. Both were victims of circumstances beyond their control. Both were prisoners of different ideologies, but both men served their country to the best of their ability. They clasped hands in a final gesture of appreciation.

Early that afternoon, the prisoners were divided into three groups and marched aboard the *Oryoku Maru.* Commander Warner Portz was placed in charge of the first group of 850 men. The prisoners were pushed, shoved, and jammed into the aft cargo space (hold #5). The guards met the men with bamboo sticks and brooms as they descended the ladder and forced the first few hundred back against the ship's bulkhead. By the time Commander Portz's men had been packed into the hold, there was neither room to stand nor sit comfortably. The opening for light and air was the eight-by-ten hatch.

The second group of over 500 men was under the command of Lieutenant Colonel Curtis Beecher of the Fourth Marine Regiment. His men were forcibly pushed down into the forward cargo compartment (hold #1). This space was only 60 by 100 feet and the Japanese had installed a horizontal platform about four feet from the floor in order to double the space in the hold. The platform was nine feet deep and the prisoners were forced to sit four men to a row, each man's back against his neighbor's knees. The men in the center had no choice but to stand, packed like sardines against each other. They were then ordered to "sit down."

Commander Hayes and his medical crew, along with the chaplains, were shoved down the hold amidships (hold #2). Grain was stored on three sides of the compartment. This cargo space had been used to transport horses to Manila and it contained an air conditioner for the comfort of the animals. Toshino refused to turn on the cooling unit for the prisoners.

Hayes and his group were also cramped for space and a "watch" routine of four hours standing and four hours sitting was placed in effect.

The heat in the holds below deck was overpowering and bulkheads on all sides cut off any air circulation. Wooden platforms had been built over the hatch openings, allowing very little light or air to enter the cargo spaces. Japanese guards, peering down into the dark pits, were able to see the masses of human bodies staring upwards with bulging eyes, their shallow chests heaving for air. Commander Frank Bridget tried to convince the half-crazed men to take off their shirts and fan the stale atmosphere.

About five o'clock in the afternoon, the *Oryoku Maru* hoisted anchor and joined a convoy of four other Japanese merchant ships. All were unmarked and of the same type and tonnage as the prison vessel. They were escorted by a cruiser and several destroyers. The convoy was blacked out as it slipped out of Manila Bay and hugged the coast of Luzon.

The suffocating prisoners shouted for more air and water but the ruckus only angered Wada. He threatened to close the hatches completely. However, the clamor of the men only became louder and more insistent. Wada finally slammed the hatch cover shut over hold #5.

Shortly before dark, the guards lowered a few wooden buckets of rice and seaweed into the dark holds. The men who had mess kits scooped up the food while others grabbed blindly with their hands, taking whatever they were able to carry. One canteen of water for about every forty-five men was distributed. Each man received three teaspoonsful.

Along with the food containers, the Japs sent slop buckets (*benjos*) down at the same time and both pails circulated together in the darkness. The men were unable to tell which bucket was being passed to them—food or excrement. Certain prisoners would whisper to a neighbor that one bucket was another, and considered the joke hilarious if a hand was dipped into the toilet bucket, or the food bucket was used as a toilet.

Within the dark spaces, the prisoners soon lost all sense of time and direction. Insane screams, from men already cracking under the strain, terrorized the ones who had any sanity left.

Wada was continually upset by the disturbance and advised the prisoners that he would batten down all the hatches if the racket persisted. Wada complained that the uproar was disturbing the women and children above decks, and if the commotion did not stop, he would instruct the guards to fire into the holds.

An unearthly quiet, born of exhaustion and death, settled over the cargo spaces. The floors were covered with excrement and urine. The prisoners stripped their bodies of clothing so that their pores would be able to breathe.

In hold #5, the scramble for food and air created numerous personal feuds and hatreds. Occasionally a man would awake out of his mind and begin yelling at his tormentors. A prisoner later said: "The others, afraid the hatch would be closed, shouted, 'Knife him! Knife the son of a bitch!' Someone screamed, 'Denny, you get him!' There was a scuffle, and then a sharp cry in the dark. Somebody else yelled, 'Get Denny! He did it! Get him! There was another struggle, and then a tension-filled silence. Men who owned jackknives unclasped the large blade and prepared to defend themselves if attacked."

All through the terrible night the men in hold #5 fought, clawed, and tore at each other for a breath of air. Madness, induced by the lack of oxygen, caused many men to pair off and attack their comrades in the dark. They slashed the wrists of the weak and drank the blood. Others urinated into their own canteens and drank the fluid.

A haunting fear began to grip the deranged masses below decks. Several of the prisoners heard (or imagined they heard) people plotting against them. Chief Pharmacist's Mate, Dudley Hensen, stumbled through the dark steaming aisles to a group of officers. He pleaded with them that the men in his bay were intending to kill him. He was told that it was nonsense and to return to his place. The next morning they found Hensen, his belly slit open.

Another prisoner awoke to find five men in a circle around him. They sat naked and doubled up, as if in prayer, but they were stone cold, and dead.

The first light of day revealed the horror of the night. Fifty men had died, and their bodies had been stacked like wood against the bulkheads. Most of the victims were those who were farthest from the source of air.

A surviving officer recalled the night of death: "Once you passed out, you were gone; but only those nearby could tell if you were dead. The temperature must have been at least 130 degrees, and it took a long time for a body to grow cold. One man, who had gone mad, pestered me by pressing his mess kit against my chest. He kept repeating, 'Have some of this chow, it's good.' I smelled the stuff, but it wasn't rice. 'All right,' he said, 'If you don't want it, I'm going to eat it.' A short time later, I heard him eating as he sat beside me. Another person, who talked perfectly normal, continually ran his hands up and down my arms, as if trying to make sure that we were both alive."

It was not long before the Japanese refused to allow the *benjos* to be handed up the ladder for emptying. Overfull as they were, the buckets still circulated.

Occasionally a prisoner would call out: "For God's sake, take this thing! I can't hold it and have no place to set it down!" He would be ignored. Nobody was willing to give up space in order to take the *benjo*. If angry or irrational, the tormented man would simply overturn the bucket on his neighbors.

In hold #2, amidships, Commander Hayes managed to maintain discipline. He also kept one bucket each time the Japanese sent down food. In this way, the men soon accumulated enough *benjos* for their own toilet facilities. In the other cargo spaces the prisoners were using mess kits and hats for latrines.

Below decks the search for water became a mind-boggling obsession. Moisture from their lungs had collected on the bulkheads, and the men lapped like dogs at the beads of water. Their fingers were thin and wrinkled, as though they had been soaking for a long time in water. The prisoners were in the first stages of dehydration.

The morning of December 14 dawned hot and muggy. The Japanese barely had time to dispose of the dead and send a breakfast of rice into hold #2, when American planes appeared overhead.

Commander Bridget climbed the ladder in hold #5 and pushed a few hatch planks aside. He began to give the men a play-by-play report of the screaming aircraft as they dove down toward the convoy. The prisoners stirred apprehensively, knowing that a successful attack might be their death knell. The entire ship vibrated as each bomb straddled the vessel. After their bombing runs, the planes made wide circles and returned, strafing the ship from one end to the other. In hold #2, ricocheting bullets splattered into the doctors and corpsmen.

The strafing planes wreaked havoc with the Japanese gun crews. As soon as one crew was killed, another took its place, then another, and another. The blood of hundreds of Japanese civilians poured across the decks, and the screams of the wounded ripped the air like witnesses to Armageddon.

When the air attacks ceased, the shock of death settled over the ship. Hayes and his medical personnel were ordered topside to care for the Japanese wounded, but when he asked for permission to treat the wounded Americans, the request was denied. Wada said he would do nothing for the prisoners, and then ordered the medics severely beaten because "Americans were sinking Japanese ships."

Even though the planes brought terror to the captives, they also brought light and air. Many hatch and deck planks were broken, and the sudden rush of fresh air did wonders to improve the morale of the prisoners.

While Commander Hayes and his men were topside, they noticed a large transport burning in the distance, but the other ships in the convoy had vanished.

The bombings had shattered the *Oryoku Maru*'s steering gear, and the vessel's captain, Shin Kajiyama, attempted to head back to Subic Bay. Among the Japanese civilians there was terror and confusion. The decks were covered with dead and wounded. Blood continually seeped down through the broken deck planks and dripped on the naked prisoners, giving the men a spotted appearance.

Later that afternoon, as the prison ship edged close to shore, Captain Kajiyama announced that he intended to disembark the passengers. Wada notified the prisoners that they would be evacuated as soon as guards could be arranged to control the men and keep them from escaping.

During the evening, the *Oryoku Maru* ran aground 300 yards off-shore from the Olongapo Naval Station, and shortly before midnight the civilians left the stricken ship.

The prisoners with any sanity left were fearful that the irrational men might rush the ladder and try to escape. Navy Lieutenant James O'Rouke tried to make a dash for freedom, but Boatswain's Mate Jesse Lee pulled him down before the guards fired their weapons.

Commander Bridget tried to maintain order. "For God's sake, men, don't leave your place. Every move you make generates heat. Keep fanning the air. There are people in the back who are going to die unless you sit still and keep fanning."

After all the passengers had been removed, Wada informed the prisoners that they would be allowed to swim for shore at sunrise. The men were told that they could wear shirts and pants, but no shoes; barefoot captives could not get very far if they tried to escape.

The hatch cover of hold #5 was opened and dead bodies were hauled topside by the dozens. The living shouted for water but their cries fell on deaf ears. A few deranged men managed to elude the grasp of their fellow prisoners and dashed for the ladder. The guards met them with rifle fire.

When morning finally arrived, the *Oryoku Maru* was dead in the water off Olongapo Point. Boatswain's Mate Clarence Taylor pleaded with Wada that there were twenty-five men in his hold that were either badly wounded or unable to swim. Wada consulted with Toshino and returned to announce that a boat would be ready for the men. Pharmacist Emmet Hogan designated the patients and attending medical personnel. A lifeboat was soon lowered, but only six prisoners and eight Japanese guards were allowed to enter the craft.

As Hogan was about to return to his hold, several American planes flew over the ship. Toshino frantically signaled Taylor's boat to shove off. Hogan scrambled for cover in a passageway on the main deck. On all sides he noticed the mangled bodies of hundreds of Japanese.

One of the planes raced for the lifeboat and opened fire. Taylor recalled: "Six of the eight guards were killed. As I sat in the stern, the Jap on my right was hit in the face, and his whole head simply disintegrated. The Jap on my left was struck in the chest and died instantly. Someday I'm going to find that pilot and tell him that he did the fanciest trick shooting since 'Wild Bill' Hickok."

Only the guards on the strafed boat were supplied with life jackets. The prisoners stripped the jackets from the dead, put them on the nonswimmers, and headed for shore. Taylor, floating on his back, watched the planes dive on the ill-fated prison ship.

A bomb exploded on the stern of the *Oryoku Maru*, raining shrapnel into hold #5. A steel girder supporting the hatch collapsed into the cargo space, killing many men. Coal dust in the compartment suddenly ignited, and there was a mad dash for the ladder. One of the guards fired into the hold. Captain Ted Parker fell backward, shot through the head.

Lieutenant Russell Hutchinson stated: "Everywhere around us were dead bodies, with blackened faces and purple lips. I soon noticed that the guards had disappeared, so we grabbed the shaky ladder and climbed topside through the smoke. We scooped up sugar from some broken baggage and ate what we could before jumping over the side."

The prisoners in the other cargo spaces remained below for several minutes before realizing that they were no longer being guarded. The men cautiously climbed to the main deck. Most of them stripped down to their underwear and dived into the water.

The nonswimmers threw overboard anything that would float, while others searched the passenger cabins for life jackets. All they found were the bloodied bodies of dead Japanese. Several men, taking advantage of the chaotic confusion above decks, fought their way through the smoke and flames to the ship's storeroom. They looted American Red Cross food and cigarettes in the officers' pantry. Toshino discovered William Brewster in one of the supply rooms and shot him dead.

Many of the prisoners climbed out of the holds and wandered about the decks dazed. Japanese guards ordered them to abandon ship, but some were too confused to understand. They were shot as they staggered around like zombies.

Pharmacist's Mate Eugene Rogers jumped into the sea and dived deep to avoid the strafing aircraft. It was not until he reached shore that he remembered he had failed his swimming test in boot camp.

One lifeboat was lowered. It contained Toshino in full dress uniform and Wada. Captain Kajiyama remained on the bridge of his ship and in faltering English warned the prisoners to leave quickly.

By noon, most of the captives had left the burning vessel. The passengers had taken all the life preservers, leaving hundreds of men floundering in the water, grasping anything that would float. American planes continued strafing the *Oryoku Maru,* but their pilots soon noticed the number of white bodies in the water and waved in recognition.

One swimmer yelled to a prisoner still aboard, "Hey, throw us down some shoes!" He was tossed four pair which he tied around his neck, and headed for the beach.

The shoreline was not a beach at all, but only ankle-deep water below an eight-foot seawall. As the first exhausted prisoners stumbled ashore and stretched out on the seawall, they were met with machine gun fire. The men were stunned, but then realized that the Japanese wanted them back in the ocean until all the swimmers had reached the beach.

For more than two hours the men huddled at the base of the wall. Commander Hayes organized a first aid station and the wounded men were treated with whatever supplies were available.

Only a few guards had lived through the air attacks. A detachment of Japanese Marines soon arrived and Toshino motioned for the prisoners to crawl up the wall. Over 250 Americans had died on the *Oryoku Maru* and the remaining captives were marched to the north gate of the Olongapo Naval Station. The path was over sharp coral rock, and the bare feet of the men were cut and bleeding. If a prisoner even looked as if he was about to stop, the nearest Japanese would club him with a rifle or bamboo pole.

The line of march ended at a tennis court, about 500 yards back of the seawall. The court was a single concrete slab with a ten-foot-wide strip of sod extending along each side, enclosed by a chicken wire fence about twelve feet high. There was a gate at one corner and a single hydrant of trickling water along one side of the fence. A referee's stand stood inside the compound. It was about ten feet high with a small platform on top.

As the prisoners filed into the tennis court, they were divided into rows of fifty-two men each. Individual groups were forced to occupy a space four feet wide by fifty feet in length. There was no room to lie down and the men were compelled to sit, with knees drawn up, and fit themselves between each others' legs.

The weary men had no sooner settled down than three American planes flew over the court. One of the aircraft silenced an antiaircraft battery beyond the compound and another dropped a bomb on the *Oryoku Maru*. The ship began to burn fiercely and sank two hours later.

The referee's platform was moved to the center of the court, where it became a lookout and command post. The Japanese appointed Colonel Beecher and Major Ridgely in charge. They sat aloft on the platform and tried to establish quiet and order among the prisoners.

Commander Hayes established a hospital along a fifteen-foot-wide strip of the court, beyond one of the base lines. The sick bay consisted of sheets and a couple of raincoats that were stretched between the fence at one end and bamboo poles at the other. Hayes, along with Clyde Welsh, Art Barrett, and Army Colonel Jack Schwartz, worked valiantly to care for the sick and wounded.

The Japanese refused to furnish medical supplies and, because of the hot concrete deck, many men soon became victims of sunstroke. At night the temperature dropped rapidly, and the prisoners huddled together for warmth. Only the guards had blankets and warm clothing.

No food was issued the first day, even though the nearby Japanese Marine barracks had sacks of rice and vegetables stacked alongside the buildings. The starving prisoners were informed that the food belonged to the Japanese who were occupying the naval station. The only men who had anything to eat at all were those who had raided the *Oryoku Maru* before they left and brought food to shore with them.

Tall cassava plants grew on three sides of the court and provided shade for the guards. The Japanese, on the west side of the compound, soon discovered that they were able to acquire an American wristwatch in exchange for a dozen edible cassava roots and a leather wallet could be received for six roots. Prisoners sitting in the center of the enclosure, or on the far side, took their chances on passing trading items across the court. They had no choice but to accept whatever amount of cassava roots finally reached them, after being passed through many hungry hands.

The water problem was acute, even though the faucet alongside the fence kept running day and night. The rows of men rotated at the hydrant, but the stream was so slow that a man could consider himself lucky if he was able to have a drink every eighteen hours.

On the second day at the tennis court, the Japanese served the prisoners their first meal: two tablespoons of raw rice. The same portion was allocated each day, even though cooking facilities were within sight of the men.

Colonel Beecher requested larger food rations, but he was informed by Wada that this was impossible. Now that the men were on shore, they came under the jurisdiction of the Japanese Army. While they were aboard ship, the Japanese Navy was in charge. Regulations prohibited this form of cooperation between the services.

After three torturous days under the broiling sun, the Japanese permitted twenty-four of the sickest prisoners to be moved to a shady area outside the compound. The men were brought inside the enclosure at night.

Commander Hayes and his medical unit worked around the clock and miracles of surgery were performed with nothing more than knives and razor blades. Marine Corporal Carl Logan had a gangrenous arm that had swollen to an astonishing size. Colonel Schwartz amputated the arm with a sterilized razor blade, and without the benefit of anaesthesia. Roland Stickney and Charles Towne held Logan down during the operation.

[There has been much controversy regarding the correct name of this Marine. Most reports say that the man whose arm was amputated was Corporal Eugene Specht. However, Fourth Marine Regiment records indicate that Specht was killed on December 15. Commander

Arthur Beale reported that he had visited Logan and talked with him a few hours before Logan's arm was amputated.]

The prisoners on the tennis court were allowed to build a small straddle trench latrine directly opposite the gate, but they were required to obtain permission in order to use the facility. However, most of the men had diarrhea and the half hour wait to receive permission was of little use. Many of the men used an area inside the court near the gate. They tried to keep the place clean, but it still remained a mess.

Beecher and Ridgely spent most of their time on the referee's platform. Every morning a roll call was made and a burial party was formed for those who had died during the night. The dead were stripped of their clothing and hauled outside the gate. They were buried in an improvised cemetery down by the seawall.

American aircraft appeared daily over the tennis court, at times flying as low as 500 feet while blasting enemy gun emplacements. The prisoners were often sprayed by empty fifty-caliber cartridge cases as skimming planes made low-level strafing runs on nearby targets. The pilots signaled their recognition to the mass of men packed in the tiny space below them. The prisoners were given new hope, even if it was to be only temporary.

During the fifth day on the broiling concrete, a supply of cast-off clothing from Bilibid was delivered to the compound. Every man was outfitted with at least one item—trousers, shirt, or a hat.

The next morning, December 20, 1944, nineteen trucks rambled up to the tennis court. Half the prisoners were crammed into the lorries and driven sixty miles to the provincial jail at San Fernando, Pampanga. The following day the trucks returned for the rest of the men. They were also transported to San Fernando, but were unloaded at the local movie house.

The prison yard at the city jail was a fenced-in area, about sixty by eighty feet. A lemon tree was growing in the center of the courtyard. Within five minutes the prisoners had devoured all the lemons and most of the leaves. The jail contained two small cell blocks, and the sickest men were moved inside. The others rested on the hard ground. The site was as hot as the tennis court but water was available from broken indoor toilet pipes.

The old movie house had long since been converted to other uses and all the seats had been removed. A single water faucet was discovered in the lavatory and over 500 men lined up for a drink of the brackish fluid. Many fell asleep before their turn at the faucet came around.

The following day the men in the theater were permitted to dig a ditch latrine, but were lucky if they were able to use it once a day. There was barely room to lie down inside the musty old building, and the air was polluted with the odor of sickness and death. Corporal Logan had died during the night.

At San Fernando, the prisoners were fed their first hot food since leaving Bilibid: a meal of rice, served on two large sections of corrugated roofing.

For the next few days the city was a beehive of military activity. Japanese troops were constantly moving south to meet MacArthur's advancing army, and American planes continually bombed the town and surrounding areas.

On the afternoon of December 23, Wada informed the prisoner group commanders that he wanted fifteen of the sickest men selected for return to Manila. Among those chosen were Lieutenant Dwight Edison, Lieutenant John Elliot, Lieutenant Colonel Ulysses Peoples, Jr., Lieutenant Colonel Samuel Freeney, Second Lieutenant Herman Sherman, and Major Wendell Swanson.

At about seven o'clock, a truck arrived and the suffering men were placed inside. Pharmacist's Mate Deenah McCurry was sneaked aboard the vehicle, in hopes he would eventually reach Bilibid and relate the fate of the prisoners.

Instead of proceeding to Manila, however, the truck stopped at a small cemetery on the outskirts of San Fernando, where a group of soldiers had dug a grave about fifteen feet square. The prisoners were forced to kneel at the foot of the hole while their captors took turns bayoneting and beheading them—one at a time.

Besides Toshino and Wada, the Japanese guards who participated in the execution included Kazutane Aihara, Suketoshi Tanoe, Jiro Ueda, Sho Hattori, and Risaku Kobayashi.

About three o'clock in the morning of December 24, the prisoners at the jail and movie house were roused from their quarters, served a meal of cooked rice, and then marched to a bomb-wrecked train station. On the siding sat a battered locomotive and a line of boxcars. It was a narrow-gauge railroad and each car was only six feet wide and twenty-six feet long. The first few boxcars were loaded with ammunition, and the next seven were designated as prisoner cars.

The captives were pushed aboard the train and packed one hundred men to a car. The wounded, wearing bandages, were ordered to sit on the roofs. Wada instructed the men to wave their bandages at any attacking planes. By using this ploy he reasoned that the ammunition train would not be bombed or strafed.

Three Japanese were stationed in the doorway of each car and two more on the roof. The foul air inside was stifling. The only ventilation was virtually cut off by the guards blocking the open side doors. If a prisoner collapsed unconscious, he was passed from hand to hand toward the entrance, in hopes he would revive.

The line of boxcars headed north, away from the liberating armies. That evening the train stopped at Tarlac, in order for the Japanese to eat supper. No food or water was offered to the prisoners.

The wounded, sitting on top of the boxcars, shivered with cold and begged to be brought down as night approached. A few of the guards did permit an exchange of prisoners between the men on the roof and those inside the cars.

About three o'clock in the morning, Christmas Day, the train arrived at the town of San Fernando del Union on the Lingayen Gulf. The prisoners were unloaded and marched to a small one-story elementary school building. The sick and wounded were moved inside the structure, while the other men collapsed from exhaustion on the schoolhouse grounds.

During the afternoon, the prisoners were served Christmas dinner: a half cup of rice and one cup of water for every two persons.

A hibiscus hedge had been planted around the school building, and in no time at all the hungry men discovered that the pretty red blossoms were good to eat. Even the green leaves were devoured. Other prisoners stumbled across several banana stalks on the ground. They had been cut more than a month before, but were greedily gobbled down, even though the taste was horrible.

Commander Hayes held sick call for the weary men, but with only meager medical supplies available there was little his men could do to alleviate the enormous suffering.

Early in the evening, the captives were rousted from their rest by the guards and ordered to move out. For almost an hour, the straggling column was marched over a paved road in a westerly direction. The beleaguered group was then turned northward over a coral shell path. The roadway was soon red with the blood of many shredded feet. If a prisoner stopped for a moment, he was struck with a rifle butt across the kidneys.

A sudden air raid alert halted the column and the men dropped to the ground, nursing their swollen, lacerated feet. The captives had hoped that they might be headed for a prison camp on Luzon, but no such luck. As the prisoners surveyed their surroundings, it was evident that they were in a port area. Japanese soldiers were rushing madly about, unloading ammunition and supplies from ships in the nearby bay.

When the alert was over, the men were marched to a narrow strip of beach jutting into the water. The ankle-deep sand was to be their bed for the night. The sharp sea air was bitter cold, and the wind felt as though it was slicing clear through the half-naked prisoners. Some of the men dug foxholes and covered themselves with a blanket of wet clammy sand. As the men clawed into the sand for protection, they discovered that they were resting on hundreds of drums of high-test gasoline buried beneath them.

About seven o'clock that evening, a truck drove up to the beach with a supply of rice balls, barely enough to feed half the men. The rice was not rationed, and only the prisoners with enough strength to fight their way to the truck managed to grab whatever they could hold in their hands. Some men had two rice balls, others had none at all.

The next morning the rising sun turned the cold sand to a pit of fire. There was not a drop of shade anywhere. The men broiled like lobsters in a cast iron kettle. Their wretched bodies were so dehydrated that they did not even perspire. The cries of the heat-crazed men sounded anything but human. Several of the prisoners became mentally unbalanced and had to be forcibly restrained.

Late in the afternoon, the Japanese permitted the prisoners to bathe themselves for a brief period of five minutes in the cooling waters of the bay. A few of the men were so dehydrated that they drank the salt walter without any thought of the consequences.

It was not until men began dropping from sunstroke that Wada allowed a guard to accompany two prisoners to a nearby sump and dip out a bucket of stagnant water. He was finally persuaded to increase the supply but still only allocated one bucket of water for every hundred men—three teaspoonsful for each prisoner.

All through the day and night of December 26, the men sat on the sandy beach and watched enemy reinforcements and supplies being ferried ashore.

Early in the morning of December 27, the prisoners were marched to a pier and forced to jump from the wharf into two landing barges about twenty feet below. If a man hesitated, a guard would push him off the pier. Several prisoners broke their legs when they hit the deck. One man missed the craft completely and struck his head on the side of the barge. When he was dragged aboard, he was dead.

Both landing craft headed out into the bay toward a 10,000 ton cargo vessel—the *Enoura Maru*. Several hundred sick and wounded Japanese soldiers had climbed aboard the ship shortly before the prisoner barges came alongside. The Japanese officer in charge of the loading procedure impatiently ordered the prisoners to hurry and board quickly. Many of the Americans were so weak that they had to be helped up the gangplank. The Japanese officer soon became exasperated and ordered the second barge, with 236 prisoners still aboard, to move to another ship in the bay. The vessel was the 12,000 ton *Brazil Maru*.

As soon as both ships were loaded they hoisted anchor and proceeded in convoy with four other vessels. They were escorted by destroyers and steamed north along the Luzon coast.

A small trickle of greasy water dripped from the deck winches of the *Brazil Maru*. A few of the prisoners lapped at the fluid, but they were spotted by the guards and savagely beaten across the arms and backs with rifle butts.

The last cargo carried by the *Enoura Maru* had been horses. The Japanese forced the prisoners to climb down into the hold amidships and make the space habitable for humans. No brooms or shovels were furnished and the men were compelled to scoop up the manure with their bare hands. The "stables" were filthy, but at least there was room to lie down—even if it was on a bed of horse manure.

Buckets of rice were lowered into the hold, but the guards insisted that the buckets be emptied immediately. The frustrated and hungry men dumped the rice on straw mats and on the dirty floor. They ate from their hats, from their shirts, and from their hands. The horse flies were vicious, biting the men and swarming all over the rice.

The convoy was soon attacked by an American submarine. Two torpedoes were fired but both passed ahead of the *Brazil Maru* and exploded on the beach.

Aboard the *Enoura Maru*, a man died almost every hour from dehydration, diarrhea, or untended wounds. The bodies were wrapped in straw and hauled topside by the Japanese. However, as the number of bodies multiplied, the captors decreed that the corpses could not be lifted from the hold immediately. The dead had to be laid on the floor where they could be seen from above by Toshino or Wada. After eight bodies accumulated, Wada would give permission for the dead to be hoisted topside.

Conditions were as bad aboard the *Brazil Maru*. Occasionally the guards amused themselves by tossing a cigarette into the cargo space and watching the prisoners scramble for the tobacco. The first food that the men received amounted to a teaspoon of rice per person; it was the leavings, scraped from the plates of the Japanese, after they finished their meal. The prisoners notified the Japanese commander that if they were not soon given food and water he would have a cargo of corpses. The reply was: "We don't care if you do starve! We hate you! Your submarines are sinking our ships!"

As the convoy rounded the southern coast of Formosa, American submarines closed in for the kill. Shipboard guns blasted throughout the night and the upturned faces of the prisoners were splattered with rust and iron scale. The men sat quietly, in terror, waiting any minute for the crash of a torpedo against the hull.

Miraculously, the two prison ships were the only survivors of the convoy that steamed into the harbor at Takao, Formosa on New Year's Eve.

On New Year's Day, 1945, the prisoners on the *Brazil Maru* were allotted four pieces of hard tack and one-fourth cup of water per man. The ship was carrying dozens of drums of drinking water on the forecastle, but no amount of begging could convince the Japanese to issue one single drop more to the thirsty captives.

While the *Enoura Maru* was anchored in Takao, Formosa, sacks of coarse brown sugar were loaded into the aft cargo space. They were separated from the prisoners by heavy cargo netting.

The temptation was too great for some of the men and they began to steal and eat the raw sugar. However, even a small amount caused severe diarrhea and sometimes death.

The Japanese soon became aware of the looting but, despite repeated warnings, the thefts continued. Each morning they found another sack missing, but not one guard could be found willing to spend a night in the hold to catch the thieves.

Finally, tired of the insubordination, Toshino and Wada appeared at the hatch opening and gazed angrily down into the dark space below. They demanded to know who had been stealing the sugar, and announced that unless the guilty culprits gave themselves up, there would be no more rice or water issued to the prisoners.

Colonel Beecher realized the seriousness of the situation and asked for two volunteers to take the blame. He promised that, if they survived the Japanese reprisals, he would do everything in his power to make sure that they would not go without food or water during the remainder of the trip to Japan.

Sergeant Arda M. Hanenkrat, of the Thirty-first Infantry, and Sergeant Edwin Trapp, of the British Army, volunteered to take the rap for their fellow prisoners.

The men in the hold held their breath as the two sergeants climbed up the ladder. Most of the captives expected that a volley of rifle fire would greet the men when they reached the main deck.

The Japanese proceeded to slap, kick, and bludgeon the volunteers for several hours, then shoved them back down the hold, more dead than alive.

The sick and wounded Japanese soldiers were transferred from the _Enoura Maru_ to hospitals in Takao. The British prisoners were also taken off the ship and sent to prison camps in Formosa.

On the morning of January 6, the Americans aboard the _Brazil Maru_ were transferred to the _Enoura Maru_. Some of the men attempted to carry straw mats with them for warmth, but these were taken away by the guards.

The cargo space on the _Enoura Maru_ was already packed with almost 1,000 men and there was virtually no room for 200 more. As the men from the _Brazil Maru_ descended the ladder to their new quarters in hell, no one moved to make room for them. Each man was forced to fight and worm his way into the hold.

Late in the afternoon, a small portion of rice and soup was served. The thin greasy fluid acted as a laxative on the men and they frantically pushed and shoved their way to the horse troughs.

The following morning, the Japanese opened the forward hold and moved 500 men, including Commander Hayes and most of his medical crew, into the compartment. More men were also moved into the aft cargo space.

The prisoners knew that Formosa was within range of American bombers operating from the China mainland, and their alarm increased when a Japanese destroyer tied up alongside.

Early on the morning of January 9, antiaircraft batteries were heard pounding away and moments later American planes screamed across the dock area, heading for the warship and the _Enoura Maru_. A bomb exploded against the side of the prison ship, ripping the partition between the amidships and forward cargo spaces. A second bomb blasted directly into the forward compartment and another brought the hatch planking crashing down into the aft hold, crushing bodies like eggshells.

Theodore Lewin picked himself up and peered through the dust and debris into the forward hold. "I could see bodies all scrambled up. Almost nobody was moving. In my compartment, the whole place was covered with corpses."

Lieutenant Robert Russell reported, "A Navy doctor, only a foot away from me, lost the right eye out of his head. The man on my left had the back of his head blown clean off."

Yellow fumes poured from the bilges of the *Enoura Maru*. The ship was carrying a cargo of ammonium picrate, and the chemical turned the hair of the prisoners an unearthly yellow color.

In the aft hold, forty men were killed instantly and about 200 were wounded. The forward compartment resembled a butcher shop. Approximately 250 prisoners were blasted to eternity and the wounded were tumbled together with the dead and dying. Nearly all the medical corpsmen and doctors, including Commander Hayes, were killed when the bomb exploded in the forward cargo space.

Despite the fact that the *Enoura Maru* was in a heavily populated harbor, with doctors and hospitals in the vicinity, the Japanese refused to give any aid to the wounded Americans. The few medical personnel still alive pleaded for medicine and bandages—but to no avail. The prisoners tore their own clothing in strips to be used as bandages for the wounded.

A section of the aft hold was set aside as a hospital space and the medics treated the wounded as best they could. The dead were stripped of their clothes and stacked like sacks of grain in the center of the hatch area. The doctors and corpsmen were also sick and wounded, yet they carried out their duties until they dropped from exhaustion—many dying in their sleep.

On January 11, two Japanese medical corpsmen climbed aboard the "death ship." They announced that they would be allowed to treat the men with minor injuries. They arrived with a few bandages and Mercurochrome, but only painted a couple of lacerations and then left the ship. One glance into the forward hold was enough for them. The sight of thousands of flies, contorted bodies, broken limbs, dried blood, and excreta was more than their stomachs could take. One of the Japanese heaved his guts on the spot.

For three days and nights, the living shadows of men wandered shocked and dazed among the decaying corpses. In the crowded holds it was not uncommon to see men sitting on stacks of dead bodies. Dysentery was rampant and the horse troughs were soon overflowing, but Wada refused to allow the prisoners to empty the "toilet."

Finally, on January 12, Toshino granted permission to remove the dead from the cargo spaces. In the aft compartment, the corpses were tied to ropes and dragged topside. However, the sheer number of bodies in the forward hold made it impossible to haul them up individually. A cargo net was rigged and the dead were tumbled into the carrier. As the net was raised, arms and legs dangled through the mesh openings like stalks of vegetables. An attempt was made to identify the bodies, but the condition of the corpses made identification virtually impossible.

A short time later, a small barge tied up alongside the *Enoura Maru,* and as many bodies as it could carry were unceremoniously dumped on the deck. Toshino ordered a burial detail of thirty prisoners to climb aboard the overloaded craft. When the barge reached shore, the men were too weak to carry the bodies. They were compelled to tie ropes around the naked feet of the dead and drag the corpses to the beach.

The next morning, another load of bodies was hauled ashore and stacked next to the others. Among the pile of cadavers was the broken body of Commander Thomas Hayes.

Before returning to the ship, the burial party stood at attention and gave their dead comrades a farewell military salute. The 300 corpses stacked on the beach were taken by the Japanese to a nearby crematorium and burned.

The war, for Commander Hayes at least, was now over. His prophecy had been fulfilled. He had died a stranger in a strange land. Many of the lives he saved were but futile gestures in an endless parade of death. But the saving of life was his sacred obligation, and every extra breath was worth whatever the cost. He had fought the battle and lost, but his story lives on. He was indeed a "chronicler" of history.

There were still 900 starved and battered American prisoners aboard the *Enoura Maru,* however, and their voyage to Japan was about to resume.

V.

The Death Cruise
January 13, 1945 to January 30, 1945

During the afternoon of January 13, Wada informed the remaining American prisoners that they were to be transferred to the *Brazil Maru*.

The very sick and the wounded were hoisted from the holds of the *Enoura Maru* by means of improvised stretchers—broken wood planks and straw mats. The able-bodied prisoners were so weak that it required sixteen men to haul one stretcher to the main deck.

The fracture cases screamed in pain as their broken bones grated against each other. Their pain and suffering only increased as the stretchers were dropped into barges, then hauled up the hull of the *Brazil Maru*, only to be dropped again into another pit. A dozen brave men died during the transfer operation.

The aft hold of the *Brazil Maru* was designated as the prison quarters. The compartment was divided into bays separated by stanchions. Each bay comprised a space of about ten by twelve feet but with less than four feet of headroom. Thirty prisoners were assigned to each bay, and the men had either to sit with legs stretched out, or lie down with their knees drawn up. Diarrhea cases slept on a twenty-by-forty foot lower hatch cover in order to be near the *benjo* buckets.

As soon as the sun set, the *Brazil Maru* slipped out of the harbor at Takao, Formosa and headed for Japan. As the prison ship plowed northward, the weather became increasingly bitter. There were straw mats in the hold, but only enough for one-third of the prisoners.

A freezing draft blew continually through a ventilator shaft astern of the Japanese living quarters, and cold air and snow whipped through the opening into the cargo space. The nearly naked men sitting near the air vent were the first to die; their bodies were immediately stripped of any clothing by the shivering men still clinging to life. The first day at sea, forty-seven corpses were piled in the hold.

The dramatic jump in the death rate created some additional space per man, but the bodies were not allowed to be hauled topside immediately. A few men in each bay were assigned to the burial detail, and were responsible for carrying the corpses to the main deck and dumping them overboard.

The prisoners were jammed so tightly together that in order to lie down they all had to sleep on the same side. When one man turned over, the whole roll had to do likewise. The frigid bulkheads made staying in one position for more than a half hour excruciatingly painful.

Colonel Beecher pleaded with Wada for permission to stuff a straw mat in the ventilator, but his appeal was denied.

The *Brazil Maru* soon joined a convoy and continued north across the East China Sea. These waters were excellent hunting grounds for American submarines, and the fear of a torpedo suddenly crashing into a bulkhead was a constant threat.

The scantily clad men shook violently with the cold and pneumonia began to run rampant in the hold. The terrific blast of frigid air, swirling like a whirlpool into the tiny space, became known as the "Wind of Death."

The overhead hatch above the hold was covered with a tarpaulin. Even though it was tied down, rain and snow sifted through the cracks. Half-mad prisoners tried to catch the falling flakes in their filthy mess kits, waving the containers back and forth so as not to miss a single snowflake or drop of rain.

The lower hatch cover, about eight feet below the main deck, was called the "zero ward." Whenever a man felt that he could no longer go on, he would say, "Well boys, I have had enough. I'm going to sleep in the 'zero ward' tonight." Death seemed to be the only escape from the weeks of misery.

The water situation was acute. For the first two days, no liquids of any kind were issued, and only a quarter cup of rice was rationed to each man.

Americans continued to die from dehydration and starvation. Almost all open wounds had become gangrenous and the odor was nauseating. Wounds refused to heal due to the lack of body fluids.

Finally, on January 15, the men were allowed two teaspoonsful of water. It was brackish and unpalatable, but water nevertheless.

The Japanese may not have had food or water to give away, but they had plenty to sell. At the rear of the passageways, between the bays, there were two open gratings. One carried the "Wind of Death." The other was a ventilator shaft to the Japanese living quarters and soon became a trading center. The Warriors of Dai Nippon took a fancy to wedding and graduation rings. A thick solid gold ring, passed through the opening, would bring a canteen full of water, a handful of limes, or a few cigarettes. Anyone who had anything at all to trade did so.

The daily rice ration was cooked in a large steam kettle on the main deck. A single guard did the cooking. His recipe called for a combination of rice and kafir corn. The grain was covered with a coarse shell that did not soften with cooking. The hard substance could not be digested by many of the men and the grain passed through their intestines whole. Those who were able to chew the mixture, until it was completely pulverized, fared a little better.

A few curious prisoners sneaked into the lower hold, under the "zero ward" hatch cover, and discovered sacks of sugar. Successful forays into the lower cargo space were carried out. Distribution was not on a regular basis, however, since the sugar was only passed around by men who had strength enough to climb in and out of the hold.

The sugar was unrefined and may have helped those who ate it sparingly, but many gorged themselves. This action only brought on severe thirst and diarrhea. One man, who had not had a bowel movement for twenty-six days, gulped down several cupfuls of sugar. He immediately developed diarrhea, and was dead within a matter of hours.

Along with the madness, induced by deprivation, a cunning fight for survival "at any cost" began to manifest itself. A few prisoners learned to slip down beside a sleeping man, silently open his canteen, and drink all the water without making a sound while swallowing.

Frantic, pathetic men tried to sleep with hands locked tight around the tops of their canteens; but every morning someone would wake up screaming, "Where's the son of a bitch that stole my water!"

Insane men continually roamed about the hold, stepping on dead bodies, and calling for a drink of water from a friend who had died the day before. The death rate climbed hour by hour, until it reached forty men per day by the time the *Brazil Maru* dropped anchor at Moji, Japan. Commander Joses, the senior medical officer aboard, died on the fifth day at sea.

The search for water became a twenty-four-hour obsession. Chief Yeoman Theodore Brownell recalled: "I crept up the ladder and sneaked on deck. Suddenly I saw the most beautiful sight in the world—a long thick icicle. But as I reached for it, a Jap sentry spotted me. He rushed toward me with his bayonet. I scooped up a snowball, hoping to grab something for my efforts. However, while trying to avoid the bayonet, I lost the snowball and fell back into the hold—empty-handed and thirsty as ever."

One resourceful individual adopted the habit of going topside to use a box latrine that had been slung over the side of the ship. While on deck, he would stall the guards as long as possible by exercising, in order to keep his blood circulating. Occasionally, if no one was looking, he would scoop up a handful of the dirty snow that blanketed the deck.

Commander Frank Bridget was wandering about the deck, dazed and incoherent. He was discovered by the Japanese and severely beaten. He was thrown back down the hold where he died the same night.

All the prisoners were filthy. Their hair was matted and a four-week growth of beard gave them a ferocious appearance. Eyes were sore, dry, and glassy. Colorless skin was drawn tightly over their bones, and they were smeared with one another's filth. Lice and other vermin infested their bodies.

The dead presented a more gruesome, unforgettable appearance; lips were drawn back, revealing snarling teeth, and ribs seemed to burst from the ashen bodies. Where a stomach should have been, was now only a hollow depression. Arms and legs protruded like narrow, bent pipe stems and sunken eyes stared, unmoving, at the frightened men who would soon be joining them.

Chaplain William Cummings was a tower of religious strength for the men. Every evening he offered short sermons and prayers; for a few moments the captives forgot their suffering as Father Cummings spoke to them in welcome words of encouragement. Only three days out from Japan, dysentery finally caught up with the priest. But even in his weakened condition, Father Cummings insisted on being lifted up so that he could deliver his evening sermon. That night he lay down in the "zero ward" and passed away. His frail body, like the others, was hoisted to the deck and tossed unceremoniously into the sea by the Japanese. A dark cloud of loneliness and despair settled over the men still alive in the dark hold.

Navy hospital corpsmen and doctors cared for the sick and wounded as best they could. The Japanese refused to supply any medicine or pain-killing drugs. They appeared to revel in the misery of their captives.

The corpsmen were assigned the "night shift" for the duration of the voyage. Although many were sick and wounded themselves, they stayed awake night after night, giving whatever comfort they could to the doomed men.

The very weak prisoners had to be fed, and even carried to the *benjo* bucket. Many men who were too weak to move were shifted so that they would not remain in the same position for hours at a time.

The medical personnel attempted to sleep during the day, but there was so much moving about that sleep was impossible. Patients, mad with fever and putrid wounds, demanded care that was unavailable, and expected the medics to be continually at their beck and call. One officer, out of his mind, insisted on an order of ham and eggs for breakfast.

Some of the prisoners never got up during the entire voyage, preferring to lie in their own filth until they died. Others rose only to relieve themselves. The cripples were the most unfortunate, and had to depend on the hospital corpsmen for their every need. Most of the fracture cases died before the ship reached Japan.

For more than a week, the *Brazil Maru* traveled north along the Chinese coast, dropping anchor at night behind an island or cove. At one point during the trip she towed a cargo vessel that had sustained a damaged keel, and another time assisted a ship with a gaping hole in its stern.

On January 28, the prisoners observed a large convoy escorted by Japanese cruisers, carriers, and other fleet units. They were heading south, apparently in a last ditch effort to reinforce the Philippines.

During the morning of January 30, the *Brazil Maru* crept into an inlet to hide as a flight of American planes passed overhead. The prison ship then changed course to the southeast, bound for the island of Kyushu. That night, off the entrance to the harbor of Moji, American submarines blasted the port, leaving the harbor a mass of flames.

The next morning, the *Brazil Maru* steamed into the anchorage. The two-week voyage from Formosa had finally ended. Almost 900 men had boarded the vessel at Takao, but only 425 survived the trip to Japan.

As soon as the prison ship docked, Japanese Army officers in full dress uniform scrambled aboard and asked to see the senior American officer present. A scraggly figure, clotted with filth, wearing a dirty towel around his brow and sporting a long matted beard, emerged from the dark pit into the daylight. Colonel Curtis Beecher gave a feeble salute, then leaned against the ship's bulkhead, utterly exhausted.

The Japanese were visibly shocked. They had expected a shipload of healthy, able-bodied men to be used in labor camps. As the other pitiful wrecks of humanity stumbled up from the hold, they were lined up on the deck and ordered to strip naked. The men were then sprayed with disinfectant while they shivered in the freezing cold.

A little clothing was distributed. Some of the men received their first shoes and shirts since leaving Bilibid six weeks earlier. Pharmacist's Mate Eugene Rogers was given a pair of Army shoes. They were so heavy, and he was so weak, that he carried them around for two days until he had built up enough strength to put them on.

One officer, while putting his clothes back on after the delousing, dropped to the deck and died under the very eyes of the Japanese.

After dressing, the prisoners were marched to a large warehouse. The first men to enter the building began a frantic search for water and soon discovered a "well." It was only the intake valve of a toilet, but before the Japanese were able to establish any semblance of order, more than 400 men had lined up for a drink. After much arguing and pleading, the prisoners were finally allowed to take turns at the "drinking fountain."

Buckets of rice were brought to the building, but the Japanese refused to let anyone eat until a roll call was made. Another hour went by before the famished prisoners were allowed any food.

Approximately 135 extremely sick men were transported to a local hospital, where more than eighty eventually died. The remaining prisoners were transferred to prison camps near Omuta and Fukouka. After six weeks in these brutal camps, 235 more survivors of the *Brazil Maru* had passed away.

Eugene Rogers was imprisoned at Omuta, about sixty miles from Nagasaki. He remembered the day that the second atom bomb was dropped: "The sky stayed black for two days. It was strange and frightening not to see the sun come up the next morning like we expected. The Japanese told us that the earth had been knocked out of its orbit. We finally saw a little bit of sun on the third day."

After the Japanese surrender, one of the surviving officers was asked what he thought of his captors: "Yes, the Japanese were as bad as you say, but we—the 300 living—we were devils too. If we had not been devils, we could not have survived. When you speak of the good and the heroic, don't talk about us. The generous men—the brave men—the unselfish men—are the men we left behind."

Epilogue

There was constant apprehension on the part of Commander Hayes regarding the safety of his diary and notes, and what might happen if they fell into enemy hands. For this reason, initials or fictitious names were often used to mask the identity of his underground contacts.

The real name of St. M. (or Santa Maria) is presumed to be Maria Esperanza Alvarez Sobral. Maria did volunteer nursing at Bilibid and Santo Tomas. She acted as a liaison agent, handling medicine, money, and food. Maria was continually under suspicion by the Japanese, but was very clever in her ability to stay out of the clutches of the "gestapo." Father Buddenbruch was not so lucky. He was interrogated at Fort Santiago for three months and then executed.

The "rumor" incidents mentioned throughout the diary were, in fact, clever ways for Tom Hayes to camouflage any news received from the many secret radios that were hidden throughout the prison.

Dr. Alfred Smith recalled: "A radio ham in the same building where I was located built himself a footstool. However, underneath the stool, instead of the space being open, he attached two boards and placed a battery-operated radio inside. I was no more than twenty feet away from the radio the whole time and never even knew it was there.

"This radio operator would frequently receive information, never telling a soul. But every time a new draft arrived at Bilibid, or a working party returned from the outside, rumors would suddenly flood the prison.

"This radio technician would nonchalantly mention the latest news to a prisoner returning off a work detail, or a new draft arrival. These men would then tell the information to someone else, and within an hour everybody in Bilibid had learned the latest gossip. By the time the Japanese found out what was going on, nobody knew where the rumor came from or who started it. The reason that most of the rumors were so outlandish was due to the fact that they had been embellished by word of mouth communication."

Certain prisoners on work details would steal radio components and smuggle them into camp. Soon Bilibid became a radio and rumor factory under the very noses of the enemy. The Japanese issued flashlights and batteries to the officers who made bed checks at night, and continually wondered why the batteries would wear out so rapidly. It would be difficult to estimate how many Japanese flashlight batteries ended up in illegal radios.

Dr. Paul Ashton's personal impressions reveal additional insight into the characters of Hayes, Sartin, and Duckworth. Ashton stated: "I guess you might say that Commander Hayes was a combination Errol Flynn and Douglas Fairbanks type of individual—always wearing his uniform cap at a jaunty angle on the side of his head and a rabbit's foot hanging from his belt. He was an uncompromising maker of policy, handing down edicts and rulings that were inflexible and untainted by equivocation. Whatever was best for the flag, for the Service, or for the most people was his yardstick.

"Hayes had always been this way, but he never before had an opportunity to play the part. He was a ham actor in his costume and portrayal, but did his best (as conscience dictated), and then agonized about the effect—having misgivings and fearing 'political' repercussions.

"However, I can't allow his 'Errol Flynn' estimations of Duckworth or Sartin to dilute the color or strength of their personalities. My longer acquaintance with them, under many trying situations, can not be abandoned so easily.

"Duckworth and Sartin were of a different stripe—from each other, and from Tom Hayes. Hayes had studied the role, rehearsed it, and was ready when his turn came to take charge.

"Command was thrust upon Sartin and it never did fit the costume or gentle mien of this very civilized man. He took the baton with reluctance and was forceful in his thin, quiet, elderly way. I was always proud of his persistence. But by contrast, the arrogance, roughness, and brutality of the enemy were so overpowering that they never took Sartin seriously. He was unreal to the Japanese—but the heyday of Bilibid was during Sartin's administration.

"The 'Duck' was a pure hedonist—obese, always seeking comfort and ease. He was yet another kind of rule maker. Big, Prussian, inflexible, obviously fearless, and always a leader—like a Mafia godfather.

"Following my altercation with the guard who shot Griffin, I was not allowed off the ward. Hayes's diary makes no mention of my long trial by the Japanese from September 1944 to January 1945 [Hayes's last diary entry is September 17, 1944]. Kubota helped me through this stressful period. However, I lost the case despite the testimony of patients on the ward who stated that they saw the guard shoot himself.

"During this time, I became well acquainted with Kubota who always admonished me never to sign any testimony unless he read it first and approved. Trial transcripts, written in Japanese, were often altered, Kubota said, 'Just to catch me up.' However, these delays tended to lengthen the trial until MacArthur reached Lingayen. The Japanese then got cold feet and issued orders to execute all prisoners—an 'Errol Flynn' ending for sure!

"Tom Hayes's diary is an important addition to the knowledge of our little war in the Philippines. Therein much is to be learned about the rivalry between the Army and Navy Medical Corps—though I always flattered myself that the Navy took me in as one of them. I saw the development of the Navy corpsmen and the hierarchy of warrant officers and pharmacist mates. They were a special class of people—an administrative outfit—a few of whom the Army had also in the MAC (Medical Administrative Corps)."

Opinions and impressions of Commander Tom Hayes are widely varied. He was admired by certain people and hated by others. Although he had a definite touch of paranoia, he was also a clever "game player." At every opportunity he would put the enemy on the defensive and revel in their confusion. He continually attempted to manipulate Nogi, and many times succeeded in shifting blame from the Americans to the Japanese themselves.

The voyage to Japan where more than 1,300 prisoners lost their lives is a sad commentary on the war in the Pacific. During the war crimes trials much of the blame was shifted from the Japanese commanding officers to their subordinates, and so on down the line. The "who to blame" theory was in effect. There was no way that everyone responsible could be charged, let alone convicted. The Allies grasped at straws and found a few needles, but only the top of the haystack was ever probed.

Commander Hayes was certainly prophetic when he stated, "When this war is over, it will be hands across the sea and all is forgiven!"